Student Engagement in Urban Schools

Beyond Neoliberal Discourses

A volume in
Issues in the Research, Theory, Policy, and Practice of Urban Education
Denise E. Armstrong and Brenda J. McMahon, *Series Editors*

Issues in the Research, Theory, Policy, and Practice of Urban Education

Denise E. Armstrong and Brenda J. McMahon
Series Editors

Student Engagement in Urban Schools

Beyond Neoliberal Discourses

edited by

Brenda J. McMahon
University of North Carolina at Charlotte

John P. Portelli
University of Toronto

INFORMATION AGE PUBLISHING, INC.
Charlotte, NC • www.infoagepub.com

Library of Congress Cataloging-in-Publication Data

Student engagement in urban schools : beyond neoliberal discourses / edited
by Brenda J. McMahon, University of North Carolina at Charlotte, John P.
Portelli, University of Toronto.
     pages cm. – (Issues in the research, theory, policy, and practice
of urban education)
 Includes bibliographical references.
 ISBN 978-1-61735-731-2 (pbk.) – ISBN 978-1-61735-732-9 (hardcover) –
ISBN 978-1-61735-733-6 (ebook)
 1. Education, Urban. 2. Educational equalization. 3. Neoliberalism. I.
McMahon, Brenda J. II. Portelli, John P. (John Peter)
 LC5115.S84 2012
 370.9173'2–dc23

                                                                2011048233

CONTENTS

ACKNOWLEDGEMENTS

We thank the authors for their contributions and their enthusiasm about this project. In the various stages of this project we benefited from the support that our respective institutions gave us. In particular we thank Frankie Vondrejs for her editorial assistance, and Mary Drinkwater for her assistance in contacting the authors. We also thank Denise Armstrong, series co-editor of *Equity and Inclusion in Urban Educational Environments,* and George Johnson of Information Age Publishing for supporting this project.

SERIES EDITORS' PREFACE

Denise E. Armstrong and Brenda J. McMahon

This series focuses on contemporary issues in the theory, practice, and policy of urban education. Our primary aim is create a substantive body of research and scholarship that provides critical and/or innovative perspectives on urban education and examines how urban education is currently conceived, enacted, and transformed in educational contexts. Public education is a hopeful endeavor which has the potential to transcend worlds and transform lives. Unfortunately, these possibilities for democratic transformation are lost to many of our students and educators. As rational-technical reform agendas take root and individualist agendas vie for control, today's schools are more and more likely to be experienced as sites competition and conformity than as communities of empowerment and engagement. Tensions between individual and collective rights, freedom and choice, equity and equality, compliance and agency, accountability and responsibility abound and shape educational processes and outcomes in paradoxical ways that reinforce the status quo and lead to the educational impoverishment and diminishment of less powerful individuals and groups.

This situation is particularly troubling for equity-focused educators and students who seek to engage individuals and communities in meaningful ways. *Student engagement in urban schools: Beyond neoliberal discourses* focuses how competing notions of student success impact the experience and enactment of education in public schools both locally and internationally and the ways in which this situation can be addressed. The contributors problematize the different ways in which student engagement is conceived and practiced. They describe social and historical patterns of engagement and show how diverse students and communities' needs are often at odds with external government accountabilities and standardized, homogeneous curricula. They also illustrate how neoliberal ideologies operate within hierarchical structures to determine the goals and purposes of education and to subvert democratic outcomes and processes. Often based on narrow market-driven principles of success, standardization, and accountability, these ideologies impact how schooling is enacted and experienced. These diametrically opposed notions of, and approaches to, engagement and success lead to decidedly different teaching and learning processes and outcomes. For the most part, technical-performative and efficiency models of student engagement that are based on narrowly defined outcomes, high stakes standardized testing, and competitive league tables, privilege powerful agendas. They also stifle critical and participatory approaches to democratic community, deny alternative histories and perspectives, deligitimate students' voices, deprofessionalize teachers, and polarize communities.

This book proposes a hopeful view of democracy as a communal process of being and becoming that respects difference, encourages critique, values participation and multiple voices, and engages students in authentic ways. Moving beyond neoliberal discourses requires broader and more substantive definitions of engagement, authentic dialogue, and critical action that are grounded in socially just and equitable praxis. The authors provide a number of practical examples regarding how individuals and groups can work together strategically to create democratic communities that transgress neoliberal practices and ensure critical democratic engagement for all. These include: inclusive approaches to education that promote meaningful participation in decision- and policy-making activities; democratic public spaces for student leadership and activism, and the establishment of strategic relationships; networks and alliances to disrupt the status quo; and challenges to systemic inequities that reproduce the power and privilege of dominant groups.

CHAPTER 1

THE CHALLENGES OF NEOLIBERALISM IN EDUCATION

Implications for Student Engagement

Brenda J. McMahon and John P. Portelli

There is no doubt that we live in what has been referred to as "neoliberal times." Neoliberalism, which has its roots in liberalism, has become the dominant ideology since the early 1980s both in economics and politics, but also in other areas such as education. Neoliberalism has taken different forms, and this is why we refer to "neoliberal discourses." However, these discourses rest on a certain way of life and beliefs which have impacted our daily lives including schooling. In its root sense, the term "neoliberalism" simply means a new form of liberalism. The term has not generally been used by those who are associated with neoliberal thinking and policies. It is mostly used by critics of neoliberalism. Hence it is crucial that we clarify what is meant by the term "neoliberalism."

Nineteenth century liberalism is based on two basic principles: the inalienable rights of the individual and the right to freedom of thought and action. Liberalism arose in response to the social conditions of the time: lack of workers' rights, racism, lack of women's rights, and lack of children's rights, among others. As a response to such conditions, liberalism argues for the defense of the individual rights (whoever that individual happens to be we are all equal in front of the law and all should have the same equal opportunities), and the defense of freedom or lack of constraints on the individual to exercise her or his rights. A popular liberal tenet has been expressed in the popular dictum: "One can do whatever one wishes to do as long as one does not interfere with the rights of others." In a sense, liberal thought assisted the cause of the civil movement. Such social movements had an impact on schooling and education, and hence the nature and purpose of education were among the early issues debated in the formation of compulsory schooling as it emerged in North America in the mid to late 19th century. Debates about the role of democracy in education and the democratic aims of education are not new ones; they have a long history.

Neoliberal thinking is rooted in the basic liberal thinking; however, the basic liberal beliefs have been interpreted differently than the proponents of liberalism in the 19th century. In a nutshell, the two basic liberal principles of individual rights and freedom have been taken to an extreme. In popular discourse, the plea for individual rights has been transformed to a staunch defense of a narrow and rigid form of individualism, which, in turn, led to excessive competition. Moreover, the notion of freedom has been translated to mean simply any form of choice, which, in turn, has led to the emphasis of free market and an almost absolute choice of the "client." It is exactly because of these interpretations that conceptually neoliberalism has been associated with narrow forms of utility and accountability and profit at all costs. At the same time, the fixation with narrow forms of accountability (in contrast to moral responsibility) has led to a one-size-fits-all mentality or standardization, on the basis that standardization is needed to achieve equality of opportunity. Ironically, what initially started as a defense of the fulfillment of the needs of the individuals who had different needs arising from different contexts became transformed into a standardization movement that does not take heed of different needs arising from different contexts. It is also worth noting that the major critique the West launched in the 1970s and 1980s against the communist thinking in Russia and China was exactly that of standardization. Now standardization has become the norm for the neoliberal West!

Neoliberalism as an ideology has had an impact on various areas of our lives. We have all experienced the handing over of basic institutions to private businesses, the emphasis on the so-called "free market economy," and the association of democracy to simply free choice. In education, neoliberal thinking has brought about an increase on high stake testing usually of a standardized form, a standardized curriculum, an ethos of narrow instrumentality that has reduced the arts and humanities to second class subjects, and an encroachment of consumerism in schools (Norris, 2010; Nussbaum, 2010). Such a mentality has had an impact on how educators and students conceive of and experience engagement in learning. Student engagement has been impacted by a narrow notion of success that primarily, if not exclusively, identifies learning with test results rather than deep understanding and inquiry.

Conceptions of student success influence beliefs about and practices of student engagement. While it is self-evident that no one wants to argue against student engagement, it is crucial to note that different views about success determine how one views student engagement and what actions go with it. Different notions of success lead to different aims and different ways of achieving those aims. How one views success will influence how one acts and what one considers to be worthwhile objectives. This is a general truism about human life. For example, if one believes in good health and that good health can be achieved by exercising, all things being equal, one would do one's best to exercise. The same holds for educational matters. Narrow notions of success or notions of success that are limiting will invariably lead to narrow understandings of student engagement. If we are really interested in achieving the different needs and expectations of all, then a broader and more varied notion of success is called for. The points being made here are twofold: first, that it is crucial to determine one's purpose of student engagement since not all aim for the same kind of learning, and secondly, that such purposes are determined by one's notion of success, and hence it is a moral imperative to identify and justify one's notion of success.

Within neoliberal agendas that protect individual rights and seek to reinforce the status quo, student engagement is often configured in behavioral terms.[1] Student engagement has been conceived and practiced in a variety of ways. One form constrains engagement strictly to behavior of the students; for example, are students performing well on tasks, completing their homework, appearing to be involved in their school work. These technical or performative conceptions of student engagement are consistent with standardization and envision student engagement as measurable with an emphasis on aspects of schooling such as student performance and time on task (Steinberg, 1996). This position raises several conceptual problems. For example, it reduces learning simply to what is observable and measurable, and it disregards student voice and contributions. It reinforces authoritarian notions of school and the role of the teacher and does not question the prescribed curriculum and its purpose. From several empirical studies, it has been shown that this form of engagement leads to boredom and disengagement for both teachers and students (Fine, 1995; McMahon & Armstrong, 2003; Portelli, Shields & Vibert, 2007; Smith et al., 1998; Smyth, 2008).

In response to the narrow scope of these technical-performative notions of student engagement, several authors have proposed another form of student engagement based on individual growth (Cothran & Ennis, 2000; Newmann, Wehlage, & Lamborn, 1992). While still stressing the importance of behavioral aspects of student engagement by emphasizing individual interests, this conception adds independent study projects to established core curricula. What also differentiates this notion from its performative counterpart is the inclusion of a psychological component such as a sense of connectedness or belonging, which is deemed to be realized in schools through the use of group-work and membership in teams and clubs. Although this understanding of student engagement reduces the authoritarian role of the teacher, it is still problematic. For example, it continues to focus on the primacy of the individual educator, student behaviors remain the primary criterion for determining success, and it does not question the prescribed purposes of schooling or the role of the prescribed curriculum, and hence, possibly unwittingly reinforces the status quo. Both of the two major conceptions of student engagement identified thus far locate their sense in the actions of the students or the teachers and neither questions the meaningfulness of the engagement.

Student engagement from a critical democratic perspective is qualitatively different from either of the two conceptions mentioned above and includes both procedural and substantive aspects. It is embedded in beliefs about education as a vehicle for democratic transformation, where democracy is ongoing, evolving, and "associated with equity, community, creativity, and taking difference seriously" (Portelli & Solomon, 2001, p. 17). Rather than being seen as resulting from specific student and teacher behaviors, or teacher strategies and techniques, critical inquiry based on robust notions of equity and social justice is central to education for democratic transformation.

> Engagement is realized in the processes and relationships within which learning for democratic reconstruction transpires. As a multifaceted phenomenon, engagement is present in the iterations that emerge as a result of the dialectical processes between teachers and students and the differing patterns that evolve out of transformational actions and interactions. As enacted, engagement is generated through the interactions of students and teachers, in a shared space, for the purpose of democratic reconstruction, through which personal transformation takes place. (McMahon & Portelli, 2004, p. 70)

The latter position is generally critiqued for not being "practical." This is a serious charge that cannot be taken lightly. However, critiques seem to assume that what is deemed to be practical is so, in and of itself, irrespective of differences in contexts. In fact, however, the notion of "practical" is a relational term. Something is considered practical depending on certain aims and certain conditions. If one is serious about the popularly made claims about the value of democracy, then the critical-democratic stance and the practices that flow from it become very practical and relevant. They are not a waste of time if one values democracy in a robust sense. Research has shown that it is indeed possible to enact the critical-democratic stance if educators and those who support their work understand the meaning and the importance of the critical-democratic perspective (Fine, Torre, Burns, & Payne, 2007; McMahon, 2003; Mills & Gale, 2002; Munns, 2007; Portelli & Vibert, 2002; Smyth, 2008). If the aims and conditions of schooling and leadership are changed accordingly, then the critical-democratic perspective becomes more achievable. Such a change requires that student engagement be construed and practiced in different ways other than those imposed by neoliberal beliefs and practices.

CHAPTER OVERVIEWS

This book incorporates a variety of perspectives on "student engagement" inside and outside of classrooms in democratic contexts. Democracy, voice, resistance, and compliance are themes that appear throughout the collection. As befitting the international and ideological natures of this volume, in addition to multiple viewpoints, the authors utilize different formats and writing styles in examining theories and practices of student engagement.

Envisioning schools as public spaces, Fielding provides a philosophical analysis of differing conceptions of democracy and their relationship to notions of educational engagement and student voice. Contrasting representative and participatory approaches, Fielding equates the former with high-performance school initiatives that narrowly define measurable outcomes and cast students in the role of consumers with teachers and students alike valued for their contributions to high-stakes test scores. While he identifies both individual and collective perspectives consistent with this notion of democracy and schooling, both are market-driven and lack communal perspectives necessary for the creation of an inclusive, creative society. Fielding provides examples of schools that modeled participatory democracy and functioned as public spaces for identity development and democratic renewal. He calls for educators to reclaim radical traditions of democratic education as a means of attaining socially just and equitable societies.

McMahon furthers this discussion by linking notions of democracy and educational leadership to beliefs about student engagement and the roles of student voice and identity in schools. Using data from interviews with students who experienced both marginalization/failure and inclusion/success in schools, she differentiates between student voice in schools preparing students *for* democracy and student voice in schools existing at least to some extent *in* or *as* democracy. With a narrow focus on elements of schooling, educational leadership for democracy reinforces hegemonic structures, enforces compliance, and silences voices that are inconsistent with institutional agendas. Conversely, focusing on broader aspects of schooling, educational leadership as democracy is emancipatory and creates spaces and means within which students are involved in meaningful decisions and democratic processes are continuously enacted.

Mitra and Kirshner continue to develop the connection between student engagement and student voice by providing a framework for analyzing the strengths and weaknesses of specific youth leadership and social activism initiatives inside and outside of educational institutions. Consistent with neo-liberal agendas, youth leadership occurs in existing structured organizations inside and outside of schools where adolescents are given permission to be involved in planning and decision-making about issues supportive of the organizations. Contrariwise, although these are not, at a practical level, mutually exclusive stratagems, youth social activism initiatives are aimed at changing social injustices and inequities, and seek to disrupt the status quo. Although successful youth activism organizations depend on leadership development for their success, because this form of youth involvement seeks to bring about democratic transformation, its ideologies and purposes are fundamentally different from initiatives that work to maintain the status quo.

Smyth addresses questions about which issues are important to marginalized students and the conditions needed to foster meaningful student engagement in the schools that have served to disadvantage these students. Embedded in neoliberal ideologies, singular approaches and narrow foci to schooling and student engagement create environments that are unwelcoming to and disengaging for large numbers of urban and otherwise minoritized students. Alternatively, when students reclaim the voice and power that has been stripped from them by policies and practices that have turned urban schools into vocational training grounds, there are radical possibilities for education. Using the language of "students speaking back" as illustrative of respecting and welcoming resistance as a means of developing student resilience, Smyth presents a framework whereby critical democratic engagement and student voice are realized in schools. He expands on how meaningful learning, socially just lives, and contested ideas intersect and overlap in such environments.

Sellar and Gale deconstruct "aspirational" approaches to student engagement that attempt to engage students by illustrating how education offers them a means to economic ends and challenge notions that working-class and low-income teenagers are essentially materialistic. They analyze "aspirational" policies developed to increase enrollment in higher education programs and interview teachers who work with the targeted populations to determine the meanings of and suppositions behind aspiration as a tool for student engagement. Sellar and Gale contend that policies and practices within this neoliberal paradigm employ outsiders' evaluations of student engagement and aspiration, and that their narrow focus on preparing workers for the market is antithetical to socially just forms of student engagement with and in schools and universities.

Zyngier describes the elements of a multi-school Australian project aimed at providing engaging, student-centered learning by building social competencies, skills, and knowledge through community action research projects. The "ruMAD" (Are You Making a Difference) program is inquiry based and incorporates values education into school curricula that focus on enacting social change in disadvantaged schools and communities. Following an outline of the tenets of the ruMAD organization, Zyngier provides an in-depth description of one of its environmental projects that demonstrates that students and teachers alike are transformed by the educational process. Hence this chapter provides examples of alternatives to neoliberal practices.

Munns triangulates data gathered from student focus groups with classroom observations and teacher interviews focused on student engagement in low socio-economic communities in Australia. While Munns is clear that this is not the definitive approach to student engagement, his research identifies the importance of pedagogical approaches that consist of high cognitive, affective, and operative learning experiences concurrent with the conscious creation of learning environments that shift away from compliance to shared ownership of all aspects of the learning process and increased student voice. He provides examples of ways in which the purposeful design of learning experiences and the crafting of classroom practices can engage and achieve academic success with students who might otherwise be disengaged and academically at risk.

Seltzer-Kelly's autoethnography argues against efficiency models of schooling that inform effective school movements. She focuses on the need to shift student-teacher interns' beliefs away from the dichotomy inherent in either pathologizing students and their families in urban and otherwise designated as at-risk communities or blaming themselves for their failure to teach disengaging curricula. The former disposition is prevalent in students selected by faculties of education who because they have experienced success in school systems have difficulty identifying the problematic nature of standardized curricula and more importantly the strengths and knowledges that marginalized students possess. To counter these dominant discourses, Seltzer-Kelly presents a philosophical and empirical argument for student–teacher relationships based on empathetic engagement in the pursuit of conjoint inquiry in education.

Cooper and Portelli deconstruct the concept of controversial issues in education in a qualitative study conducted with student leaders and their staff advisors during an annual student leadership conference in Canada. They argue that addressing matters related to social diversity that do not have universally accepted points of view provides opportunities for meaningful student engagement and democratic transformation in schools. Moreover, these conversations are essential if we are to enact critical democratic processes that require subversion against inequitable social structures within and outside of schools. Schools continue to reinforce societal hegemonic ideologies and structures, and equity concerns are fundamentally related to which students succeed or fail in schools. As Cooper and Portelli illustrate, teachers and students have the potential to dismantle and confront inequitable structures and be agents of democratic transformation.

These essays, which represent different though conceptually supportive views about student engagement, arise from different international contexts: Australia, Canada, England, and the United States of America, countries that have contributed a lot to the development of neoliberal beliefs and practices. But the authors from these very countries have shown through theoretical and empirical evidence that the neoliberal hegemony can be meaningfully questioned, and alternative beliefs and practices are indeed possible and real. Such examples do not lessen the need to continue to struggle for a robust democratic way of life, but they also offer hope for others to continue the struggle that aims for fulfilling the needs of all rather than some.

NOTE

1. For a detailed examination of the student engagement paradigms mentioned here, please see McMahon and Portelli (2004).

REFERENCES

Cothran, D., & Ennis, C. (2000). Building bridges to student engagement: Communicating respect and care for students in urban high schools. *Journal of Research and Development in Education, 33*(2), 106–117.

Fine, M. (1995). The politics of who's "at risk." In B. Swadener & S. Lubeck (Eds.), *Children and families "at promise": Deconstructing the discourse of risk* (pp. 76–94). Albany, NY: State University of New York.

Fine, M., Torre, M. E., Burns, A., & Payne, Y. A. (2007). Youth research/participatory methods for reform. In D. Thiessen & A. Cook-Sather (Eds.), *International handbook of student experience in elementary and secondary school* (pp. 805–828). New York, NY: Springer.

McMahon, B. (2003). Putting the elephant in the refrigerator: Student engagement, critical pedagogy and antiracist education. *McGill Journal of Educational Research, 38*(2), 257–273.

McMahon, B. & Armstrong, D. (2003). Racism, resistance, resilience: The 3rs of educating Caribbean students within a Canadian context. In T. Bastick & A. Ezenne (Eds.), *Teaching Caribbean students: Research on social issues in the Caribbean and abroad* (pp. 249–284). Kingston, Jamaica: UWI.

McMahon, B., & Portelli, J. (2004). Engagement for what? Beyond popular discourses on student engagement. *Leadership and Policy in Schools, 3*(1), 59–76.

Mills, C., & Gale, T. (2002). Schooling and the production of social inequalities: What can and should we be doing? *Melbourne Studies in Education, 43*(1), 107–125.

Munns, G. (2007). A sense of wonder: Student engagement in low SES school communities. *International Journal of Inclusive Education, 11*, 301–315.

Newmann, F., Wehlage, G., & Lamborn, S. (1992). The significance and sources of student engagement. In F. Newmann (Ed.), *Student engagement and achievement in American secondary schools* (pp. 11–39). New York, NY: Teachers' College Press.

Norris, T. (2010) *Consuming schools: Commercialism and the end of politics.* Toronto, ON: University of Toronto Press.

Nussbaum, M.C. (2010). *Not for profit: Why democracy needs the humanities.* Princeton, NJ: Princeton University Press.

Portelli, J., Shields, C., & Vibert, A. (2007). *Toward an equitable education: Poverty, diversity, and 'student at risk.'* Toronto, ON: Centre for Leadership and Diversity.

Portelli, J., & Solomon, P. (Eds.). (2001). *The erosion of democracy in education: From critique to possibilities.* Calgary, Alberta: Detselig.

Portelli, J., & Vibert, A. (2002). The possibilities of curriculum of life. *Education Canada,* Summer, 36–39.

Smith, W., Butler-Kisber, L., LaRocque, L., Portelli, J., Shields, C., Sparkes, C., & Vibert, A. (1998). *Student engagement in learning and life: National project report.* Montreal, Quebec: Office of Research on Educational Policy, McGill University.

Smyth, J. (2008). Listening to student voice in the democratisation of schooling. In E. Samier & G. Stanley (Eds.), *Political approaches to educational administration and leadership* (pp. 240–251). London, UK: Routledge.

Steinberg, L. (1996). *Beyond the classroom: Why school reform has failed and what parents need to do.* New York, NY: Touchstone.

CHAPTER 2

FROM STUDENT VOICE TO DEMOCRATIC COMMUNITY

New Beginnings, Radical Continuities

Michael Fielding

ABSTRACT

Against market-led models of democracy and the educationally corrosive dominance of personalization and high-performance schooling, the case is made for person-centered education committed to the development of an inclusive, creative society. A key element of these alternative, participatory traditions of democracy is the nurturing of public spaces in schools and the iconic development of whole school meetings. Practical examples are explored, key issues identified, and the case made for the importance of prefigurative practice within utopian realist traditions.

INTRODUCTION

Democracy is, rightly, a contested notion: so too are the educational consequences of what it means for systems of public/state schooling to take democracy seriously. The argument of this chapter begins by suggesting that neolib-

Student Engagement in Urban Schools, pages 11–27
Copyright © 2012 by Information Age Publishing

eral, market-oriented notions of democracy offer an inadequate account of human flourishing and, as a consequence, encourage approaches to student voice and other forms of educational engagement that are less fulfilling and less inclusive than their supporters would wish. They exclude or marginalize accounts and practices of democratic education that offer alternative ways forward that not only address an increasing disaffection with the formal processes of representative politics, but also invite a creative, intergenerational commitment to shared opportunities and responsibilities of education in its broadest sense—that is to say, in how we lead good lives together.

One important difference between elitist, representative approaches to democracy and the contrasting classical, participatory traditions lies in the relative importance each accords to collective and communal deliberation and development. Inspired by and located within the latter traditions of participatory democracy, the argument of the second section of the chapter is that public space is a key site, both of individual identity and of democratic ways of living and learning together, and that because of its preeminent existential and political importance in human flourishing, it deserves considerably more attention than it has been accorded, either in theory or in practice, in schools within public systems of education.

Thirdly, I want to suggest that certain kinds of inclusive public space—in particular, the practice of general or whole school meetings of the kind exemplified in radical traditions of private and public/state education—are worthy of further study and development. In seeking to make such a case, I will suggest that in order to achieve the emancipatory potential to which these public spaces aspire we need to attend with care to a plurality of shared, subaltern/minority spaces within which identities, dispositions, and capacities can be negotiated, nurtured, and realized.

It is clear from the history of radical approaches to education in many countries across the world, not only that school meetings have an iconic status within the lexicon of radical democratic schooling, but also that developments of this kind owe much of their power and persuasiveness to the lived reality of future practice now. It is the capacity of radical pioneers not only to argue for more just and more creative alternatives to the status quo, but also to enact a quite different reality in the teeth of an antagonistic present that inspires our allegiance and fuels our resolve. It is this tradition of "prefigurative practice" that energizes the final section of the chapter and animates its concluding remarks.

ON THE POVERTY OF HIGH-PERFORMANCE SCHOOLING: RETRIEVING EDUCATION AS HUMAN FLOURISHING

Like other contributors to this book, I have for many years argued against the ideologies and practices of school effectiveness and what I have come to call "high-performance schooling," not just because they inevitably fail to achieve what they set out to do, but, more importantly, because they distort and marginalize education in favor of a thin and diminishing form of schooling only tangentially connected to democracy as a way of living and learning together. In reflecting on developments in the field of student voice over the past twenty years and, in particular, on the latest phase of its neoliberal incorporation, I have been struck, firstly, by the ways in which it has been drawn in to the largely atomistic discourses of personalization and, secondly, by the need for an alternative account of possibility that names quite other aspirations of young people and the adults who work together on a day-to-day basis.

Student Voice, Personalization, and High-Performance Schooling

The personalization, high-performance perspective set out in Table 2.1 is heavily influenced by market-led thinking with substantial emphasis on individual choice. Individuals are encouraged to see themselves as consumers or customers who need to make informed choices about opportunities for learning within the school, often connected with their future life chances within the jobs market. At a collective level, a school committed to this way of working also operates within a market framework. It sees its main task as one of maximizing its position in competitive league tables or their de facto equivalents by producing better outcomes, invariably in the form of high stakes test scores, for students and, indeed, for staff. Student voice is regarded as important here because in listening to students, the school perceives itself as a more accountable and more effective learning organization and thus better at meeting what it regards as its core responsibilities.

While many schools warm to this perspective, I see in it too many dangers, too much that denies what is important in education, too much that

TABLE 2.1   Personalized Schooling

Individual perspective	Collective perspective
Personalized learning	**High Performance schooling**
Driver	*Driver*
Individual ambition	Fully informed accountability
Dominant model	*Dominant model*
Consumer choice	Learning organization
Key question	*Key question*
What job do I wish to have?	How can we learn from everyone to achieve better outcomes?

has led the world to the brink of economic and social collapse. Although the personalization model's key underlying questions to do with individual employment and the school's collective capacities to achieve these kinds of outcomes for as many as possible are entirely legitimate, they are, in the end, inadequate. They fail to acknowledge or utilize other motivational dynamics that presume less individualistic, more generously conceived, more inclusive notions of what it might mean to lead a good and fulfilling life.

Because the activities and aspirations of the school as a high-performance learning organization are dominated by narrowly defined outcomes and measured attainment, such schools too often turn out to be not only educationally impoverished but diminishing rather than enabling of individuals as persons. It is especially ironic—given the mantra of "individual choice," of the "customer," of "ownership," of "empowerment," and of "personalization"—that its form of unity is collective, rather than personal or communal. The significance of both students and teachers is derivative and rests primarily in their contribution, usually via high-stakes testing, to the public performance of the organization. The high-performing school is an organization in which the personal is used for the sake of the functional: Relationships are important; the voices of students are elicited and acknowledged; community is valued, but all primarily for instrumental purposes within the context of the marketplace. Social and, indeed, personal relationships are reduced to social capital; "having relationships" moves subtly towards "doing relationships," towards relationship management. The high-performance model is, in effect if not intention, one that sails too closely to the rocks of totalitarianism: Individuals cease to have anything other than parasitic organizational worth. The tyranny of the market proscribes the possibility of alternative forms of being, insisting, in a contemporary echo of F.D. Roosevelt, that "The only thing we have to choose is choice itself."

Student Voice, Person-centered Education, and the Good Society

The person-centered perspective also starts with individuals, but its understanding of what it means to be an individual is quite different (see Table 2.2). It sees individuals as persons, not as isolated, self-sufficient beings, but as essentially the product of relationships. As the great Scottish philosopher John Macmurray (1961) once said, "We need one another to be ourselves" (p. 211). A person-centered perspective does include the responsibility to make choices, but they are choices made within the context of deeper aspirations than those of the market and are often plural or communal in their direction and mode of thinking. They concern fundamental questions to do with how we become good persons, and the means of an-

TABLE 2.2 Person-Centered Education

Personal perspective	Communal perspective
Person-centered Education	Creative Society
Driver	*Driver*
Personal development	Shared responsibility for a better future
Dominant model	*Dominant model*
Relational dialogue	Learning community
Key question	*Key question*
What kind of person do I wish to become?	How do we develop an inclusive, creative society together?

swering those questions are essentially through dialogue with others whom we care for and respect. At a communal level, a school committed to this way of working sees its main task as one of developing an inclusive, creative society that benefits everyone. Student voice is important here, not so much through representative structures (though it will have these and operate them well), but rather through a whole range of daily opportunities in which young people can listen and be listened to, make decisions, and take a shared responsibility for both the here-and-now of daily encounter and for the creation of a better future.

In contrast to the school as high-performance learning organization, the school as person-centered learning community is guided by its commitment to the functional arrangements and interactions of the school being firmly committed to wider human purposes.

Certainly, the functional is genuinely felt to be for the sake of, and at its most developed form, expressive of the personal. Invariably one sees the development of organizational forms that deliberately establish a sense of place, purpose, and identity within which emergent, fluid forms of learning are encouraged. The revival of schools-within-schools/sub-schools, an implacable opposition to "ability" grouping, and more integrated, co-constructed approaches to curriculum together with wide-ranging use of the community exemplify commitment to more exploratory modes of being and development. Such schools deliberately develop more participatory, less hierarchical forms of engagement and decision making. Distinctions between pastoral and academic become more problematic and ultimately less significant. Professional development embraces more explicitly dialogic, even narrative forms of engagement such as action learning sets and self-managed learning groups, and boundaries between status, role, and function are increasingly transgressed through new forms of "radical collegiality" (Fielding, 1999).

The key questions underlying a person-centered model—What kind of person do I wish to become? How do we develop an inclusive, creative society together?—do not ignore the instrumental necessities of getting a job and equipping young people to make their way in a competitive world. Rather, they connect with deeper issues within a wider context of human flourishing. The person-centered approach does not deny the functional; it transforms and transcends it. The same is true of its approach to student voice and to democracy. Rather than the instrumental capture and control of young people's perspectives, it is dialogic and emergent in its processes, dispositions, and intentions. Rather than the exclusions and denial of difference that invariably accompany the actualities of representative democracy, its embrace of the participatory tradition requires a richness and range of formal and informal daily encounter. As I shall argue later in connection with whole school meetings, the viability and legitimacy of communal flourishing requires a multiplicity of opportunity made real within a resolute affirmation of possibility.

PUBLIC SPACE AND PARTICIPATORY DEMOCRACY

The relational presumptions underpinning the person-centered model of student voice I have just described privilege a very different set of aspirations and practices to those of the dominant market-led, neoliberal model. Among these practices I want to pick out the development of democratic public space as of special importance to those who wish to develop student voice within the traditions of participatory democracy.

In championing public space as a key site, both of individual identity and of democratic renewal, one useful and creative tradition of thought and praxis is the republican tradition of democracy recently explored in Stuart White's contribution to his co-authored book with Daniel Leighton. White (2008) argues for six key elements, which, in contrast to representative or elitist theories of democracy, emphasize the importance of the public good, of an inclusive popular involvement in decision-making, of appropriate deliberation in that process, of the necessity of each person being free to make authentic judgments unintimidated by dominant others, of economic egalitarianism, and, most important of all, of participation in collective decision-making in public-spirited action.

John Dewey's writing on democracy and education also privileges a wide-ranging commitment to shared ways of living and learning together in which, I suggest, public space has an important role to play. For Dewey (1916), "democracy is more than a form of government: it is primarily a mode of associated living, a conjoint communicated experience" (p. 87), and, for me, part of that "mode of associated living" inevitably involves the nurturing of a vibrant public realm in schools—that is, public space where staff and students can reflect on and make meaning of their work together and agree on shared commitments to further developing the ideals and practices of life and learning to which the school aspires.

Some of the key theoretical arguments for the importance of public space go well beyond the case for democratic participation and suggest that it has a crucial role to play in our development as persons, not just as citizens. Within the field of education, one of the most eloquent and persuasive contemporary writers within this tradition is Maxine Greene (1982, 2000). Often inspired by the work of the political philosopher Hannah Arendt, she argues for what I call (1) the presumption of agency, or the development of individual identity through acting with others; (2) communal contexts of identity formation, or each person's uniqueness being a function of togetherness, of being participants; and (3) inclusive solidarity, or people perceiving what is common from different positions and against different backgrounds.

Within the field of educational leadership and management for democracy, Philip Woods (2005) argues strongly for space as a key orienting concept. Broadly speaking, he suggests that firm democratic structures within a school must be complemented by "free spaces" that minimize assumptions of hierarchy and knowledge. Free space can be found in what he calls "independent zones," two examples being (for students) playtime and peer mediation and (for staff) team working scenarios and shared leadership opportunities. While not explicitly naming inclusive public space between students and staff, he does advocate the development of what he calls "blurred status zones"—for example, informal daily encounters and student councils, where there is at least an ambivalence, if not an equity, of status within intergenerational encounters.

Interestingly, in the last couple of decades, some of the strongest challenges to notions of public space have come from the left. Within political theory, writers like Nancy Fraser (1997) have critiqued Habermasian accounts of the public sphere by pointing out, firstly, that historically situated understandings reveal important exclusions from dominant sites of public space. Secondly, they point to the key role of what she calls "subaltern publics" within which excluded or minority members of society develop dispositions, identities and capacities which enable solidary forms of encounter and, should they wish it, a more confident and challenging entry into hegemonic pubic spaces which, in practice if not intention, remain persistently exclusive in terms of both process and outcome. Thirdly, and as a cautionary aside to overly inward approaches to the creation of "counter publics," Fraser reminds us of the dangers and challenges of creating separatist enclaves without the dispositions or capacities to engage with dominant publics and the wider social and political contexts that frame present realities and future possibilities.

Within the field of education, one of the most insightful and powerful writers who has taken forward the work of people like Maxine Greene, Hannah Arendt, and Nancy Fraser is Aaron Schutz. Formerly one of the very few strong advocates of public space in schools, Schutz is now sceptical, not of its desirability, but of our capacity to create spaces within which subaltern publics can negotiate and transform the pathways of power and so lead to genuinely democratic engagement and action. In his more recent writing, Schutz (2001) argues that the "challenge of 'difference' means we must...acknowledge the effects of power and oppression on individuals' ability to participate in even the smallest of communities....The creation of a single common public space may be fundamentally oppressive to those groups" (p. 294).

In some of my recent work I have been trying to explore the lived realities, as well as the theoretical resonance, of these concerns. Certainly, we need to ask (1) How can schools co-create, especially with disadvantaged young people, a range of spaces where they can develop their own identities and capacities? (2) How can we find out more about whether some safe spaces unwittingly foster dependency and others are more able to bridge to other groups and wider public spaces, cultures, and practices in schools? (3) How do we help dominant assumptions, cultures, and practices within schools to be more open to alternative perspectives and understandings? (4) How might we create circumstances, occasions, and on-going practices that help individuals and groups to re-see each other?

Certain kinds of public space, and the subaltern practices we need to make them vibrant and inclusive, can form part of a response to these questions, just as they can to Nick Stevenson's companion insistence that "in our short-term and disposable society there need to be spaces where young people can discuss what it means to live a good and meaningful life and the kinds of people they wish to become" (Stevenson, 2008, para. 8).

Despite its dangers and limitations, I do not want to give up on the possibility of inclusive public space: For me it is at the heart of what lived democracy is about. To give up on this is to give up on too much of what makes democracy worthwhile, on democracy as a communal process of becoming that honors and depends on its continuing capacity to listen attentively to difference, both for its vitality and its legitimacy as a life-enhancing, socially just way of life.

RADICAL EDUCATION, WHOLE SCHOOL MEETINGS, AND THE PUBLIC PRACTICE OF DEMOCRACY

Perhaps the best known example of strong commitment to public space within radical democratic traditions of education is the General School

Meeting developed at Summerhill School in England a radical democratic private school set up by A.S. Neill in the 1920s, still going today under his daughter, Zoë Readhead. At the meeting, matters of importance to do with the daily running and future development of Summerhill are raised, discussed, and decided together by the whole school, students, and staff. According to Neill (1968) its importance is crystal clear: "In my opinion, one weekly General School Meeting is of more value than a week's curriculum of school subjects" (p. 68). For other schools within the radical tradition of private education, the general meeting also held a place of preeminent importance, as, for example, in the work of John Aitkenhead at Kilquhanity House School, Castle Douglas, Scotland. It was also central to the disgracefully forgotten radical tradition of special education in the private sector as exemplified in the pioneering work of, for example, Homer Lane, David Wills and George Lyward, and in the public sector by Howard Case at Epping House School (see Weaver, 1989 for a good overview).

Within the public sector of mainstream education, examples are, unsurprisingly, even more sparse. In the U.S. the best researched and most sophisticated examples are to be found in the pioneering work of Lawrence Kohlberg (1980) and the Just Community Schools that flourished in the 1970s (Oser, Althof, & Higgins-D'Alessandro, A., 2008). In my own country, England, currently, the best known, though as I shall argue later, not the best developed, post-war example of something roughly equivalent to the general meeting is the Moot at Countesthorpe Community College, Leicestershire where from 1970 to 1985, despite the fact that it had a headteacher, all key decisions of policy and practice, including the appointment and payment of staff, were taken by the Moot. This was a communal gathering open to all in the school, including non-teaching staff and students. All attending had one vote each and anyone was entitled to call a Moot. With one or two significant exceptional occasions, student participation was minimal and often confined to a small number of sixth form/12th grade students and, for many teachers, the informal structures and very significant way in which students were involved on a day-to-day basis about their learning was what really mattered (Gordon, 1986).

Alex Bloom—Pioneer of Radical State/Public Education

In my view, the most outstanding example of a general meeting operating successfully within the radical publically funded tradition of education is to be found in the work of Alex Bloom at St George-in-the East Secondary School, Stepney, London (Fielding, 2005). In the decade between 1945 and 1955, Bloom's development of the whole school meeting brought together one of the most imaginative and most sophisticated unions of democratic learning and democratic governance England has ever seen. Its success depended in part on the values it strove to realize in all aspects of daily encounter, in part on the nature of the curriculum it provided, and in part on the depth and detail of its democratic structural hinterland. It is to each of these three aspects of its supporting context to which I now turn.

In marked contrast to the national norms of secondary schools at the time, Bloom (1948) described what he set out to build as "[a] consciously democratic community... without regimentation, without corporal punishment, without competition" (p. 121). The work of the school was guided by an orienting set of perspectives that became known as "Our Pattern." Fundamentally, this was about the eradication of fear and the creation of a context for human flourishing that valued the contribution of each person and worked hard to develop a creative and responsive school community worthy of the loyalty and commitment of all its students.

The majority of the formal curriculum was co-constructed within the context of thematic work culminating in a school conference in which work was celebrated and reviewed in both mixed-age and in form groups. The remainder of the curriculum was negotiated through mixed-age electives in which "children make up their own timetable." There was thus substantial emphasis both on continuity of relationships with a class teacher and on multi-faceted communal engagement with other students and staff. In addition, there was strong commitment to learning outside the physical confines of the school. Lastly, students' own evaluations of their curricular experience in both its broad and narrow senses was sought and acted on through weekly reviews in which each student commented on any aspect of learning and teaching they felt appropriate.

The formal democratic organization of the school was expressed through three core channels of work, comprising the staff panel, the pupil panel, and, at school level, the joint panel. The staff panel met every Monday at lunchtime and included all staff (i.e., about 10 people). The pupil panel was comprised of the head boy and head girl, their two deputies, and the secretary, all of whom were elected by students. It also included elected form reps. The panel met every Friday morning in school time and considered all school matters. There were reports from form reps and business sent by staff. It also appointed a range of pupil committees that took responsibility for running various aspects of school life. The joint panel met on the last Friday of the month. It was comprised of members of both staff and pupil panels and chairs of all pupil committees. Reports were given by a member of staff for the staff panel, by the head girl or head boy for the pupil panel, and by chairs of the various pupil committees. On the Monday following the joint panel meeting, there was a school council/school meeting presided over alternately by a member of staff and by a member of the pupil panel agreed at the previous full school meeting.

The School Meeting

Space does not allow a rich description of the conduct of a School Meeting (see Fielding, 2009 for a fuller account). Suffice to say here that it typically involved a framing of purposes and aspirations, both by Bloom and by the head boy/girl before each class offered a celebration of its learning. This was then followed by reflection and open dialogue between students and staff on any matter of concern or delight in the school. This would invariably challenge traditional hierarchies, with all ages and identities contributing before the proceedings were brought to a close by Bloom's affirmation of pride and joy in the work of young people.

Such practices and traditions take seriously the importance within a democratic society of creating a public space within which members of the community (in this case a secondary school of about 200 students and 10 staff) can make meaning of their work and their lives together in ways which are rigorous and respectful, challenging and caring, and utterly committed to a way of being that sees individuality and community as both the condition and purpose of living our lives well together.

Sixty years ago, in this small secondary school in one of the toughest and poorest areas of London, we saw glimpses of both the challenges and possibilities of developing a school meeting as an iconic democratic practice. Many of the proper and continuing concerns we have about the possibility of developing an inclusive public space can be interrogated and understood not only in the different strands of its main narratives, but also in the "petit ecrits," the little stories of subaltern spaces, exploratory practices, and felt egalitarian encounters that provide a necessary preliminary to the larger community conversation.

Thus, contemporary concerns that the language of participation hides manipulative or disciplinary intent are countered by explicit, public commitment to inclusive democratic values and practices. Worries that there is little opportunity or desire to develop and name peer identities are ameliorated by a hinterland of subaltern publics, inclusive practices, and person-centered relationships. Individual apprehension about speaking out is countered by the articulate solidarity of representing the views of others, not merely or only one's own, and by daily opportunity for dialogue and discussion. Dangers that adults use complex language and abstruse or boring topics to alienate, obscure, or dominate are countered by discourses and processes that elicit the engagement of all. Hectoring or admonitory uses of public space so typical of traditional schools is replaced by celebratory content chosen and articulated by students and confirmed by Bloom's closing remarks. Potential marginalization of student contributions is countered by traditions of democratic procedure that ensure parity of status and the insistent foregrounding of student experience. Subtly corrosive effects of the multiple, often covert, realities of power are, often and unpredictably, met by the spontaneous leveller of laughter or by Foucauldian parrhesiastic practices of fearlessness and risk taking (Foucault, 2001), in which individuals, known and respected within the school community, tell truth to power. Dangers of demagogic persuasiveness are met by the companion parrhesiastic interrogation of integrity by meeting participants through shared community knowledge of the fidelity between the speaker's words and deeds. Finally, the dangers of institutional inaction are countered by the explicitly stated, empirically matched commitment to shared responsibility for future action.

IN PRAISE OF REFIGURATIVE PRACTICE—
"MAKING SOMETHING THAT MIGHT BECOME THE
MEANS TO MAKING SOMETHING MORE"

One of the difficulties of valorizing the work of Alex Bloom and other pioneers of radical democratic education within state/public systems of schooling is the often remarked observation that their work did not survive them. While a full response merits a chapter in its own right, a preliminary engagement might include at least three broad points. Firstly, as William Morris (1968) reminds us, there can never be closure on the struggle for social justice and the development of a more creative, more humanly fulfilling society. We will inevitably and properly reflect on "[h]ow men (sic) fight and lose the battle, and the thing that they fought for comes about in spite of their defeat, and when it comes turns out not to be what they meant, and other men have to fight for what they meant under another name" (p. 53). Not only does the struggle continue, it does so in important part through radical traditions of democratic education that prefigure quite different realties to those dominating contemporary norms at the time.

Secondly, in addition to our reclamation and renewal of radical traditions of democratic education in our own countries and across the world, as advocates and chroniclers of radical education like Nigel Wright (1989) have argued, we need to be more committed to developing rich research knowledge that can provide us with, among other things, a more strategic understanding of how we might engage with and influence dominant systems of schooling.

Thirdly, and integrally linked to these first two desiderata, I wish to argue for the importance of prefigurative practice, both as a tradition of radical praxis worthy of renewed respect and development and as a key element in the development of a wider understanding of the nature and practice of education in and for radical participatory democracy.

"Some Changes Have to Start Now, Else There Is No Beginning for Us"

A key text of the New Left that subsequently influenced writers such as Wini Breines (1980) and, within the field of education, Roger Dale (1988), was a paper on prefigurative practice by the Gramscian scholar Carl Boggs. Boggs (1978) describes "prefigurative" as "the embodiment within the ongoing political practice of a movement, of those forms of social relations, decision making, culture and human experience that are the ultimate goal" (p. 100). One of the reasons practices like Neill's and Bloom's school meetings are powerful and important has to do with what one might call the existential integrity, the reciprocity of felt encounter that helps democracy transcend the limits of procedural justice and begin to open us up to the lived realities of the other as a person, not just a citizen or as a "learner." As I have argued earlier, for school meetings to work well, they must draw not just on the procedural machinery of democratic decision making, but also and as importantly on daily opportunities to explore the world together with a freshness and openness that exemplify the joys and responsibilities of democratic living and learning. This is why school meetings are iconic—they are a litmus test both of democratic aspiration and integrity.

Prefigurative practice is important because it unites transcendent longing with courage and resolution and the need to act as a means of knowing, learning, and living a radically different future now. It is about the need to "release the imagination of what could be. The effort to go beyond what we know now has to be part of our experience of what we might know" (Rowbotham, 1979, p. 147). For many 1970s feminists like Sheila Rowbotham (1979) it was not only about "making something which might become the means to making something more"; it was also driven by an insistence that "some changes have to start now else there is no beginning for us" (p. 140).

This insistence that we "release the imagination of what could be," this anticipation of future modes of being through processes and relations, not just structures, that exemplify and embody the viability and desirability of radical alternatives is one of the most important past and continuing contributions of the radical traditions of publically funded education to the furtherance of democracy. Thus, Roger Dale (1988) argued:

> The more radical, recent and professionally initiated concepts of comprehensive education ... contain ... a view of education's role in social change which sees it as prefigurative. That is to say, rather than waiting until all the necessary social engineering has been done, and the planned widespread social change brought about, this approach to social change suggests that education through its processes, the experiences it offers, and the expectations it makes, should prefigure, in microcosm, the more equal, just and fulfilling so-

ciety that the originations of comprehensivism aimed to bring about. Schools should not merely reflect the world of which they are a part, but be critical of it, and show in their own processes that its shortcomings are not inevitable, but can be changed. They aim to show that society can be characterized by communal as well as individual values, that all people merit equal treatment and equal dignity, that academic ability is not the only measure of a person, that racism and sexism are neither inevitable not acceptable. (p. 17)

Utopian Realism—Creating the Future Now

Perhaps the most compelling attraction of prefigurative practice is its utopian realism, its insistence both on the necessity of a radical break with the present and its companion commitment to a transitional practice that enables significant aspects of future ways of being to happen now, or, in the syndicalist phrase, "to build a new world in the shell of the old." Perhaps its most enduring challenges rest on its capacity to distance itself, on the one hand, from the unwitting or disingenuous accommodations of humane reformism that, in Quintin Hoare's incisive words, "has failed to do more than salvage a minority from being broken by the system" (Hoare, 1965, p. 47) and, on the other hand, from the charge of exotic irrelevance. These are matters I pursue at length elsewhere (see Fielding & Moss, 2011) arguing for twelve dimensions of a prefigurative practice of democratic state education, three of which are briefly considered below.

The first concerns the need for profound change. At a time when there is much talk about innovation, step change, 21st century thinking, and other exhortations to transgress boundaries and create new opportunities for consumption, it is important to underscore the ideological and actual distance between prefigurative practice and what, for example, the English "innovation unit" calls "next practice." While next practice often has much to recommend it, what it currently does not do is seriously challenge the deep presumptions of its host society. Prefigurative practice is not about ameliorative social and political processes or faddish articulations of extended consumerism that characterizes much of the resurgence of contemporary student voice. While radical change can be cumulative and incremental advocacy, it has also to address and challenge what Roberto Unger (1998), in his description of "democratic experimentalism" calls "the basic arrangements of a society" (pp. 18–19), not just its surface features or relational conventions.

The second dimension concerns the need for strategy. Without wider strategic engagement, whether through social movements, political alliances, or local, regional, national, and international networks, prefigurative practice is unlikely either to be successful in keeping the formal and informal intrusions of the status quo at bay or to learn from solidary organizations and movements and thus sustain the necessary processes of learning how to live and work differently, how to enable the future to grow in the present.

Thirdly, in order to fulfill its emancipatory potential, prefigurative practice must illustrate the grounded possibility of doing things significantly differently. Counter-hegemonic institutional practices and aspirations—prefigurative practices—are likely to have pride of place in any radical strategy because they have the power of presence, the irrefutability of contemporary reality, that gives the lie to the familiar fabrications of "there is no alternative." When we actually encounter convincing radical alternatives, it is in large part their brute reality, their enacted denial of injustice and inhumanity, and their capacity to live out a more fulfilling, more generous view of human flourishing that in turn moves us to think and act differently.

NEW BEGINNINGS AND RADICAL CONTINUITIES

There are, of course, many things we might fruitfully do to develop convincing, sustainable, radical democratic alternatives to an increasingly sophisticated and resourceful status quo. I have argued, firstly, that we need to work within alternative, participatory traditions of democracy which offer different, more inspiring, more demanding and more humanly fulfilling possibilities of what it means to live and learn democracy than neoliberal, market-led models allow. I have also suggested that within these alternative traditions there is an important recognition of public space as a key site, both of individual identity and of democratic ways of living and learning together and that the practice of whole school meetings offers a particularly important site for their development.

My valorization of prefigurative practice is a small contribution to the traditions of utopian realism that currently seem to me to be among the most promising intellectual and practical resources at our disposal within the fields of education and democratic renewal. Not only do these traditions excite our imagination, they urge us to act in ways that affirm the practical possibility of a more just, more creative, more humanly fulfilling way of being and becoming in the world. They insist, as Gandhi did, that "You must be the change you want to see in the world." They insist, as Sheila Rowbotham (1979) did, that "some changes have to start now else there is no beginning for us" (p. 140). But they also insist that for those beginnings to flourish, for us to sustain and develop our daily enactment of being the change we wish to see in the world, we must ally passionate commitment with strategic acumen. Without wider strategic engagement, whether through social movements, political alliances, or local, regional, national, and international networks, prefigurative practice is unlikely either to be successful in keeping the formal and informal intrusions of the status quo at bay or to learn from solidary organizations and movements and thus sustain the necessary processes of learning how to live and work differently, how to enable the future to grow in the present.

Finally, we must be mindful of Russell Jacoby's warning that "society has lost its memory, and with it, its mind. The inability or refusal to think back takes its toll in the inability to think" (Jacoby, 1997, pp. 3–4). A preeminently important strand of our advocacy must argue strongly for the necessity, not just of history, but of history's pluralities, for a radical chosen genealogy. The ahistorical presumptions of neoliberalism are a consequence both of its millennial arrogance and its fearful insistence on denying the possibility of alternative ways of being. The practices we prefigure are also practices rooted in a chosen past whose radical continuities we wish to explore celebrate and extend together.

REFERENCES

Bloom, A.A. (1948). Notes on a school community. *New Era, 29*(6), 120–121.

Boggs, C. (1978). Marxism, prefigurative communism, and the problem of workers' control. *Radical America, 12*(1), 99–122.

Breines, W. (1980). Community and organization: The new left and Michels' "iron law." *Social Problems, 27*(4), 419–429.

Dale, R. (1988, April). *Comprehensive education.* Paper presented at the Madrid Conference, Madrid.

Dewey, J. (1916). *Democracy and education.* New York, NY: The Freedom Press.

Fielding, M. (1999). Radical collegiality: Affirming teaching as an inclusive professional practice. *Australian Educational Researcher, 26*(2), 1–34.

Fielding, M. (2005). Alex Bloom: Pioneer of radical state education. *Forum, 47*(2), 114–134.

Fielding, M. (2009). Public space and educational leadership: Reclaiming and renewing our radical traditions. *Educational Management Administration & Leadership, 37*(4), 497–521.

Fielding, M., & Moss, P. (2011). *Radical education and the common school: A democratic alternative.* Abingdon, UK: Routledge.

Foucault, M. (2001). *Fearless speech,* (J. Pearson, Ed.). Los Angeles, CA: Semiotext(e).

Fraser, N. (1997). *Justice interruptus: Critical reflections on the 'postsocialist' condition.* London, UK: Routledge.

Gordon, T. (1986). *Democracy in one school? Progressive education and restructuring.* London, UK: Falmer Press.

Greene, M. (1982). Public education and the public space. *Educational Researcher, 11*(6), 4–9.

Greene, M. (2000). Lived spaces, shared spaces, public spaces. In L. Weiss & M. Fine (Eds.), *Construction sites: Excavating race, class, and gender among urban youth* (pp. 293–303). New York, NY: Teachers College Press.

Hoare, Q. (1965). Education: Programmes and men. *New Left Review, 1*(32), 40–52.

Jacoby, R. (1997). Revisiting 'social amnesia.' *Society, 35*(1), 58–60.

Kohlberg, L. (1980). High school democracy and educating for a just society. In R. L. Mosher (Ed.), *Moral education: A first generation of research and development* (pp. 20–57). New York, NY: Praeger.

Macmurray, J. (1961). *Persons in relation.* London, UK: Faber.

Morris, W. (1968). *Three works by William Morris.* London, UK: Lawrence & Wishart.

Neill, A.S. (1968). *Summerhill.* Harmondsworth, UK: Penguin.

Oser, F., Althof, W., & Higgins-D'Alessandro, A. (2008). The just community approach to moral education: System change or individual change? *Journal of Moral Education, 37*(3), 395–415.

Rowbotham, S. (1979). The women's movement and organizing for socialism. In S. Rowbotham, L. Segal, & H. Wainwright (Eds.), *Beyond the fragments: Feminism and the making of socialism* (pp. 121–155). London, UK: Merlin Press.

Schutz, A. (2001). John Dewey's conundrum: Can democratic schools empower? *Teachers College Record, 103*(2), 267–302.

Stevenson, N. (2008). Living in 'x factor' Britain: Neoliberalism and 'educated publics.' *Soundings.* Retrieved from http://www.lwbooks.co.uk/journals/soundings/class_and_culture/stevenson.html

Unger, R.M. (1998). *Democracy realized.* London, UK: Verso.

Weaver, A. (1989). Democratic practice in education: A historical perspective. In C. Harber & R. Meighan (Eds.), *The democratic school: Educational management in the practice of democracy* (pp. 83–91). Ticknall, UK: Education Now Books.

White, S. (2008). The emerging politics of republican democracy. In S. White & D. Leighton (Eds.), *Building a citizen democracy* (pp. 7–22). London, UK: Lawrence & Wishart.

Woods, P.A. (2005). *Democratic leadership in education.* London: Paul Chapman.

Wright, N. (1989). *Assessing radical education: A critical review of the radical movement in English schooling 1960–1980.* Milton Keynes, UK: Open University Press.

CHAPTER 3

EDUCATION IN AND FOR DEMOCRACY

Conceptions of Schooling and Student Voice

Brenda J. McMahon

ABSTRACT

Contrasting notions of democracy and educational leadership can be linked to beliefs about student engagement and the roles of student voice in schools. Tensions exist between identity as defined by students and by the schools they attend. They are also present in the dichotomy between voices that educational institutions allow, respect, and/or listen to or at least do not castigate and the voices that are punished by and in them. Keeping in mind that legitimized voice in schools has long been in the domain of holders of power, in this chapter, I draw links between notions of democracy and student voice. Student voice in schools preparing students *for* democracy is contrasted with student voice in schools existing at least to some extent *in* or *as* democracy.

Toni Morrison's (1987) *Beloved* highlights the importance of names as symbols of identity. The novel, set in a time and place of questionable democ-

Student Engagement in Urban Schools, pages 29–48
Copyright © 2012 by Information Age Publishing
All rights of reproduction in any form reserved.

racy, is based on a historical incident following the passage of the Fugitive Slave Laws in the United States. In *Beloved,* names represent either obscurity or identity, freedom, strength, and individuality. I am haunted by the choice of the name Schoolteacher for the character who enslaves and abuses the African American people. The relationship of schoolteachers to students is shown when one minor character dares to use his voice: "Clever... [answered], but schoolteacher beat him anyway to show him that definitions belong to the definers—not the defined" (Morrison, 1991, p. 234). This characterization is troubling precisely because it captures a sense of the silencing of student voices within the undemocratic configurations of schools.

Education—or more specifically schooling—is frequently under attack for not achieving desired results. Although meanings of the desirable vary with the definer, successive governments attempt to respond to charges from certain quarters that schools are failing to graduate literate, numerate, productive citizens. Without seriously attending to questions of the meanings of democracy, the purposes of education, or education according to whom, and for whom, massive reforms have been implemented in Canada, the United States, and England. Research conducted in all three of these countries (Leithwood, Fullan, & Watson, 2003; MacKinnon, 2001; Nieto, 2000; Taylor, 2001) reports that the overt goals of these reforms have not been realized. In spite of being touted as the solution to promote excellence, success, and high achievement for all students, they have had the opposite effect (Gillborn & Youdell, 2000; Haberman, 2003, 2004; King, 2004). Across urban school districts, this failure exists in the form of disproportionate numbers of students from less advantaged and diverse student populations (Dei & Karunmanchery, 2001; Gillborn & Youdell, 2000; Haberman, 2003).

Educational reforms and their attendant theories and practices in North America are embedded within conceptions of democracy that are based on a market economy. The narrow visions of democracy underlying these reforms can be categorized as "minimalist, protectionist and marginalist" (Portelli & Solomon, 2001, p. 17). They see society as static and schools as sites to perpetuate compliance and prepare students to fit in to a world as it exists. Adopting top-down and paradoxically named transformational leadership models (Bush, 2003; Leithwood, Jantzi & Steinbach, 1999; Starratt, 2004), schools prepare students for a deferred version of democracy where meaningful student voice is decidedly absent. These models assume not only that formal leaders have *a* moral vision but that they have *the* moral vision into which the school community needs to be transformed.

This is in stark contrast to emancipatory (Corson, 2000; Ryan, 2003), transformative (Anderson, 2004; Foster, 1986), and polyfocal (McMahon & Armstrong, 2006) leadership paradigms that cohere with education *as* or *in* democracy. These models are imbued with beliefs that educational leaders are responsible for facilitating the active participation of all members of the school community in decisions impacting on the organization, structure, and operation of schools. They are also informed by conceptions of critical pedagogy (Fernandez-Balboa, 1993; Freire, 1998; Martin, 1992) that include action for democratic transformation. Notions of democratic schooling based on these ideals of leadership and pedagogy are informed by conceptions of democracy as "participatory, public, and critical" (Portelli & Solomon, 2001, p. 17). This understanding of democracy sees society as contested and changing and schools as sites for democratic transformation where formal leaders facilitate the creation of space and means through which democratic processes are enacted.

Contrasting notions of democracy and educational leadership can be linked to beliefs about student engagement and the roles of student voice in schools. Voice can be configured as discourse, encompassing one's thoughts, beliefs, values, talk, actions, and attitudes (Armstrong & McMahon, 2004). Related to this and extending beyond discourse, voice can also be seen as being, answering questions of identity such as "who am I?" and "who defines me?" Tensions exist between identity as defined by students and by the schools they attend. They are also present in the dichotomy between voices that educational institutions allow, respect, and/or listen to or at least do not castigate and the voices that are punished by and in them. Keeping in mind that legitimized voice in schools has long been in the domain of holders of power, in this chapter, I draw links between notions of democracy and student voice. Student voice in schools preparing students *for* democracy is contrasted with student voice in schools existing at least to some extent *in* or *as* democracy.

POLICY CONTEXTS OF SCHOOLING FOR DEMOCRACY

Paradigms grounded in education *for* democracy envision the purpose of schooling as primarily for cultural capital (Portelli & Solomon, 2001). Within this worldview, schools serve to maintain, reproduce, and perpetuate existing social inequities (Boyd, 1996; Solomon, 1992). Because they are located within narrow definitions of democracy, the results are contrary to articulations that public education systems serve as vehicles for the attainment of equity. Instead as mirrors of the economic, political, and ideological stratifications of the society in which they exist, by normalizing and idealizing White, middle class, male, heterosexual experiences and worldviews, schools perpetuate the inequities of the larger society that is "structured by class and status, as well as by race, ethnicity, gender, and sexual orientation" (Marshall & Rossman, 1999, p. 6). Schooling for cultural capital identifies it as belonging to members of the dominant groups. As Ryan

(2006) contends, the cultural capital valued by and in schools is based within a specific class, race, gender, and sexual orientation. As a result, students whose life experiences are outside of those thought to be desirable "are routinely excluded from learning activities because they do not bring to school the same kinds of language and interaction skills that are required in the classroom context" (Ryan, 2006, p. 7). By privileging the knowledges and experiences of the already advantaged over others, this education *for* democracy configures society as a static entity into which students must fit and is consistent with conservative or traditional notions of student engagement that equate engagement with behavioral manifestations involved in doing the work of schooling (McMahon & Portelli, 2004).

Adopting this perspective, educational institutions focus on preparing students for two functions; firstly, as workers for global market economies and secondly, as citizens for life in democratic societies. The motivation and ideology behind the reforms are similar across Canada, the United States and England. As one example of this, the Ontario Ministry of Education is now under the umbrella of the Ontario Ministry of Education and Training. The addition of training to the educational mandate provides a clear indication of its emphasis on job readiness schooling. As such, the Ministry's vision of education is articulated as a "goal . . . to help develop the intellectual, emotional and physical potential of our children and young adults so they become the best contributing citizens they can be" (Ontario Ministry of Education, 2004, p. 2). Although the term contributing is ambiguous, schools are structured to produce job-ready graduates. In addition to competency in literacy, numeracy, physical health, and music and arts education, the onus is on the student to "reach the highest level of achievement that his or her ability and willingness to work hard will permit" (Ontario Ministry of Education, 2004, p. 2). Although students are also expected to "appreciate the rights and obligations of good citizenship and learn about character values" (p. 2), the meanings of good citizenship and character are not deconstructed (Ontario Ministry of Education, 2004). These conceptions of student engagement are consistent with Steinberg's (1996) claims that "engaged students attend their classes, try reasonably hard to do well in them, complete the homework they are assigned, and don't cheat" (p. 67).

A brief overview of the Ontario Ministry of Education's policy website provides a clear although unarticulated understanding of the ministry's conceptions of the goals and purposes of schooling, the teaching/learning process, and the role of educators, parents, and students within educational communities. Buried near the bottom of listed policies is Antiracism and Ethnocultural Equity in Schools. Of greater predominance are a myriad of documents including Violence Free Schools Policy, Provincial Model for a Local Police/School board Protocol, Trillium List of approved textbooks,

OSS Program and Diploma Requirements, and Who Is Responsible for Your Child's Education? This last policy document states that students are to be compliant, which is demonstrated by "attending classes and taking examinations; and exercising self-discipline and behaving courteously toward their teachers and their fellow students" (Ontario Ministry of Education, 2006, 'Students' section). The sole responsibility that parents are accorded is to "ensure their children attend school...compulsory between the ages of 6 and 16" (Ontario Ministry of Education, 2006, 'Parents' section).

As a consequence of educational reforms in Ontario, King (2004) reported that 49% of secondary school students were no longer able to graduate within the requisite four-year timeframe, if at all. Specifically, King's research found that at the end of their third year, within this regime only 42% of students had earned their full 24 credits, 16.9% had earned 23 credits, 8.9% had earned 22 credits, 5.4% had earned 21 credits, and 26.4% had earned 20 credits or less. As a response to these statistics, and without examining their ideological, racial, and economic underpinnings, or consulting with the students who comprise the population of concern, the province launched subsequent addenda variously called "Pathways to Success," "Success for All," and "Choices for Success" (Ontario Ministry of Education, 2004). Under the guise of choice and student autonomy, this scheme camouflaged another sorting and slotting venue through which the holders of power continued to determine school curriculum and potential life chances for marginalized students. Ministry and school board personnel define schools and consequently students' experiences through the creation and implementation of policies and procedures which, by guiding certain students into service sector jobs, function to reinforce existing hegemonic structures.

A Ministry communiqué celebrating the success of these educational reforms reported that 60.5% of secondary school students had currently completed 16 credits at the end of their second year (Ontario Ministry of Education, 2006). This surreptitious shift in data collection from grade 11 results in 2004, to grade ten results in 2006, meant that any accurate comparison of student credit accumulation within this initiative was impossible.

Even if it were possible to compare these results, it is difficult to fathom how a failure rate of approximately 40% is indicative of an educational system's moral obligation to all students within its care. These numbers are even more troubling when the data are deconstructed, finding that for Black students, high school graduation rate remains at 60% (Dei, Holmes, Mazzuca, McIsaac, & Campbell, 1997; McMahon & Armstrong, 2003; Solomon & Palmer, 2006). Research also finds that Black students born in Canada and elsewhere have similar levels of student achievement (Brown & Sinay, 2008). Aboriginal students who identify as 1st Nations have a high school graduation rate of 50% when living off reserve, and 40% when living on reserves (Richards, 2008).

STUDENT VOICE

In Ontario and other contexts, student voice is noticeably absent from academic research, practice, and policy formation. The utilization of dominant perspectives of knowledge and knowledge creation "helps create a great divide between those who regularly produce specialized forms of knowledge and those who are supposed to be informed by that knowledge" (Gitlin & Russell, 1994, p. 184). Furthermore, as Seidman (1998) contends, within educational contexts in particular, even though there is an abundance of research conducted on schooling in North America, "little of it is based on studies involving the perspective of students [etc.] ... whose individual and collective experience constitutes schooling" (p. 4). Student voice is considered legitimate when it reinforces compliance with school structures and systems or more often is ignored. Like "Clever" in Morrison's *Beloved*, students are not considered creators of school policies, procedures, and reform initiatives but instead are constructed as "products of the school system" (Taylor, 2001, p. 243). Democratic participation for students is limited to elections held to nominate various student council representatives who are relegated duties at the discretion of the school administration, such as raising funds or negotiating special dress up days, carnivals, or dances. The school administration to an extent controls who is able to seek office as these positions are generally limited to students who attain a certain grade point average. As Glass (2005) reports "students' identities are conformed to norms and standards that favour the status quo and make them more or less like anybody else of their race, class, gender, or abilities" (p. 84). Furthermore, within this deferred notion of democracy, even the students' elected representatives are not given voice in any meaningful decisions in the life of a school such as curriculum, pedagogy, hiring, and promotion. Rather than existing as forums for participatory democracy, "the social and academic practices of public schools mostly develop forms of identity that undercut the kind of self-understanding required for critical democratic citizenship" (Glass, 2005, p. 84).

From this narrow perspective of democracy, positive student voice is framed as compliant, furthering the school's agenda and confined to "suggesting that school reform will be more successful if students participate" (Mitra, 2005, p. 521). Other research finds this notion of student voice currently existing in schools, and contends that when student voice is solicited it "is sought primarily through insistent imperatives of accountability rather than enduring commitments to democratic agency" (Fielding, 2001,

p. 123). Within this context, student engagement is understood primarily in conservative or traditional terms and becomes "almost exclusively identified with a certain conception of academic achievement or a process identifiable by behavioral traits and/or observable psychological dispositions" (McMahon & Portelli, 2004, p. 62).

Schools operating within limiting and deferred definitions of democracy serve to either silence and make invisible or magnify and emphasize those voices which do not appear to support existing hegemonic structures. When asked, urban students identify schools as sites where they are muzzled and their concerns not taken seriously (Dei, 1996; McMahon & Armstrong, 2003; Solomon, 1992). Silencing venues include: irrelevant curriculum, inconsistency in the application of school rules between students and teachers as well as among students from different groups; having no say in school policies and procedures which impact on them; and being treated as criminal and deviant (McMahon & Armstrong, 2003).

METHODOLOGY

In this chapter I enrich relevant literature on student engagement and voice with information from participants' narratives of their experiences of marginalization and inclusion within educational institutions. Data were derived from a larger study (McMahon, 2004) which sought to understand how students who have encountered both academic success and failure made sense of their lived experiences. In order to gain an understanding of their lived journeys, I analyzed responses and obtained information that was "richly descriptive" (Merriam, 1998, p. 8), I conducted in-depth audio-taped interviews using semi-structured questions as a means of "understanding the experience of other people and the meaning they make of that experience" (Seidman, 1998, p. 3). This was consistent with Clandinin and Connelly's (1994) contention that "experience, in this view, is the stories people live. People live stories, and in the telling of them reaffirm them, modify them, and create new ones" (p. 415). As McCabe, Capron, and Peterson (1991) suggest, "Narrative and memory have a complicated relationship" (p. 137). The fact that during these interviews adults were reflecting on their experiences both as adults and as adolescents raises a question of voice identified by Clandinin and Connelly (1994) with their claim that "the stories we tell of our experience change over time. An adult person speaking of her experience as a child . . . for the most part, expresses a current voice rather than a historical voice" (p. 424). Although it was the voice of the student experiencing both academic success and failure that I was seeking to understand, it is only through the lens of their later success that I was able to access this information.

In order to access potential participants who fit this criterion, I contacted directors of transitional and articulation programs that admit students into university preliminary programs who are believed to have the potential and who have not yet consistently demonstrated the knowledge, skills, and/or self-confidence required for successful completion of university curriculum. Participants were drawn from both a university transitional program and a college/university articulation program in a large metropolitan center in Ontario. To assure anonymity, potential respondents were contacted through a blind mailing sent out by the transitional or articulation program they had attended. They were invited to contact me with questions about the study and/or to arrange to be interviewed. Following a series of telephone conversations and/or email correspondences, each respondent was interviewed for between 60 and 120 minutes in order to establish a climate of trust and to understand experiences with educational institutions as they reflected on them. In addition, I conducted and transcribed follow-up discussions of between 30 and 60 minutes with respondents for purposes of clarification and of obtaining further information. Participants' confidentiality was assured and maintained throughout the process.

For the purposes of this discussion I focused on eight adults registered in university programs who had successfully completed either a transitional or an articulation program. The general question relevant to this discussion sought to identify how student voice was enacted or silenced within schools. In order to protect the identities of the participants, the following pseudonyms are used throughout this discussion: Anthony, Barbara, Carol, Deanna, Elaine, Frank, Greg, and Jennifer.

FINDINGS AND DISCUSSION

The participants recounted instances of silencing and of having a voice within three overlapping and at times competing spheres: the overt curriculum, the covert curriculum, and identity. The overt curriculum consists of formal curricular documents, the texts and content of what is taught in schools. The covert curriculum is comprised of all other facets of schooling, including written and unwritten policies and procedures. Identity as it is used here encompasses both how students are defined and who has power to define them.

Student Silence and Schooling for Democracy

Analysis of the formal curriculum of schools consistently demonstrates that the voices of marginalized students are decidedly absent. This is particularly true of core curriculum in academic streams where Eurocentric notions determine what constitutes valid and invalid knowledge and in doing so replicate racial, cultural and class inequities (Dei & Karumanchery, 2001). Through meaningless and irrelevant curriculum, instead of being equitable sites which mitigate risk, schools further alienate students who are not members of dominant groups.

These contentions were supported by the participants in the study. For example, Anthony said,

> I was looking for [Black] Canadian role models.... It would have given me identity. It would have made me feel that I could be part of the system knowing that there were other Black professionals who were part of the system and they struggled and they're there now.

Similarly Frank, who was successful in university, speculated that one reason he quit school in grade 10 was that "everything in school just seemed irrelevant. I never saw myself going on to university and so I thought, 'why do I have to know any of this?'"

The expectation in schools is that to be seen as academic, students are to "engage" in and with whatever curriculum is prescribed. Rather than expanding notions of who the school configures as academic, in an attempt to be relevant, reform "success" initiatives are based on primarily preparing students for service sector employment. Ruddock and Flutter (2000) challenge similar conceptions of relevant curricula that continue to be based on adult rather than student views of what is meaningful. Extending beyond the overt curriculum, students' voices are silenced in much more dangerous ways. As Glass (2005) reports, students "who cannot or will not conform are marginalized into nobodies, people not expected to contribute to the school and community, to be intelligent or know much of value, or to be articulate or say much that anybody wants to hear" (p. 83). Although theorists such as Mitra (2006) state that "student voice can consist of youth sharing their opinions of problems and potential solutions" (p. 459), within deferred conceptions of democracy students who are configured as "school failures" are either highly visible if they were seen as not fitting in to the school agenda or are rendered invisible.

The latter was the case in Carol's grade nine experiences of disengagement when, in spite of being two years younger than the legal age to leave school, she said, "I don't know if anyone even paid attention, but I went to half of Grade 9 and dropped out and worked full-time." Of teachers and administrators she suggested, "They could have noticed that I wasn't showing up and even pulled me aside and 'say you know, you haven't been here for two weeks and now you show up today, what's going on?'" Jennifer also experienced this callousness when an upheaval in her home life had repercussions for her academic performance. Her feelings about this were evident when she said, "If you see a kid going from honor roll down to 30% you would think that they would notice something and nobody, counselors nobody did anything." The experience of being devalued and made to disappear was echoed by Deanna, who in high school was a member of a "Section 19"[1] class. Isolated from the rest of the student population, these students who live in group homes are sometimes simply warehoused in school classrooms or portables and the concept of engagement is generally believed to be irrelevant. Because they are perceived as problem students, unlikely to attend post-secondary academic institutions, even less attention is paid to their education and more to control of behavior than is the case with students who are believed to be part of the normal school community. She recalled one of the teachers in this program: "You could smell alcohol on him and it was so obvious that the teachers knew—the whole school knew and there's no way for them not to know... [and] the administration didn't get rid of him."

Policies that are derived from perspectives that objectify students, although they may be well-intended, are unsuccessful because they lack an understanding of the lives of students (Anderson & Herr, 1993). Rather than looking within to draw on the strengths and needs of their students, urban schools are inundated with what Haberman (2004) calls "projectitis." Governments and central office bureaucracies in charge of urban school districts call on schools to implement one-size-fits-all curricula while "administrators are pressured to try out new programs against drugs, violence, gangs, smoking, sex, etc." (p. 3). These initiatives disservice students in multiple ways, as experienced teachers know that they do not have to take curricula initiatives seriously because they will pass when the next "flavor of the month" comes through. More importantly, negative portrayals of marginalized students as non-academic and violent are reinforced by and in schools. Attention is thus diverted away from institutional and societal factors by blaming students and their families for the compounding effects of racism and poverty on their lives (Books, 1998).

As an example of being made visible as Black and poor, Elaine recalled how her grade nine principal stigmatized her. "He knew the area I was coming from and I think he believed.... You're supposed to not come to school. You're supposed to not want anything. He basically pigeonholed me and didn't give me any encouragement." At the same time, in attempting to gain control where they have none, urban students become inadvertently complicit in negative depictions of themselves (Anderson & Herr, 1993; McMahon & Armstrong, 2003). As Ruddick and Demetriou (2003) report,

> [F]rom an early age in school young people are capable of insightful and constructive analysis of social institutions and if their insights are not harnessed

in support of their own learning then they will use them strategically to avoid learning in school and conspire unwittingly in their own underachievement. (p. 276)

As a response to not seeing themselves represented in the overt or covert curriculum of schools, students often "act out" as in an attempt "to force their visibility onto the consciousness of institutions that fails to 'see' them" (Anderson & Herr, 1993, p. 59).

Anthony recounted his early high school encounters with school personnel as highly visible and decidedly negative. "I felt like I was always targeted, especially by vice-principals, principals, and teachers." This was magnified by external societal hegemonic structures. "It's every day, day-to-day people and how they treat young, especially young Black adolescents are the most targeted. To be young, Black and 16, you are a target, 24 hours a day, 7 days a week." This stereotyping serves to further exacerbate the consequences of glaring failures to incorporate student input in educational decision making. Even for school leaders who are concerned with issues of safety and control, Freire (1998) contends that "true discipline does not exist in the muteness of those who have been silenced but in the stirrings of those who have been challenged, in the doubts of those who have been prodded, and in the hopes of those who have been awakened" (p. 86). His observations are inconsistent with theories and practices of education that are configured to prepare students *for* democracy. They are consistent, on the other hand, with educational praxis *in* or *as* democracy.

Student Voice and Schooling As and In Democracy

Contrary to education conceived within democratic paradigms that are passive and deferred, Glass (2005) contends that "[d]emocratic citizenship does not simply prepare students for a future citizenship, but rather builds critical citizenship into the social and academic practices of the school" (p. 86). Education that can be defined as being *as* or *in* democracy is based on beliefs about the evolving nature of democracy that envision it as a way of life as opposed to merely a form of government (Portelli & Solomon, 2001). The primary purpose of education within this paradigm is democratic transformation. Integral to this vision of democracy in education, is the need to address inequities arising from dominant ideologies which exist in the current curriculum, policies, practices, and structures of schooling. It is by acting to reverse these injustices that "democratic education directly struggles to transform the inequities in the immediacy of everyday life in schools" (Glass, 2005, p. 86).

An emphasis on struggle is significant in that the evolution of democratic processes is often uncomfortable and conflicted from individual, organizational, or institutional perspectives. Any ensuing discomfort is however necessary if educational theorists and practitioners are serious about their espoused commitments to democracy. In the words of Frederick Douglass (1849/1991),

> Those who profess to favour freedom and yet depreciate agitation, are people who want crops without ploughing the ground; they want rain without thunder and lightning; they want the ocean without the roar of its many waters. The struggle may be a moral one, or it may be a physical one, or it may be both. But it must be a struggle. Power concedes nothing without a demand; it never has and it never will. (n.p.)

Educational leaders' responsibility for providing the spaces and facilitating processes that involve the students in dialogue and action for change includes realizing the potential that students have "for contributing their opinions on a variety of levels, including sharing their views on problems and potential solutions in their schools" (Mitra, 2003, p. 289). Education in and as democracy is not reserved for the students who are already seen as academic and cultural leaders being given opportunities to mentor those from 'poorer' communities. Rather, it involves all students in challenging and reconstructing the very curriculum, policies, practices, and structures of schooling which impact on their lives. Breault (2003) contends that in order for schools to generate meaningful democratic change, educators "need to recognize their institutions and attitudes as oppressive and learn to see themselves as potential oppressors rather than as beneficiaries of a pre-existing, inevitable system" (p. 2). Student engagement in this context is aligned with democratic transformation and is experienced as "a multi-faceted phenomenon, engagement is present in the iterations that emerge as a result of the dialectical processes between teachers and students and the differing patterns that evolve out of transformational actions and interactions" (McMahon & Portelli, 2004, p. 70).

At the curricular level, this translates into action that requires that educators and students engage in the enactment of curriculum that is relevant and meaningful to their lives and their lived experiences. Reporting on one of the sites that the participants in the study attended, Allen (1996) claims that one of its strengths is that "the course content is specially selected to fit the multi-cultural orientation of the [Transitional Year Program] TYP and the diversity of backgrounds of the students" (p. 244).

The respondents commented on the curricular differences between this type of environment and traditional schools. Anthony stated, "I just love knowledge. I like to learn. Especially being within this environment that I am right now there are so many things." Likewise, Barbara reflected, "I loved the books we were being asked to read and I wanted to talk about them and I wanted to be involved." Carol recalled that one of the things she most enjoys about university is "the actual things we talk about in that class, and I learn in that class. I think I actually apply them to my life." These comments were juxtaposed with others that emphasize struggles with formal curriculum that exposes existing hegemonic structures. Anthony described his encounters with investigations into the realities of competing societal forces:

> Sometimes what you learn really pisses you off and you think that 'this is the way things are going. This is what governments are doing.' But it's politics and economics and you have to deal with it and learn as much as you can and just go with it.

These reports support Saul's (2005) findings that identify being granted the license to be involved in their own learning or the freedom to speak as a motivating factor in student learning.

Mitra (2003, 2006) identifies three purposes served by implementing democratic processes in schools which involve students and encompass both overt and covert curriculum. Each of these can be seen as components of education for democratic transformation where "engagement is not viewed simply as a matter of techniques, strategies or behaviors"; rather, "engagement is realized in the processes and relationships within which learning for democratic reconstruction transpires" (McMahon & Portelli, 2004, p. 70). Firstly, they "help re-engage alienated students by providing them with a stronger sense of ownership in their schools" (Mitra, 2003, p. 290). Secondly, involving students in the identification of "school problems and possible solutions reminds teachers and administrators that students possess unique knowledge and perspectives about their schools that adults cannot fully replicate without this partnership" (Mitra, 2006, p. 459). Thirdly, through the process of "involving students—and particularly students failing subjects or rarely attending school—school personnel cannot easily shift the blame of failure onto students" (Mitra, 2006, p. 459). The enactment of democratic processes cannot be realized in the absence of educators who respect their students as learners.

Participants in the study all recalled teachers and administrators who treated them as having strengths and abilities as opposed to deficits and as partners in the learning process. Deanne encountered a teacher who told her about the transitional program that would enable her to attend university in spite of receiving very low marks in high school. Similarly, Elaine found someone she experienced as a different type of secondary school administrator. She said she was shocked when, in her words,

> I went for an interview to go to the school. The principal was kind and encouraged me ... it was refreshing. They encouraged me to come to school. They noticed me and said, 'You're 18 years old and have 3 credits so it's going to be an uphill climb.'

This understanding of students was informed by high expectations. Barbara expressed admiration for one professor: "He was so helpful, he was so kind and considerate and gracious. I was just so grateful for people like him who saw something in me and had faith in me, and it was people like him who made me think I could do this." Similarly, according to Frank, "I would go to some professors after class and meet with them and I became really engaged in the papers that I wrote." Likewise, Anthony described his experience with educators who supported him:

> They were very good, vice-principals, guidance counselors, teachers. It seemed like there was a strong community of teachers ... that all teachers were on the same page when it came to me. Everyone knew 'he's trying to do something.' Most important of all, everyone treated me with respect.

Although all of the respondents support Saul's (2005) findings on the importance of positive relationships with educators and a sense of belonging, they exemplify Douglass' observations of change and are not realized in interpersonal or intrapersonal environments free form tensions and struggle.

Jennifer recalled the anger she felt generated her increased awareness within the learning environment as she reflected, "Sometimes I'd get mad as hell at a professor but they brought the best out in me. They forced me to do well." More significantly, even within educational environments that function primarily in or as democratic institutions, educational background remains a significant force and competition is present. For Anthony, his high school preparation impacted his university experiences as he described the factors that led to his being placed on academic suspension in university. "Over that time I would feel that my writing isn't up to par because I didn't do writing like everyone else did from grade 12 to OAC.[2] I couldn't take certain courses because I didn't have the math background or the science background." Deanna articulated the tension inherent in juxtaposing democratic process within the competitive environment of a university as she says that you are told, "you're going to go to university, they're going to welcome you. . . . You're just a new budding mind, and then you get there and they want you out. They're going to do their best to weed you out." However, of individual educators she said, "Everyone seems real there. They seem genuine and seem aware like, if you come to them and say, I'm going through a lot of difficulties because of this, they're like, okay, we understand, you're not the first."

Ruddick and Dimitriou (2003) claim that meaningful active participation in democratic processes within schools act as learning communities that are committed to enacting as opposed to merely teaching about democracy "enables young people to develop positive identities as learners" (p. 276). It is also not only the students who benefit from education as or in democracy, however. Fielding's (2001) research finds that "teacher learning is both enabled and enhanced by dialogic encounters with their students in which the interdependent nature of teaching and learning and the shared responsibility for its success is made explicit" (p. 130). For students, this form of democratic education that "facilitates the formation of somebodies-in-particular, citizens who intentionally embody their power to make history and culture in the quest for a just pluralistic society" (Glass, 2005, p. 86).

The participants' struggles with their identities concurrent with their changes in academic achievement personify the enactment of engagement for democratic transformation at least at an individual level. According to Mitra (2003), this identity formation is a paradigm shift that "occurs when hearing their voices in the formal curriculum, and being taken seriously within the covert education structures where their voices are welcomed, students are empowered by their own definitions of themselves" (p. 289). The tensions that are inherent in democracy as evolving are mirrored in the participants' narratives of their changes in identity resulting from their involvement in democratic educational institutions. For example, Carol reflected, "Emotionally I mean it's still hard every day and some days I just want to give up and I don't want to be a thinking person—I have to fight to not want to go back there." In spite of these struggles, the participants were overwhelmingly positive about the impact that being involved in forms of schooling in democracy has had on their feelings about themselves and interactions with others. They easily identified changes in their self-concept concurrent with their success in university. Deanna said that she has "become more self-assured, more self-aware, self-love—all that positive stuff ... and I've become less angry, less judgmental—less of all the negative things and more of all the positive."

Her optimistic outlook was echoed by Elaine who claimed that success in school "gave me a lot of confidence. It gave me a lot of willpower. It let me know that I could do anything I really want to do and if I'm doing it for myself it makes it a million times better." Greg's experience was similar as he indicates, "I think I feel a lot better about myself. . . . I'm a lot more motivated now and happy about my life than I would have been before." As well, Carol linked her increased confidence within academic spheres with other aspects of her life. She credits her accomplishments as giving her "self-worth probably more than anything," and Jennifer declared, "I have better faith in people." Anthony said of his active participation in democratic processes in educational institutions, "I really learned that there is so much more out there in life than just your little community area or your neighbourhood... That definitely changed my outlook, my perspective on life.... It's made me a positive person." These reflections were consistent with Glass' (2005) contention that "[i]f we cannot authentically participate in the direction of society, we cannot be full citizens" (p. 85).

CONCLUSIONS AND RECOMMENDATIONS

Without examining the role that researchers play in the creation of student silencing, Fullan (2005) lays responsibility at the feet of practitioners with claims that the failure of educational reforms is due to a lack of systems thinkers and to the speed of reform implementation. However, according to Ruddick and Demetriou (2003) "over the last twenty years or so—and despite extensive programs of mandated reform—schools have changed less in their deep structures and patterns or relationships than young people have changed" (p. 275). Unfortunately, current educational reforms may more appropriately be called reframes or retreads as ideologies regarding democracy, purposes of schooling, and student voice are recycled and remain unchallenged and unchanged. Analogous to a hamster in a wheel, whether we focus on the landscape in front or the shavings and droppings below, we are confined to the same circle. However quickly or slowly we run in the wheel, unless we change the system and shift the paradigms of democracy and student voice that inform educational theory, policy, and practice, we will continue on the same path.

Participating in democratic processes is based on active involvement. Schools prepare students for reading by practicing reading, and classrooms are envisioned as places to take risks and learn from mistakes in this area. At the same time, schools purport to prepare students for democracy while removing them from ownership of and/or involvement in democratic processes. This can be seen as analogous to having students certified to drive cars by reading and hearing about what is involved. By giving them only the theoretical background of operating a motor vehicle we could defer students' participation in driving until after they graduate from driver's education programs. We are unlikely to trust an important task such as driving to such a deferred or limited notion of what it entails. Yet this is precisely what educational reframes continue to do by claiming to prepare students for the important role of acting as citizens while restricting them from involvement in, and ownership of, democratic activities.

If educational theorists and practitioners are sincere in their efforts to create equitable socially just schools there is a need for radical revolutions enacted within participatory notions of democracy. Within theory and practice this calls for critical pedagogy as envisioned by educators such as Fernandez-Balboa (1993), Freire (1998), and Morrell (2006). Enacting education in and as democracy requires that emancipatory and transformative school leaders provide space and facilitate processes for student voice in meaningful issues related to curriculum, policies, and procedures that impact on their education and life chances.

NOTES

1. Section programs are named after the section of the Education Act pertaining to education within hospitals and institutions. The Section program Deanna was in was a segregated class designed for students, generally living in group homes, who are deemed for behavioral reasons unable to attend "regular" classes.
2. Ontario Academic Credits (OACs) were required for admission to university programs during the previous educational reforms.

REFERENCES

Allen, K. (1996). The transitional year programme at the University of Toronto: A life-line for Blacks seeking a university education. In K. Brathwaite & C. James (Eds.), *Educating African Canadians* (pp. 234–250). Toronto, ON: James Lorimer.

Anderson, G. (2004). William Foster's legacy: Learning from the past and reconstructing the future. *Educational Administration Quarterly, 40*(2), 240–258.

Anderson, G. L., & Herr, K. (1993). The micro-politics of students' voices: Moving from diversity of bodies to diversity of voices in schools. In C. Marshall (Ed.), *The new politics of race and gender* (pp. 58–68). Washington, DC: Falmer Press.

Armstrong, D., & McMahon, B. (2004, May). *Pedagogical practices: Creating possibilities for students at risk.* Paper presented at the Ontario Ministry of Education/ Faculties of Education Conference, Toronto, ON.

Books, S. (1998). Speaking of and against youth. In S. Books (Ed.), *Invisible children in the society and in the schools* (pp.183–199). Mahwah, NJ: Lawrence Erlbaum.

Boyd, D. (1992). The moral part of pluralism as the plural part of moral education. In F. C. Power & D. Lapsley (Eds.), *The challenge of pluralism: Education, politics and values* (pp. 141–167). Notre Dame, IA: University of Notre Dame.

Breault, R. (2003). Dewey, Freire, and a pedagogy for the oppressor. *Multicultural Education, 10*(3), 2–6.

Brown, R., & Sinay, E. (2008). *Research report: 2006 student census: Linking demographic data with student achievement.* Toronto, ON: Toronto District School Board.

Bush, T. (2003). *Theories of educational leadership and management 3rd Edition.* London, UK: Sage.

Clandinin, D. J., & Connelly, F. M. (1994). Personal experience methods. In N. Denzin & Y. Lincoln (Eds.), *Handbook of qualitative research* (pp. 413–427). Thousand Oaks, CA: Sage.

Corson, D. (2000). Emancipatory leadership. *International Journal of Leadership in Education, 3*(2), 93–102.

Dei, G. (1996). Listening to voices: Developing a pedagogy of change from the narratives of African-Canadian students and their parents. In K. Brathwaite & C. James (Eds.), *Educating African Canadians* (pp. 32–57). Toronto: James Lorimer.

Dei, G., Holmes, L., Mazzuca, J., McIsaac, E., & Campbell, R. (1997). *Reconstructing "drop-out": A critical ethnography of the dynamics of Black students' disengagement from school.* Toronto, Ontario, Canada: University of Toronto Press.

Dei, G. & Karunmanchery, L. (2001). School reforms in Ontario: The marketization of education and the resulting silence on equity. In J. P. Portelli & P. Solomon (Eds.), *The erosion of democracy in education* (pp. 189–215). Calgary, AB: Detselig Enterprises.

Douglass, F. (1991). Letter to an abolitionist associate. In K. Bobo, J. Kendall, & S. Max (Eds.), *Organizing for social change: A mandate for activity in the 1990s.* Washington, DC: Seven Locks Press. [originally published in 1849] Retrieved from http://www.buildingequality.us/Quotes/Frederick_Douglass.html

Fernandez-Balboa, J. (1993). Critical pedagogy: Making critical thinking really critical. *Analytic Teaching, 13*(2), 61–72.

Fielding, M. (2001). Students as radical agents of change. *Journal of Educational Change, 2*, 123–141.

Foster, W. (1986). *Paradigms and promises: New approaches to educational administration.* Amherst, NY: Prometheus Books.

Freire, P. (1998). *Pedagogy of freedom: Ethics, democracy, and civic courage.* New York: Rowman & Littlefield.

Fullan, M. (2005). *Leadership & sustainability: System thinkers in action.* Thousand Oaks, CA: Corwin.

Gillborn, D., & Youdell, D. (2000). *Rationing education: Policy, practice, reform and equity.* Philadelphia, PA: Open University.

Gitlin, A., & Russell, R. (1994). Alternative methodologies and the research context. In A. Gitlin (Ed.), *Power and method: Political activism and educational research* (pp. 181–202). New York, NY: Routledge.

Glass, R. (2005). What is democratic education? In W. Hare & J. Portelli (Eds.), *Key questions for educators* (pp. 83–86). Halifax, NS: EdPhil.

Haberman, M. (2003). Who benefits from failing urban school districts? *EducationNews.org.* Retrieved from http:www.alcert.org/research.asp?article=Benefits& page=Research October 21, 2006

Haberman, M. (2004). Urban education: The state of urban schooling at the start of the 21st century. *EducationNews.org.* Retrieved from http:www.educationnews.org/urban-edcuation-the-state-o-furb.htm

King, A. (2004). *Double cohort study: Phase 3 report.* Toronto, ON: Ontario Ministry of Education.

Leithwood, K., Fullan, M., & Watson, N. (2003). *The schools we need: Recent education policy in Ontario and recommendations for moving forward.* Toronto, ON: OISE/UT.

Leithwood, K., Jantzi, D., & Steinbach, R. (1999). *Changing leadership for changing times.* Philadelphia, PA: Open University.

MacKinnon, D. (2001). A wolf in sheep's clothing: A critique of the Atlantic provinces education foundation program. In J. P. Portelli & R. P. Solomon (Eds.), *The erosion of democracy in education* (pp. 117–144). Calgary, AB: Detselig.

Marshall, C., & Rossman, G. (1999). *Designing qualitative research 3rd Ed.* Thousand Oaks, CA: Sage.

Martin, J. (1992). Critical thinking for a humane world. In J. Norris (Ed.), *The generalizability of critical thinking* (pp. 163–180). Boston, MA: Teachers College Press.

McCarthy, C. (1995). Multicultural policy discourses on racial inequality in American education. In R. Ng, P. Staton, & J. Scane (Eds.), *Anti-racism, feminism, and critical approaches to education* (pp. 21–43). Toronto, Ontario, Canada: Ontario Institute for Studies in Education.

McMahon, B., & Armstrong, D. (2003). Racism, resistance, resilience: The 3Rs of educating Caribbean students in a Canadian context. In T. Bastick & A. Ezenne (Eds.), *Teaching Caribbean students: Research on social issues in the Caribbean and abroad* (pp. 249–284). Kingston, Jamaica: University of the West Indies.

McMahon, B., & Armstrong, D. (2006). Framing equitable praxis: Approaches to building socially just and inclusionary educational communities. In D. Armstrong & B. McMahon (Eds.), *Inclusion in urban educational environments: Addressing issues of diversity, equity and social* justice (pp. 191–212). Greenwich, CT: Information Age.

McMahon, B., & Portelli, J. (2004). Engagement for what? Beyond popular discourses on student engagement. *Leadership and Policy in Schools, 3*(1), 59–76.

Merriam, S. (1998). *Qualitative research and case study applications in education.* San Francisco: Jossey Bass.

Mitra, D. (2003). Student voice in school reform: Reframing student-teacher relationships. *McGill Journal of Education 38*(2), 279–304.

Mitra, D. (2005). Adults advising youth: Leading while getting out of the way. *Educational Administration Quarterly, 41*(3), 520–553.

Mitra, D. (2006). Youth as a bridge between home and school: Comparing student voice and parent involvement as strategies for change. *Education and Urban Society, 38*(4), 455–480.

Morrell, E. (2006, April). *Critical pedagogy in a summer research seminar.* Paper presented at the Annual Meeting of the American Educational Research Association, San Francisco, CA.

Morrison, T. (1987). *Beloved.* New York, NY: Knopf.

Nieto, S. (1992). *Affirming diversity: The sociopolitical context of multicultural education.* New York, NY: Longman.

Ontario Ministry of Education (2004). Building the Ontario educational advantage: Student achievement. Toronto, ON: Author. Retrieved from http://www.edu.gov.on.ca/eng/document/nr/04.03/building.pdf

Ontario Ministry of Education (2006). Whose responsible for your child's education? Toronto, ON: Author. Retrieved from http://www.edu.gov.on.ca/eng/document/brochure/whosresp.html

Portelli, J. P. & Solomon, R. P. (Eds.). (2001). *The erosion of democracy in education.* Calgary, AB: Detselsig.

Richards, J. (2008). *Closing the Aboriginal/non-Aboriginal education gaps.* C.D. Howe Institute. Retrieved from http://www.indianz.com/News/2008/011705.asp

Ruddick, J. & Demetriou, H. (2003). Student potential and teacher practices: The transformational potential. *McGill Journal of Education 38*(2), 274–288.

Rudduck, J., & Flutter, J. (2000). Pupil participation and perspective: Carving a new order of experience. *Cambridge Journal of Education, 30*(1), 75–89.

Ryan, J. (2003). Principals and inclusive leadership for diverse schools: Vol. 2. Studies in educational leadership. Hingham, MA: Kluwer.

Ryan, J. (2006). Exclusion in urban schools and communities. In D. Armstrong & B. McMahon (Eds.), *Inclusion in urban educational environments: Addressing issues of diversity, equity and social justice* (pp. 3–30). Greenwich, CT: Information Age.

Saul, D. (2005). Education unplugged: Students sound off about what helps them learn. *Education Canada, 45*(2), 18–20.

Seidman, S. (1998). Dislodging the canon: The reassertion of a moral vision of the human sciences. In S. Seidman (Ed.), *Contested knowledge: Social theory in the postmodern era* (2nd ed., pp. 171–343). Malden, MA: Blackwell.

Solomon, R. P. (1992). *Black resistance in high school: Forging a separatist culture.* Albany, NY: SUNY.

Solomon, R. P., & Palmer, H. (2006). Black boys through the school-prison pipeline: When "racial profiling" and "zero tolerance" collide. In D. E. Armstrong & B. J. McMahon (Eds.), *Inclusion in urban educational environments: Addressing issues of diversity, equity and social justice* (pp. 191–212). Greenwich CT: Information Age.

Starratt, R. (2004). Responsible leadership. *The Educational Forum.* Retrieved from http://www.kdp.org/archives/files/edforum/forum_w05_124-133.pdf

Steinberg, L. (1996). *Beyond the classroom: Why school reform has failed and what parents need to do.* New York, NY: Touchstone.

Taylor, A. (2001). *The politics of educational reform in Alberta.* Toronto, ON: University of Toronto Press.

CHAPTER 4

INSIDERS VERSUS OUTSIDERS

Examining Variability in Student Voice Initiatives and Their Consequences for School Change

Dana Mitra and Ben Kirshner

ABSTRACT

The purpose of this chapter is to provide a typology for understanding the range of student voice initiatives in the United States. The chapter examines the relationship between the *locus of change* strategy (inside vs. outside schools). We use the term *outsider* to refer to social organizing efforts for school reform based in community or intermediary organizations outside of schools. In contrast, *insider* student voice efforts work within school auspices, often as a school class or a club. We layer this spectrum with a second spectrum focusing on the *focus of change,* ranging from a focus on individual youth leadership to social activism strategies. This typology can help practitioners and activists to articulate their own goals/intended outcomes and processes. It can also help researchers to articulate the meaning of the student voice research they are exploring in more specific terms.

The term "student voice" encompasses a range of opportunities for youth to participate in school decisions that shape their lives and the lives of their

Student Engagement in Urban Schools, pages 49–72

peers (Fielding, 2001; Levin, 2000; Mitra, 2009a). Through student voice opportunities, students can work with teachers and administrators to co-create the path of reform. This process enables youth to meet their own developmental needs and will strengthen student ownership of the change process. All types of student voice, from limited input to substantial leadership, are considerably different from the types of "leadership" roles that students typically perform in U.S. schools (such as planning school dances and holding pep rallies). Student voice can range from the most basic level of youth sharing their opinions of problems and potential solutions, to allowing young people to collaborate with adults to address the problems in their schools, to youth taking the lead on seeking change.

Far from homogenous, student voice approaches reflect a range of reform intentions and reform strategies. This chapter examines the relationship between the locus of change strategy (inside vs. outside schools) with the focus of change (leadership vs. activism). We use the term *outsider* to refer to social organizing efforts for school reform based in community or intermediary organizations outside of schools (Kirshner, 2008; Oakes & Rogers, 2006; Warren, Mira, & Nikundiwe, 2008). In contrast, *insider* student voice efforts work within school auspices, often as a school class or a club. Figure 4.1 illustrates this spectrum. Such student voice initiatives operating inside schools may be partnered with broader reform efforts happening in the school overall, or they may be independently trying to draw attention to change that needs to occur in the school.

FOCUS OF CHANGE: YOUTH LEADERSHIP AND SOCIAL ACTIVISM

The goals and intended outcomes of student voice research ranges from a focus on boosting individual competencies, and particularly *leadership*, to broad societal critique and change that is often labeled as *activism*. In

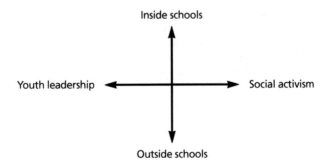

Figure 4.1 Focus and locus of change.

the realm of student voice, this distinction ranges from a focus on youth leadership to a focus on social activism. A colleague once described this distinction with a tongue-in-cheek comparison of "short haired" (leadership) versus "long haired" (activist) research. Research on youth leadership and social activism often operates in very separate fields. Figure 4.1 illustrates the spectrum of the focus of change in student voice initiatives from youth leadership to social activism.

Youth Leadership

Researchers tend to focus on developing young people to become active participants in society. For the purposes of this chapter, we will use Kress's (2006) definition of youth leadership, which defines it as "the involvement of youth in responsible, challenging action that meets genuine needs, with opportunities for planning and decision making" (p. 51). The focus is on helping young people to become the best they can be and to translate these talents in terms of service to their communities. Much of the research on this topic occurs in the domains of human development, prevention science, and agricultural extension education.

Social activism works from a social justice foundation and attempts to teach young people to critically assess the institutions in their lives, to identify injustices, and to take steps to highlight and to remedy these injustices. The goal in social activism is to identify the systemic causes of deep-rooted social problems and to highlight these challenges more broadly to the world. Often called "youth activism," student voice initiatives focused on social change tend to do so from organizations located *outside* of school auspices. These student voice initiatives often maintain a separation from school administration; this independence helps them to heighten awareness of problems in the school system. Such strategies are sometimes confrontational. Such efforts have flourished in regions of the country with a strong tradition of social protest, including major cities such as New York, Chicago, Los Angeles, San Francisco, and Oakland. These type of initiatives question inequities in the broader system of schooling (Colatos & Morrell, 2003; Fine, Burns, & Payne, 2004) and often participate in broader community organizing efforts beyond the school setting (Kwon, 2006). The language in such organizations focuses on "acting on" organizations, including schools, to raise awareness of injustice (Catone, 2009).

The remainder of the chapter will explore each of these spectra to highlight the differences in approaches and speculate about comparative strengths and weaknesses. Table 4.1 details the two dimensions of focus in this chapter—focus on leadership versus activism, and insider versus outsider strategies. We will highlight conceptually the stance of the student voice

TABLE 4.1   Types of Student Voice Efforts Based on Philosophy of Change and Locus of Change

	Youth leadership focus	Blended focus	Social activism focus
Working from inside schools	Student Councils, student projects focused on changing things within a school	*Emphasis on structural change and developing youth skills*	Students working on school reform, often in partnership with school personnel and/or skill development for students.
Blurred locus	Community Based Organizations working within chools/ partnering with schools		When activism leads to change and the activists get a seat at the table
Working from outside schools	Community-based organizations such as 4-H, Boys and Girls Clubs	*Emphasis on structural change and developing youth skills*	Social change/social protest focus, driven by youth and community organizing

initiatives in each box and provide examples that illustrate them in practice. To avoid oversimplification, we also present examples of organizations that blur the lines between each of the types as well as examples that fit each type. Layering these concepts together can help to illuminate the conditions that enable and constrain student voice initiatives. Through increased awareness of the intentions and strategies of change efforts, student voice initiatives can be strategic about their change strategies and assist researchers in clarifying their conceptual and evaluative claims.

YOUTH LEADERSHIP: FOCUSING ON BUILDING STRONG KIDS

Student voice work often focuses on a goal of enabling "youth leadership," which tends to prioritize the goal of providing experiences for young people to learn how to become leaders and change agents within their schools and communities. While these efforts usually have a project or goal attached, developing youths' skills is typically more important than the projects that are ultimately completed. A common thread among youth leadership efforts is a focus on interpersonal skills and communication (Conner & Strobel, 2007). Fostering leadership among youth is a common outcome of student voice as well (Mitra, 2004).

Often a focus on youth leadership tends to be paired with the term "youth–adult partnerships" rather than student voice initiatives. Indeed student voice initiatives can be considered youth-adult partnerships that occur in school settings (Mitra, 2009b). Youth–adult partnerships are defined as relationships in which both youth and adults have the potential to contribute to decision-making processes, to learn from one another, and to promote change. Collaboration comes with an expectation of youth sharing the responsibility for the vision of the group, the activities planned, and the group process that facilitates the enactment of these activities (Jones & Perkins, 2004). A focus on mutual teaching and learning develops in youth–adult partnerships as all parties involved assume a leadership role in some aspects of their shared effort (Camino, 2000).

A youth leadership focus is also often related to research on "civic engagement," which is an active interaction with democratic society. In such initiatives, students have the agency to participate in discussions about the core operations of schools, including teaching and learning and class or school wide decision making practices. Student voice efforts therefore not only to prepare students for a democratic society, but they also offer opportunities to transform schools and classrooms into democratic settings in which young people can gain necessary skills in understanding how to participate in pluralistic communities (Darling-Hammond, 1996; Gutmann, 1987). Student voice initiatives with a leadership focus have been shown to lead to the development of competencies linked to involved, productive citizenry and can increase the belief of young people that they can make a difference in their lives and the lives of others (Eccles & Gootman, 2002; Kirshner, O'Donoghue, & McLaughlin, 2003; Mitra, 2004). In this context, youth leadership fits with the "participatory citizen" typology in Joel Westheimer and Joseph Kahne's (2004) research on civic engagement. Such young people organize collective, community-focused efforts such as clothing collections, fundraising campaigns, and voter registration drives.

Inside Schools

Youth leadership projects located within school auspices may include traditional student council organizations, especially if the goals have some service mission associated with them. For example, one high school group developed a school program called "Just like Me," in which group members were paired with special needs students to engage in social activities such as bowling, roller skating, and other casual interactions (Mitra, Sanders, & Perkins, in press). The goals of this program exemplify the goals of a program with a youth leadership focus. The program provided leadership opportunities for the organizing students to facilitate the programming for the organizations. It also offered opportunities for both special needs and mainstreamed students to enhance their interpersonal and communication skills with individuals different than themselves.

Another example of an insider approach occurred at McGuire High School (pseudonym) in the San Francisco Bay Area. Their project focused on peer mediation and conflict resolution (Mitra, 2006). A youth in the project explained the need for the project by explaining that McGuire "is actually a continuation school, and some of the kids here have a lot of problems...with their friends and with their family outside of school [because of] drugs, fighting, and stuff like that." Student volunteers for the program received 16 hours of training to serve as mediators. An adult advisor of the group described the delicate nature of preparing youth for conflict resolution. She explained:

> It's one thing to teach them how to do it. But a lot of it is doing it and making the mistakes. So we do a lot of mock situations and they've been able to see [what] could happen. It's been an excellent opportunity to address issues that already affect them personally and then also to train them how to deal with those things both as a peer but also as a member of a family or [as a] student.

Through direct experience, students both faced their own problems and learned how to help others. Fitting with the definition of youth leadership, this program focused directly on helping individuals to develop the strategies for improved interpersonal communication.

Outside Organizations

Many youth leadership organizations exist *outside* of school auspices. Community-based organizations, church groups, and civic organizations provide a wide range of opportunities for youth to develop individual skills and talents as well as connecting young people with the needs of their broader community. In rural areas, 4-H clubs and Future Farmers of America are two common focus points for youth leadership. In urban areas, Boys and Girls Clubs tend to be a locus of working with youth. Nationwide in all settings, scouting programs, sporting organizations and a wide range of clubs and organizations serve to develop youth talents and capacities.

Research by Sanders, Movit, Mitra, and Perkins (2007) examined a summer conference sponsored by a regional Council of Governments organization. The conference was an outsider strategy—a training opportunity for young people away from school—that was designed to enhance the capacity for youth leadership in the region. The Reach for Change program (pseudonym) consisted of a four-day training institute that young people attended free of charge.

Youth who participated in the Reach for Change conference were selected to represent a broad array of youth with leadership potential—not just youth who already possessed strong leadership skills and roles in their communities. Upon arrival, they were placed immediately into teams of ten youth. A majority of these young people did not know their team members, nor did they come from the same school—in fact, not knowing anyone proved to be a critical part of the structure of the conference. Young people reported being able to break out of their defined roles at their schools, to take risks, and to try out new skills and personalities precisely because no one knew who they were back home. One student expressed amazement because he "didn't know so many people cared about the same things [he] did"; he felt that one of the most positive things about the conference was that "I met so many people I would have never even talked to before if we were in the same school."

Youth who attended the Reach for Change conference gained many skills they would need as future leaders in their communities. Through the conference, they reported that they became comfortable with the idea of sitting down with strangers, of learning about what they have in common, and of creating an interdependency that allowed them to tap into and harness the power of teamwork. Youth also improved their ability to communicate in small groups. They learned the importance of listening to and learning from others when trying to solve problems. In this way, they were learning to think outside of the box. According to the director, what youth most commonly acknowledged was their increased self-confidence. With these skills in hand, youth were prepared to become leaders when they returned home.

BLURRING THE LINES BETWEEN INSIDER AND OUTSIDER YOUTH LEADERSHIP

Some community-based organizations provide external training and support to within-school student voice efforts. For example, in Pennsylvania, the Go the Distance (pseudonym) offers a Leadership Institute in which over 50 schools attend a five-day training institute free of charge each year. Unlike Reach for Change, this training institute focused on building strong team cohesion among students from the same schools. Each school brings five students (preferably sophomores) and an advising teacher to the institute. Through lectures, interactive activities, small group work, and discussions, students strengthen their leadership and teamwork skills while creating individualized team projects designed to benefit their home schools or communities. Student teams then implement their projects at their school with the guidance of their faculty mentors and Go the Distance staffers during the following academic year.

The organization's theory of action focused on the development of four specific components of a young leader, which included team building, understanding oneself, understanding diversity, and developing a sense of accountability. Individualized school projects tended to focus on non-controversial improvement projects. They generally fit within four categories: (1) school beautification projects, (2) mentoring and orientation programs; (3) cultural diversity programs, and (4) school spirit projects.

While most schools focus on a limited goal, some groups choose to bring about a school-wide change, such as the team that decided to change its school mascot. The original mascot of this urban school was the Pegasus. The students hated their mascot, and the boys, in particular, were reluctant to join in school activities that publicly linked the Pegasus to their school. To change the mascot, the institute team recruited students from across the school to make suggestions for mascot alternatives, the art club designed possible logos for these alternatives, and the entire school then voted for their favorite mascot among the available choices. This project served as a unifying force of the school, providing multiple opportunities for enhancing interpersonal collaboration, group discussion, problem solving, and communication among the students working on the project.

The Go the Distance example provides a positive example of an outsider organization providing technical assistance that facilitated leadership development within schools, but such blurring of boundaries is not always so successful. A contrasting case can be seen in a collaboration between a community-based organization, local parents, and a student voice initiative at Highland High School (pseudonym) in the San Francisco Bay Area. This effort sought to improve the self-esteem of Polynesian students, who had the highest dropout rate in the school.

The group decided that painting a mural would be a key first step toward building a stronger and more positive identity for Pacific Islander students. The mural would symbolize the inclusion of Pacific Islanders in the school community. An adult advisor with the group explained:

> The kids chose the mural project, because they feel that they have nothing there at Highland.... Through the mural, hopefully, they will feel like they are identified as someone, so, hopefully, that will get them back in school and get them back on track.... After the mural, they can ... do other things, positive things and look at that instead of robbing people, bullying people.... We're stereotyped as that kind of people, especially the males, so I'm hoping through that mural, it might change their attitude sometime in the future.

The community-based organization hoped that the mural project would serve as a starting point for rebuilding the youth identity among Pacific Islander youth and increasing their sense of belonging to the school. The project culminated in a *Polynesian Day* to reveal the mural and to offer many other events to celebrate heritage and culture.

The blurring of the insider–outsider boundaries became a problem for the Polynesian Club when school district grading policies prevented the group from moving forward with its work. The Club faced a challenging paradox of wanting to create activities that could help to boost the sense of identity and sense of self-worth among Pacific Islander students in the school but not having enough students academically eligible to participate. A parent working with the project explained that the group usually had "a Polynesian Day, which they didn't have [this year] because of the... district policy." The district did not allow students to participate in extracurricular activities without a 2.0 grade point average or better, and only a handful of Pacific Islander students at Highlands met that requirement. The parent concluded, "Usually for that day, they have their dances, the parents bring food and feed the staff and administration. [We] share some of the culture and the history with the Highland High School community. They missed out on Polynesian Day." This group's work was impeded by a bureaucratic contradiction. Through participation in positive activities, the group was trying to break the cycle of delinquency and to increase academic achievement among Pacific Islander students, but the district requirements barred youth from participating in activities until they could demonstrate academic success.

Implications

In this section we reviewed examples of student voice initiatives that focus on youth leadership development. As our examples suggest, youth leadership efforts can be based in schools, community agencies, and hybrid combinations of the two. Although it is not our purpose in this chapter to review studies that compare outcomes across these settings, we draw on our research experience to offer some conjectures about advantages and disadvantages of school-based versus community-based settings.

The principal advantage of schools is that, by virtue of their mandatory status, they are attended by a wide range of youth. Unlike community organizations, which rely on voluntary attendance and therefore have a self-selected population, leadership efforts housed inside schools have the potential to make an impact on large numbers of students who walk through their doors every day. The unfortunate irony, however, is that schools have a bad history of tracking not only in academic classes but also in terms of extracurricular options (Eckert, 1990). Student councils are typically restricted to those who are already getting high grades or playing sports; even within schools where student voice is supported, such opportunities are often limited to high-achieving students (Fielding, 2004). In contrast, some community organizations make it their mission to recruit and design programming for struggling or marginalized students. By virtue of their outside status, they may be more likely to appeal to interests not met in conventional classes, such as hip hop, murals, poetry slams, and the like.

This is not an argument that one setting is better than another, but instead an effort to identify some of the comparative opportunities and constraints.

SOCIAL ACTIVISM:
CHOOSING A SOCIAL MOVEMENT STRATEGY

The social activism change strategy is less common than the youth leadership approach. Researchers of social movements in sociology define social movements as "collective challenges, based on common purposes and social solidarities, in sustained interaction with elites, opponents, and authorities" (Tarrow, 1998, p. 4, as cited in Giugni, 1999, p. xxi). Pockets of youth activism across the country tend to be centralized in urban communities with a strong tradition of social movement and broader social action. These types of collective movements have been examined by sociologists studying social movement theory. Westheimer and Kahne (2004) describe this type of action as a "justice-oriented approach." Instead of only preparing meals at a soup kitchen for example, a justice-oriented perspective would examine the causes of hunger, draw attention to the injustices that create the inequities, and seek to effect larger-scale changes that could help to lessen these inequities.

Outsider Strategies

The principal justification for outside approaches to student voice is political and pragmatic. It borrows from analyses of community organizing as a force for equity-based reform in communities of color (Fruchter, 2007; Lipman, 2004; Oakes & Rogers, 2006). According to this line of research, equity-focused reform is not merely a set of technical challenges solved through rational deliberation or incremental change. Instead, substantive equity reform confronts normative and political barriers to change, or what Renee, Welner, & Oakes (in press) call the "zone of mediation." Youth organizing groups based outside of schools have sometimes shown their ability to hold political decision-makers accountable to constituents and thereby promote equitable reforms (HoSang, 2006; Oakes & Rogers, 2006; Warren et al., 2008). For example, Kwon (2006) described how a pan-ethnic coalition of youth groups successfully defeated a plan to build a "super jail" for juvenile offenders in California. In Los Angeles, youth organizing groups partnered with community organizations to persuade the school district to make college-level classes the default for all students. From this standpoint, equity-based reform requires the participation of those who are its targets and who have been most affected by inequitable policies.

Traditional social protest efforts have adopted disruptive tactics focused on public embarrassment of institutions. Some social change efforts have tried to generate public pressure on institutions through media exposure and mobilizing ordinary people affected by the issue. The goal of such efforts is to draw attention to injustices occurring in a system and to place public pressure on these institutions to change their tactics to avoid future negative attention and, in strike and walkout situations, to resume operations of the organization (McAdam, McCarthy, & Zald, 1996). Media exposure is critical to such a strategy, since the goal of most of these tactics is to increase pressure on these organizations by encouraging the broader public to pay closer attention to the problems with the organization or school system.

One example of youth activism aimed at generating community-wide pressure on a school district can be observed in the campaigns of Students United (pseudonym), which was a non-profit youth organizing group whose leadership and membership was comprised of low-income youth of color. Students United sought to develop young people's capacity to impact policies in education, school finance, school discipline, police accountability, and juvenile justice systems. It had several successes in its eight-year history that focused around equity and civil rights for students of color. For example, student authors published two reports that exposed racial tracking at one school and the failure of desegregation efforts at another. Both reports were aimed at exposing inequities experienced by students of color and creating publicity that would create pressure on the district to act.

Students United's approach was also reflected in its response to the school district's decision to close a neighborhood high school, Jefferson (pseudonym), which several of its members attended. Jefferson High School went through a series of tough years leading up to its closure in 2006. A spiral of inadequate resources and declining enrollment fueled problems at the school, culminating in the school board's decision in 2006 to close Jefferson's three small schools for one year and re-open in 2007 for 9th graders only.

The closure decision was controversial, and provoked widespread anger and protest from student groups. According to students speaking at public meetings, what was pitched as a rescue felt more like an attack. Students reported feeling "blindsided," "stunned," and "crushed" by the board's decision. Students United was at the forefront at efforts to organize a coherent push-back against the closure. Members spoke at public meetings, saying, "You're putting barriers in front of us instead of removing them." Students United released talking points that viewed the closure as racist and part of a broader effort at gentrification of the neighborhood. Students United members organized a "walkout" via text messaging in which they marched to the school district headquarters. They produced and distributed T-shirts declaring "not down with the shut down." Students United also used the news media in creative ways. For example, after the list of transfer schools had been offered by the school district, they decided to see how long it would take for students from the Jefferson neighborhood to get to the furthest school on the list. Students United invited school board members, television news reports, and print journalists to follow the student on his trip to school. The following day there were several news reports about the experiences of the student, which chronicled the fact that it took 90 minutes for him to get to his new school on public transportation.

Students United's ability to organize students and publicize their opposition kept public pressure alive about the controversial decision. At a school board meeting roughly one month after the decision had been announced, a group of community members, the Minister's Coalition, announced its collective opposition to the closure in solidarity with the Jefferson students, alleging it was a racist decision that evoked memories of the 1960s Civil Rights movement. Although Students United's organizing generated community support and put pressure on the district, ultimately some of its tactics antagonized leadership within the district as well as some local community education organizations, which had in the past supported Students United. Within one year of its activism about the closure, Students United, and its parent organization, had closed their doors because funding for their operations had dried up.

The case of Students United illustrates the diverse tactics that outsider groups adopt. Members of Students United successfully organized Jefferson students as well as broader coalitions of community groups. These efforts exemplify the common phrase that when ordinary people join forces they can gain "power in numbers" (Kirshner, 2009). For reasons linked to the particulars of Jefferson, however, Students United struggled to gain traction with school board members or administrators, and ultimately the closure decision stood.

Insider Strategies

Recent scholarship in social movement theory offers a theoretical avenue for understanding how student voice initiatives can help to improve the success of school change efforts. In the late nineties, scholars began to broaden the application of social movement theory to examine efforts to seek change from within institutions (Burstein, 1999; Katzenstein, 1998). Through a focus on building alliances and support inside institutions and working collaboratively to shift the roles of disempowered groups (McAdam, Tarrow, & Tilly, 1996; Moore, 1999), including students themselves, this shift in strategy brings with it a stronger emphasis on shifting the culture of institutions by creating new norms, developing new relationships, and transforming organizational structures within them (Della Porta & Diani,

1999; Oakes & Lipton, 2002). For example, an insider strategy can allow for opportunities for students to build partnerships with teachers to tackle such problems as improving student learning, exploring the negative stereotypes associated with the school, and improving relations between students and teachers (Mitra, 2006, 2008b).

Insider strategies require that the student voice organization has established a level of legitimacy and respect with school decision makers. In such instances, the challengers must establish alliances and find support among school personnel in positions of power. A greater ability to develop support and networks inside the system often leads to greater success for challenger groups (Katzenstein 1998; McAdam, Tarrow, & Tilly 1996; Mitra, 2006; Moore 1999). Insider strategies tend to fit within notions of school reform and change, focusing on incremental improvement and voice within existing decision making structures. Within this vein, a growing body of research documents ways in which student voice initiatives can improve student learning and classroom practice (Cook-Sather, 2002; Jones & Yonezawa, 2008; Kincheloe, 2007; Mitra, 2004; Rudduck & Flutter, 2004).

Whitman High School (pseudonym), in the San Francisco Bay Area, served a community comprised of first-generation immigrants from Latin America and Asia as well as working-class African-Americans and European-Americans. With the school graduating just over half (57%) of the students that start in ninth grade and with one-third of its teachers electing to leave each year, Whitman High School staff felt compelled to make changes. In 1998, Whitman received a major grant to launch a three-year reform effort from the Bay Area School Reform Collaborative (BASRC), a $112 million education initiative in the San Francisco Bay area that was supported by the Annenberg Challenge and the Hewlett Foundation. As a part of deciding where to focus their reform efforts, the school's reform leadership team made the unusual decision of asking students what they felt needed to be improved.

The student voice initiative emerged out of the school's overall reform work. An English teacher, Amy Jackson (pseudonym), selected students to participate in focus groups on how improve the academic success of ninth graders. The students not only shared their opinions but then worked with Jackson and other reform leaders at the school to analyze the data and to develop a reform goal—improving communication between teachers and students. Student Forum developed two complementary strategies for building communication between students and teachers that can be classified as "teacher-focused" activities and "student- focused" activities (Mitra, 2008a).

In teacher-focused activities, students joined in the reform work that teachers were conducting, such as participating in staff trainings and research groups on reform. As youth participated in these activities, they gained a greater understanding of the perspectives of teachers and of how the school operates. Other activities developed by Student Forum were student-focused activities in which the group helped teachers to gain a better understanding of student perspectives. Unlike the activities in which students changed their own roles and perceptions, during student-focused activities, students asked teachers to expand their current perceptions of their students, the school, and their own practice. Student Forum focused on two such activities: student-led tours of their neighborhood so that teachers could gain an understanding of their lives and forums on the ramifications of being a "ghetto school." By developing this two-pronged strategy, both teachers and students taught each other about their perspectives, and both learned to be open to the other's point of view. Through open conversations deconstructing concepts such as *ghetto* and *standards,* the student voice initiative served as a catalyst to help the school to engage in rare dialogues about ways to seek equity within the school walls. The insider strategy allowed for the development of such initiatives focused on norms, relationships, and discourse within the school context. An outsider strategy in the Whitman context most likely would have built walls rather than working to break them down.

BLURRING THE LINES BETWEEN INSIDER AND OUTSIDER ACTIVISM

Perhaps the most common form of youth activism follows from the "relational" model pioneered by Saul Alinsky and continued in the 1990s and 2000s by a network of faith-based community organizing groups (Boyte, 2004; Freedman, 1993). Relational models of community organizing are typically based in organizations outside of schools, such as churches or non-profit community centers, but bet their success on their ability to form strong relationships with "insiders," such as school board members, principals, or superintendents. Essential to this blurred approach is that activists view insider officials as potential allies, rather than solely as antagonists in a political drama. Consistent with this view, community groups will publicly praise insider officials when their work supports an organization's goals, and even contribute to their election or political base of support. But they remain "critical friends," whose eye remains squarely on their members' goals, rather than the relationship. In other words, the relationship is an instrumental one, secured to the extent that it can help a group accomplish its members' goals. Often this leads community groups to work on two fronts—both within systems to reform particular policies and outside of systems to ensure that the broader context is hospitable to such changes.

Activist organizations working outside institutions tend to guard against becoming "co-opted" by the system. Such organizations work hard to maintain their stance of critique. Some believe that if they become too close with personnel within institutions, the focus of the organization's critique of injustice can become compromised due to fear of disrupting personal relationships. Yet often these organizations must blur the lines when something that they have struggled to accomplish actually comes into fruition. In such instances, activist organizations may be included in the planning of the change that they sought. A book by Milbrey McLaughlin, W. Richard Scott, Sarah Deschenes, Kathryn Hopkins, and Anne Newman (2009) examines ways in which youth activists form bridges movements and establishments. The book discusses the range of activist organizations—some working in opposition to the establishment and others willing to navigate the "between-ness" that might require collaboration in instances that reflect the values and agenda of the activist mission.

An example of such a blurring of the lines is the work of Youth on Board with Boston Public Schools. For the last 15 years Youth on Board (YOB) worked to lead organizing efforts, promote youth voice and train youth leaders to become powerful, effective decision makers. In its work with the Boston Public School District (BPS), YOB is dedicated to making sure that young people serve as key players in the planning and setting of school-wide, citywide, and nationwide education policies. In the last eight years, YOB served as the coaches/trainers of the Boston Student Advisory Committee (BSAC) and lobbied to change the school start time, institute a reasonable homework policy, eliminate a district-wide lock-out (or tardiness) policy, and implement a student rights awareness campaign, among many other successes.

YOB's focus on district-level student voice strikes an important balance between working *inside* district auspices while maintaining a separate *outsider* identity. YOB has stressed that the unique vantage point of being separate yet partnered with districts allowed YOB to help reform efforts with vision and planning for sustainability, ongoing leadership, and opportunities for securing financial resources. Rather than being co-opted, YOB asserts that it has provided BSAC with the groundwork, tools, and ongoing guidance and trainings to build engagement practice from ground zero and have experienced resounding success in this process. YOB therefore provided technical assistance to the district but kept the ownership of the initiative within district walls.

BLENDING YOUTH LEADERSHIP
AND SOCIAL ACTIVISM TOGETHER

Just as we highlighted examples of student voice efforts that fell in a gray zone between "insider" and "outsider" strategies, so too there are numerous examples of student voice efforts that combine a focus on leadership and activism, both in and outside of schools. In fact, we would be hard-pressed to find examples of successful youth activist organizations that did not also include a focus on leadership development among their members. Without talented youth leadership, activism efforts drift into advocacy, in which adult activists work on behalf of youth to secure political objectives. Ginwright and James (2002) were some of the first scholars to argue that youth organizing represents a next step for youth development. It is, in essence, a more robust form of youth development that attends not just to the developmental needs of youth but also to changing their context.

Youth organizing is consistent with positive youth development approaches (PYD) that build on the strengths and interests of young people to foster learning and development (Lerner, Almorigi, Theokas, & Lerner, 2005). Where it departs from conventional PYD programs is in its treatment of "risk." Whereas many PYD interventions aim to reduce risk by creating programs that protect youth from risks in their environment (Bolland, 2003; Eccles & Gootman, 2002; Ferrer-Wreder, 2004), youth organizing groups invite young people to take on social problems that give rise to risks (Ginwright, 2002; Watts & Flanagan, 2007). In doing so, organizing groups seek to develop participants' sociopolitical awareness (sometimes called "critical consciousness"), which includes the ability to analyze complex causes of social problems and take action to solve them (Diemer & Blustein, 2006; Freire, 1970; Watts, Williams, & Jagers, 2003).

Although research is at an early stage, studies suggest that social activism groups support the development of key developmental competencies, such as decision making, social trust, and tolerance (Flanagan, 2004). Larson and Hansen (2005), drawing on in-depth interviews and observations, found that participation in an organizing campaign contributed to the development of strategic thinking, such as how to locate information, frame messages with policymakers, and respond to unexpected contingencies. Additional studies have linked youth organizing experiences to increased civic efficacy (Gambone, Cao Yu, Lewis-Charp, Sipe, & Lacoe, 2004; Kwon, 2006) and intergroup understanding (Watkins, Larson, & Sullivan, 2007). These studies amount to a persuasive case that participation in social activism contributes to robust leadership skill-development.

Kirshner's (2008) profile of forms of adult guidance in three youth activism organizations documented the dilemmas that adults experienced when trying to balance their social change agendas with youth leadership development. After all, most youth participants were novices when it came to sustaining political campaigns, engaging in collective decision making, or speaking persuasively to local policymakers. If youth were to participate at all, they needed to develop new skills. But because these groups billed themselves as youth-driven, adults struggled to figure what kinds of roles to play—how to balance guidance and autonomy.

Kirshner observed different ways that experienced organizers, typically young adults in their twenties, supported novices' skill development and created authentic opportunities for participation and leadership. One group emphasized "facilitation," in which adults tried to remain neutral facilitators of a youth-driven campaign. This approach placed the greatest premium on youth developing skills for autonomous leadership, including how to facilitate meetings and work in teams without direct adult involvement. One group emphasized "joint work," in which experts and novices worked jointly on campaign-related tasks, but very little time was set aside for explicit instruction. Instead, novices, who were typically youth, were expected to participate at whatever level they were comfortable, ranging from peripheral to central. The third approach, called "youth-centered apprenticeship," embodied a hybrid of these two approaches. As with facilitation, adults devoted time to skill-building and invited youth to play important leadership roles. Unlike facilitation, and like joint work, adults participated in the campaigns, and in so doing modeled expert strategies and ensured a higher level of complexity to the campaign itself. The apprenticeship approach was most successful in finding a balance between organizing a complex, politically significant campaign and remaining true to youth's interests and voices.

These hybrid types of groups are most commonly based outside of schools, such as in community-based non-profits. Being based outside of schools enables them to develop their own curricula and engage in political activism, which is harder to sustain within school walls, which often maintain the expectation that teachers be politically neutral or not appear to be using the classroom to pursue political advocacy (Westheimer & Kahne, 2004).

But we are beginning to see examples emerging *within* schools and districts. Not just housed within schools, such as when schools allow community groups to meet within their walls, but actively sponsored by districts and paid for by district budgets. An early example of this phenomenon was demonstrated in the Peer Resources program of the San Francisco Unified School District, which launched student chapters at several high schools and middle schools. One such chapter, based in a middle school, focused on changing school-level policies towards sexual harassment (Kirshner, 2006). Although it was officially an "insider," group, it also embodied outsider approaches, such as by taking on the administration for not consistently enforcing the sexual harassment policies and for not providing adequate education. By the end of the year, the group had succeeded in persuading the San Francisco School Board to pass a resolution calling for a revision in its policies and procedures regarding sexual harassment. The group also sought to create greater awareness about the issue through multiple channels, including a youth conference at a local cultural center and a comic book/manual, "Sexual Harassment Hurts Everyone," that was distributed to every student in the school district.

The lines between activism and leadership can blend within school efforts as well. In a study of school-based activist groups, those that sustained their work over more than three years reported valuing the development of youth individual skills as important (and sometimes even more important) than other project goals, because the process taught youth valuable skills and life lessons that prepared them for adult lives (Mitra, 2008b, 2009c).

One group in this study, Hillside's Unity of Youth (pseudonym), demonstrates a blending of goals focused on systemic change and individual leadership development. The organization was housed in a community-based organization that worked with youth on school sites in the Oakland, CA area. Unity of Youth approached its focus on social injustice through a traditional form of organizing. They shared information and, at times, protest. A student leader at Unity of Youth explained, "We've joined the campaign to help stop the high school exit exam. We're [also] trying to help some teachers who are getting transferred out of [our school]. And we are trying to get them [the district and state] to stop the budget cuts." Hillside's Unity of Youth also tackled the problem of inadequate bathroom facilities at their school. A youth leader in the group explained, "First we did a survey on what was wrong here on campus so out [it came three top themes]—security, too many substitutes, and clean bathrooms." The group chose to focus on bathrooms because, according to the student leader, "The bathrooms here at school weren't clean and they were never open.... So we asked students what was it that they needed and what they wanted the principal and staff to do about it." The group felt that the lack of adequate facilities was inappropriate and unfair to young people.

The group achieved many victories in its attempt to challenge systems of inequity in their schools and the broader community. Yet, inherent in this bigger vision was a focus within each of the young people who worked with Unity of Youth. The adult advisor of Unity of Youth explained, "The process is definitely more important. I think it's about recognizing that changes at Hillside come with the changes within the youth themselves. Community transformation and community empowerment comes with [the youth] being empowered." When asked to provide an example in which group process needed to take priority over the other group activities, the adult continued:

> [If the youth are] arguing with each other, but they're talking about [a project focused on] racial unity and decreasing violence, I might cancel a meeting with the principal and remind them about what we're about.... We're not going in there to put out an idea that we can't live by ourselves.... I think those are the moments that they begin to internalize [our work].

Thus the group values made clear that *how* the youth–adult partnership accomplished its work mattered as much or even more than completing their proposed project of building a student unity center.

One step in this enabling process was helping youth make connections between their own personal experiences and issues of race, class, and gender. An adult advisor of Unity of Youth explained her interpretation of how identity formation inherently is related to broader understandings of social structures and inequities. She discussed the importance of helping youth to understand their identity by

> having them learn to be empowered by their race and their class and not having to be ashamed of the fact that they're working class kids. [It's about] being clear about understanding what it is to be a girl in this society, being a young boy having a single mom most of your life. How do all those things affect how you feel power? We work off of community building principles of empowering young people . . . to put out the kind of vision of the world that they want to live in. And to live in it.

Unity of Youth students also received training on specific skills related to conducting research, interacting with adults in power, goal setting, facilitation, and developing a work plan. One youth member of the successful Unity of Youth at Hillside explained that youth training in their group included "training on how to be more organized and how to organize ourselves. They have sessions like, 'You're talking to the media. How are you going to speak to them?'" An important skill that is necessary for collaborations in this study was clear communication with others. Many groups focus on how being a good leader means being a good listener. The group advisor of Unity of Youth explained, "True leadership is about working to create leaders in other people, not just promoting yourself."

Unity of Youth highlights the ways in which social activist organizations train youth in leadership skills. The focus can often be different, though, from a traditional youth leadership focus. Social activist organizations seek to make the political personal by helping young people to identify and to speak out about oppressions in their own lives, particularly those related to race, class, and gender. By identifying and discussing sources of oppression, the goal is to enable youth to become empowered in their own contexts and to embrace who they are and what they can achieve through this identity rather than despite it.

CONCLUDING THOUGHTS:
CONSEQUENCES FOR SCHOOL CHANGE

The concept of student voice initiatives represents an umbrella term that can encompass a wide range of perspectives, goals, and strategies. The purpose of this chapter was to provide a typology for understanding the range of student voice initiatives in the United States. We have identified spectra for examination.

The first spectrum examines how the *focus of change* varies across student voice organizations, ranging from a focus on individual youth leadership to social activism strategies. While these goals are distinct, they may blend together in many organizations depending on local contexts, needs, and capacity. Indeed it seems that most student voice initiatives contain at least a minimum focus on developing the leadership capacities of young people. For some organizations leadership is the primary focus; for others, social activism is a pathway through which leadership is developed.

The second spectrum highlights differences in the *locus of change* of student voice initiatives. Some are situated fully within schools; others are intentionally separate from schools. Still others blur the lines of insider/outsider approaches through partnerships between schools and community-based organizations.

Pushing from the outside can be more contentious but raises issues that are otherwise kept silent. Working from the inside allows a focus on norms, relationships, and the "nitty-gritty" of school change, yet some contend that working within schools can co-opt efforts and serve as barriers to change rather than leverage for change.

These conceptualizations of student voice offer a tentative framework that can help practitioners and activists to articulate their own goals/intended outcomes and processes. They can also help researchers to locate their own research and to articulate the meaning of the student voice research they are exploring in more specific terms. Future research will be necessary to determine if intended outcomes translate into actual outcomes that vary across these spectra.

REFERENCES

Bolland, J. (2003). Hopelessness and risk behavior among adolescents living in high-poverty inner-city neighborhoods. *Journal of Adolescence 26,* 145–158.

Boyte, H. C. (2004). *Everyday politics: Reconnecting citizens and public life.* Philadelphia, PA: University of Pennsylvania Press.

Burstein, P. (1999). Social movements and public policy. In M. Giugni, D. McAdam, & C. Tilly (Eds.), *How social movements matter* (pp. 3–21). Minneapolis, MN: University of Minnesota Press.

Camino, L. A. (2000). Youth-adult partnerships: Entering new territory in community work and research. *Applied Developmental Science, 4,* (Suppl. 1), 11–20.

Catone, K. (2009, April). *Youth 4 Change: Bridging "inside" and "outside" youth engagement in Providence.* Paper presented at the Annual Meeting of the American Educational Research Association, San Diego, CA.

Colatos, A. M., & Morrell, E. (2003). Apprenticing urban youth as critical researchers: Implications for increasing equity and access in diverse urban schools. In B. Rubin & E. Silva (Eds.), *Critical voices in school reform: Students living through change* (pp. 113–131). London: Routledge–Falmer.

Conner, J. O., & Strobel, K. (2007). Leadership development: An examination of individual and programmatic growth, *22*(3), 275–297.

Cook-Sather, A. (2002). Authorizing students' perspectives: Toward trust, dialogue, and change in education. *Educational Researcher, 31*(4), 3–14.

Darling-Hammond, L. (1996). The right to learn and the advancement of teaching: Research, policy, and practice for democratic education. *Educational Researcher, 25*(6), 5–17.

Della Porta, D., & Diani, M. (1999). *Social movements: An introduction.* Malden, MA: Blackwell.

Diemer, M. A., & Blustein, D. L. (2006). Critical consciousness and career development among urban youth. *Journal of Vocational Behavior, 68*(2), 220–232.

Eccles, J., & Gootman, J. A. (Eds.). (2002). *Community programs to promote youth development.* Washington, DC: National Academy Press.

Eckert, P. (1989). *Jocks and burnouts: Social categories and identity in the high school.* New York: Teachers College.

Ferrer-Wreder, L. (Ed.). (2004). *Successful prevention and youth development programs: Across borders.* New York, NY: Kluwer Academic/Plenum Publishers.

Fielding, M. (2001). Students as radical agents of change. Journal of Educational Change, *2*(2), 123–141.

Fielding, M. (2004). Transformative approaches to student voice: Theoretical underpinnings, recalcitrant realities. *British Educational Research Journal, 30*(2), 295–311.

Fine, M., Burns, A., & Payne, Y. (2004). Civics lessons: The color and class of betrayal Teachers College Record *106*(11), 2193–2223.

Flanagan, C.A. (2004). Volunteerism, leadership, political socialization, and civic engagement. In R.M. Lerner & L. Steinberg (Eds.), *Handbook of adolescent psychology* (pp. 721–746). New York, NY: Wiley.

Freedman, S. G. (1993). *Upon this rock: The miracles of a black church.* New York, NY: HarperCollins.

Freire, P. (1970/2002). *Pedagogy of the oppressed.* New York, NY: Continuum.

Fruchter, N. (2007). *Urban schools, public will: Making education work for all our children.* New York, NY: Teachers College Press.

Gambone, M. A., Cao Yu, H., Lewis-Charp, H., Sipe, C. L., & Lacoe, J. (2004, March). *A comparative analysis of community youth development strategies.* Paper presented at the biennial meeting of the Society for Research on Adolescence, Baltimore, MD.

Ginwright, S. (2002). *Youth organizing: Expanding possibilities for youth development* (Occasional Papers Series No. 3). New York, NY: Funder's Collaborative on Youth Organizing.

Ginwright, S., & James, T. (2002). From assets to agents of change: Social justice, organizing, and youth development. *New Directions for Youth Development, 96,* 27–46.

Giugni. (1999). How social movements matter: Past research, present problems, future developments. In M. Giugni, D. McAdam, & C. Tilly (Eds.), *How social movements matter* (pp. xiii–xxxiii). Minneapolis, MN: University of Minnesota Press.

Gutmann, A. (1987). *Democratic education.* Princeton, NJ: Princeton University Press.

HoSang, D. (2006). Beyond policy: Ideology, race and the reimagining of youth. In S. Ginwright, P. Noguera, & J. Cammarota (Eds.). *Beyond resistance! Youth activism and community change* (pp. 3–19). New York, NY: Routledge.

Jones, K. R., & Perkins, D. F. (2004). Youth–adult partnerships. In C. B. Fisher & R. M. Lerner (Eds.), *Applied developmental science: An encyclopedia of research, policies, and programs* (pp. 1159–1163). Thousand Oaks, CA: Sage.

Jones, M., & Yonezawa, S. (2008). Student-driven research. *Educational Leadership, 66*(4). Retrieved from http://www.ascd.org/publications/educational_leadership

Katzenstein, M. F. (1998). *Faithful and fearless: Moving feminist protest inside the church and military.* Princeton, NJ: Princeton University Press.

Kincheloe, J. (2007). Clarifying the purpose of engaging students as researchers. In D. Thiessen & A. Cook-Sather (Eds.), *International handbook of student experience in elementary and secondary school* (pp. 745–774). Dordrecht, The Netherlands: Springer.

Kirshner, B. (2006). Moral voices of politically-engaged urban youth. In D.B. Fink (Ed.), *Doing the right thing: Ethical developmental across diverse environments: New Directions for youth development 108* (pp. 31–43). San Francisco, CA: Jossey-Bass.

Kirshner, B. (2008). Guided participation in three youth activism organizations: Facilitation, apprenticeship, and joint work. *Journal of the Learning Sciences, 17*(1), 60–101.

Kirshner, B., O'Donoghue, J. L., & McLaughlin, M. W. (Eds.). (2003). *New directions for youth development: Youth participation improving institutions and communities.* San Francisco, CA: Jossey-Bass.

Kress, C. A. (2006). Youth leadership and youth development: Connections and questions. *New Directions for Youth Development 2006* (109), 45–56.

Kwon, S.A. (2006). Youth of color organizing for juvenile justice. In S. Ginwright, P. Noguera, & J. Cammarota (Eds.), *Beyond resistance! Youth activism and community change: New democratic possibilities for policy and practice for America's youth* (pp. 215–228). Oxford, UK: Routledge.

Larson, R.W., & Hansen, D. (2005). The development of strategic thinking: Learning to impact human systems in a youth activism program. *Human Development, 48*(6), 327–349.

Lerner, R. M., Almerigi, J. B., Theokas, C., & Lerner, J. V. (2005). Positive youth development: A view of the issues. *Journal of Early Adolescence, 25*(1), 10–16.

Levin, B. (2000). Putting students at the centre in education reform. *International Journal of Educational Change, 1*(2), 155–172.

Lipman, P. (2004). *High stakes education.* New York, NY: Routledge–Falmer.

McAdam, D., McCarthy, J. D., & Zald, M. N. (1996). *Comparative perspectives on social movements: Political opportunities, mobilizing structures, and cultural framings.* Cambridge, UK: Cambridge University Press.

McAdam, D., Tarrow, S., & Tilly, C. (1996). To map contentious politics. *Mobilization, 1*(1), 17–34.

McLaughlin, M., Scott, W. R., Deschenes, S., Hopkins, K., & Newman, A. (2009). *Between movement and establishment: Organizations advocating for youth.* Stanford, CA: Stanford University Press.

Mitra, D. L. (2004). The significance of students: Can increasing "student voice" in schools lead to gains in youth development? *Teachers College Record, 106*(4), 651–688.

Mitra, D. L. (2006). Educational change on the inside and outside: The positioning of challengers. *International Journal of Leadership Education, 9*(4), 315–328.

Mitra, D. L. (2008a). *Student voice in school reform: Building youth–adult partnerships that strengthen schools and empower youth.* Albany, NY: State University of New York Press.

Mitra, D. L. (2008b). Balancing power in communities of practice: An examination of increasing student voice through school-based youth–adult partnerships. *Journal of Educational Change, 9*(3), 221–324.

Mitra, D. L. (2009a). Student voice and student roles in education policy and policy reform. In D. N. Plank, G. Sykes, & B. Schneider (Eds.), *AERA Handbook on Education Policy Research* (pp. 819–830). London, UK: Routledge.

Mitra, D. L. (2009b). Collaborating with students: Building youth–adult partnerships in schools. *American Journal of Education, 15*(3), 407–436.

Mitra, D. L. (2009c). The role of intermediary organizations in sustaining student voice initiatives. *Teachers College Record 111*(7), 1834–1868.

Mitra, D.L., Sanders, F.S., & Perkins, D.F. (2010). Providing spark and stability: The role of intermediary organizations in establishing school-based youth-adult partnerships. *Applied Developmental Science, 12*(14), 1–18.

Moore, K. (1999). Political protest and institutional change: The anti-Vietnam war movement and American state. In M. Giugni, D. McAdam, & C. Tilly (Eds.), *How social movements matter* (pp. 97–115). Minneapolis, MN: University of Minnesota.

Oakes, J., & Lipton, M. (2002). Struggling for educational equity in diverse communities: School reform as a social movement. *Journal of Educational Change, 3*(3–4), 383–406.

Oakes, J., & Rogers, J. (2006). *Learning power: Organizing for education and justice.* New York, NY: Teachers College Press.

Renee, M., Welner, K. G., & Oakes, J. (in press). Social movement organizing and equity-focused educational change: Shifting the zone of mediation. In A. Hargreaves, A. Lieberman, M. Fullan, & D. Hopkins (Eds.) *International handbook of educational change* (2nd ed.; pp. 153–168). New York, NY: Springer International Handbooks.

Rudduck, J., & Flutter, J. (2004). *How to improve your school.* London, UK: Continuum.

Sanders, F., Movit, M., Mitra, D., & Perkins, D. F. (2007). Examining ways in which youth conferences can spell out gains in positive youth development. *LEARNing Landscapes, 1*(1), 49–78.

Warren, M. R., Mira, M., & Nikundiwe, T. (2008). Youth organizing: From youth development to school reform. *New Directions for Youth Development, 117*, 27–42.

Watkins, N. D., Larson, R. W., & Sullivan, P. J. (2007). Bridging intergroup difference in a community youth program. *American Behavioral Scientist, 51*, 380–402.

Watts, R., & Flanagan, C. (2007). Pushing the envelope on civic engagement: A developmental and liberation psychology perspective. *The Journal of Community Psychology, 35*, 779–792.

Watts, R. J., Williams, N. C., & Jagers, R. J. (2003). Sociopolitical development. *American Journal of Community Psychology, 31*(1–2), 185–194

Westheimer, J., & Kahne, J. (2004). What kind of citizen? The politics of educating for democracy. *American Educational Research Journal, 41*(2), 237–270.

CHAPTER 5

WHEN STUDENTS "SPEAK BACK"

Student Engagement Towards a Socially Just Society

John Smyth

ABSTRACT

This chapter explores theoretically and practically the rationale, approaches, possibilities, and effects of engaging with students in schools in ways that challenge injustices and that regard education as being *for* social justice. Examples and illustrations are drawn from research by the author in Australia from over 25 critical ethnographies of disadvantaged schools conducted over the past two decades. The central framing themes and ideas for the chapter focus on:

- student voice
- the relational school
- the pedagogically engaged school
- community organizing for activist reform
- community-voiced approaches to schooling
- "speaking the unpleasant" about poverty, education, and class
- beyond commodification, prescription, and consumption

Student Engagement in Urban Schools, pages 73–90
Copyright © 2012 by Information Age Publishing
73

- dismantling social hierarchies
- pursuing connectionist pedagogies
- creating spaces for dialogue, reflection and innovation
- "doing education" democratically

The chapter presents a number of ethnographic slices or portraits of students and schools that have created ways of "working against the grain" in the sense of foregrounding notions of social justice and challenging dominant, deforming, and damaging approaches to education and supplanting them with alternatives. The chapter explores what is possible when teachers, students, parents, and communities take seriously the opportunity to embrace a socially critical view of student engagement.

INTRODUCTION

Over the past few years I have written a number of papers/chapters that have addressed the broad theme of "students speaking back" (Smyth, 2006a, 2006b, 2007, 2008, 2009, 2010). After first addressing what I mean by the notion of students and schools "speaking back," what I want to do in this chapter is advance that topic in a new and urgent direction, by addressing two questions:

- What kind of social, economic, and political conditions are students "speaking back" to?
- What kind of sociological conditions need to be brought into existence in/through schools for this to be possible?

Perhaps I need to start by revealing something about why and how I came to be interested in this topic. For over a decade I have been researching and writing about what is happening in young lives when students from the most disadvantaged backgrounds euphemistically "drop out" of school (Smyth, Angus, Down & McInerney, 2008, 2009; Smyth, Down & McInerney, 2010; Smyth, Hattam, Cannon, Edwards, Wilson, & Wurst, 2000, 2004; Smyth & McInerney, 2007a). As a matter of fact, they don't actually "drop out"—that is a particular disposition and interpretation of what is going on—they are more often than not pushed out, eased out, or repelled by what is generally on offer in schools, for a variety of reasons I will come to shortly. To say that they are "dropouts" is to imply that somehow they are to blame—they have been lazy, indolent, or simply have given up trying. To be more accurate, when young people give up on school it is usually after a considerable period of careful consideration in which the final act is a positive statement that school is not for them.

When I use the phraseology of "speaking back," I am not suggesting in any sense that students should be cheeky, rude, or insolent—rather what I am saying is that in concert with their schools, they are positioning themselves in ways in which they make it clear that they are unprepared to continue to accept the current situation in schools as it is. In other words, borrowing from the title of Shor's (1996) book, *When Students Have Power*—the question is what happens when students challenge the existing state of arrangements in schools, under what set of conditions, and what occurs as a result? (For an example of this, see Smyth & McInerney, 2007b.) What is being developed then is the capacity for students to have a voice over their education, in a situation where the dominant voice is that of others who have an agenda that is a long way removed from that of marginalized students—and that, furthermore, is likely to be harmful, even damaging to their lives, interests and life chances.

Shor (1996), along with people like Fine (1989), refers to the way in which non-middle-class students "have learned socially to construct themselves as exiles" (Shor, 1996, p. 12) in an institution that is unsympathetic and indifferent to them, at best, and at worst, is overtly hostile. Shor says this takes the metaphorical form of young people freezing themselves out of school while still being there in name only—or as some quipped, as RHINOs (really here in name only). They construct themselves into a zone that Shor (1996) labels "Siberia." He argues that the "Siberian syndrome" constitutes a kind of "self-protective negative agency" (p. 14) in which students can appear to "be rejecting authority and submitting to it at the same time" (p. 12). What is being rejected, resisted or denied here is the legitimacy of school as a social institution by young people switching off, tuning out, and rejecting its largely "uncritical anti-dialogic curriculum" (p. 11). The mutual effect on teachers and students is palpable and immediate: "Empowered institutionally by the system but not constitutionally through negotiation with students, the teacher cannot escape problems of resistance and control. In such a non-negotiable regime, students are intellectual and political exiles who grow more cleverly and distant as they age" (Shor, 1996, p. 14).

SPEAKING BACK TO WHAT?

When we talk about urban schools in the U.S., inner-city schools in the UK, or schools that have been *put at* a disadvantage in the Australian context, we are speaking about schools that have, whether we acknowledge it or not, been positioned in a particular way right from the start, and to that extent we might therefore expect problems borne out of significant cultural mismatches. If we are to be blatantly honest, the institution of schooling in contemporary western societies is a demonstrably middle-class concept—it speaks to middle-class values of politeness, acquiescence, civility, and manners, and requires a deferral of immediacy that fits reasonably easily with people accustomed to deferred gratification. On the other hand, these are qualities that constitute forms of cultural socialization that may rest very uneasily with people for whom questions of relevance, meaning, and presentism loom very large in the struggle of their daily lives.

When schools present or are required to present themselves in a one-size-fits-all fashion that is deaf to culture, differential histories, aspirations, and the cultural way in which lives are led, then what we have, to use Fine's (1991) terminology, is a "frame-up" that cannot but culminate in "interactive trouble" (Freebody, Ludwig & Gunn, 1995) as groups are required to suppress their personal identities (Smyth et al., 2004, p. 132). Interactive trouble occurs when there is a breakdown in intercultural communication—and schools are cultures—in which there is considerable scope for misunderstanding cultural cues. To succeed, students and their parents need to have developed the recognizable middle-class dispositions to schooling that are considered crucial to success, or else a scapegoat has to be found—and invariably that is of a victim-blaming kind.

Where this line of argument is leading me is in the direction of saying that for non-middle-class students, engagement with learning and indeed the whole institution of schooling, has much to do with the degree and extent to which schools present as social institutions able to flex and re-invent themselves around the lives, experiences, and desires of non-traditional or non-middle-class students. This is a radical and unconventional idea in a climate deeply marked and scarred by an underlying expectation that it is students who should conform and act in ways that reflect favorably on what are deemed indicators of educational quality and achievement in contexts of national testing regimes and international league tables.

The notion of schools being *for* and in the interests of students, particularly those from poor backgrounds, is markedly at odds with the kind of three-ringed circus we regularly witness at the moment. For example, at the time of writing, Australian Prime Minister and Minister for Education, Julia Gillard, was part of an international forum sponsored by former governor of Florida Jeb Bush and shared the platform with UK ultraconservative educational policy academic James Tooley. The session was entitled "Allies in the International Education Arms Race" (Harrison, 2009). There are no prizes for being able to guess whose interests are being served by events like this!

On the contrary, when we have student engagement in the expansive rather than the narrow, diminished, or instrumental sense in which that term is used, then what occurs is the creation of an atmosphere and an approach in which schools are hospitable to the lives of those who are generally regarded as the most unwelcome in schools. In a real sense, the lives of these students, their families, and their communities are foregrounded and placed at the center of everything schools do. It ought to be the case that it is easier for students to secure and hold the moral voice with which to indignantly speak back to polices like NCLB and what they are doing to the lives of the most vulnerable young people, than it is for teachers to capture this ground. When teachers try to speak back to policy stupidity, they are punished or pilloried in public as being "political," "unprofessional," or "self-serving" in acting only to preserve sinecured self-interests. It is much harder for such accusations to be dismissed when they come from students in the most marginalized or disadvantaging contexts—in a very real sense, students are the ultimate stakeholders to whom school must be held accountable—even if that means naming and usurping stupid policies. Young people in schools are the most powerful and reliable witnesses to what is working or not for them in advancing their lives and life chances—not distant policy actors who are remote from classrooms and communities. As Sizer and Sizer (1999) so aptly put it in the title of their book: *The Students are Watching*.

At this point I want to briefly address three of the most significant issues students from contexts of disadvantage find themselves having to "speak back" to. These are not meant to be exhaustive of the range of issues, but they are somewhat indicative of a much larger number of issues emanating from the same crucible of structural inequality.

1. Lack of Respect

Urban and disadvantaged contexts are frequently portrayed as if the overarching problem is merely one of rectifying material deprivation—this is certainly a major element, but by no means the only or major aspect. As long as we think about the issue in this partial resources-driven way, then the "solutions" will reflect this diminished disposition. We are coming to understand that recognition and symbolic issues of power, voice, inclusion, and exclusion feature very prominently in contexts of disadvantaging. When it comes to educational engagement, whether learning occurs in these situations has a lot to do with how the lives of those involved are recognized as having worth and how that translates pedagogically.

A word like respect is notoriously difficult to define, but sociologist Richard Sennett (2003) in wrestling with it regards respect as growing out of a fundamental recognition of inequality. When applied to urban and disadvantaged schooling, Hodges and Welch (2003) capture what is involved here in the title of their book *Negotiating Educational Meaning and Transforming the Margins*—what they are arguing is that this constitutes undoing damage. That's a nice way of putting it. When it comes to educational engagement there are multiple forms in which disrespect does its ugly and hurtful work. Most of these, far from recognizing difference, are committed to constructing vernacular lives as being worthless/deficient and in need of programmatic remediation. For example, one of the most common approaches is to use the stigmatizing and stereotyping label "at risk" to effectively position the "other" as deviant and in need of obliteration/reconstruction. Ignoring, demeaning, and denigrating the lives, cultures, and histories of those considered inferior has long been a strategic hallmark of institutional colonizers like schools. As long as the fiction of inferiority can be maintained it is not difficult to sustain the argument around the need to laminate over local cultures, languages, and social practices by using practices like testing to develop hierarchical forms of academic tracking that lead to scripted forms of learning for subalterns that lack rigor (e.g., rote learning and direct instruction), and that end up endorsing the self-fulfilling views of diminished ineducability. These are deeply disrespectful and damaging approaches that have been allowed to masquerade for far too long as legitimate educational practices, and they are only sustainable for as long as we refuse to name and go along with their underlying premise of inferiority.

2. Absence of Relational Power

Relationships are the social fabric or glue of educational engagement, and when relationships become corrupted, corroded, or are prevented from coming into existence, then, as Bingham and Sidorkin (2004) aptly put it in the title of their book, there is *No Education Without Relation*. Relationships between teachers and students are the relays or carriers through which learning is made possible. It is at the level of the interpersonal that trust, which is crucial to learning, is created. As an assistant principal in one of our research projects put it to us in respect of the disadvantaged students in his school, "the kids need to learn you first, then they learn your stuff." In other words, these kinds of students cannot learn without first forming relationships.

Warren (2005) defines relational power as the resources with which "to get things done collectively" (p. 138), and in the process "to confront power inequalities" (p. 138). Elsewhere, I have summarized what I understand him to be saying as it relates to teaching and learning:

> This [relational power] seems appropriate when referring to an activity like learning, because it is only when reciprocal trust exists, in which students for their part, trust that their teachers will provide them with forms of learning that are worthwhile, interesting and rigorous, and teachers for their part, trust that students are intellectually and socially capable and sufficiently committed to make the necessary investment of effort, that learning occurs. (Smyth, 2007, pp. 230–231)

Another way of putting this is that teaching is fundamentally emotional work that involves getting up close to students and drawing heavily on social, emotional resources, and the energy necessary for continual improvisation. Connell (1996) put this succinctly when he said that "Good teaching... involves a gift relation. It is founded on a public rather than a private interest" (p. 6). This "gift relation" is especially important in challenging urban and disadvantaged contexts where trust may have been severely eroded. In other words, teaching and learning constitute an emotional exchange that requires the participants to go beyond their individual self-interests, even to the point of considerable vulnerability.

All of this is by way of highlighting that when relationships are institutionalized, as is the case in processes of bureaucratic accountability, where students are treated in detached and hierarchical ways that distance them from relational intimacy and view them as defective categories in need of technical remediation—then the basis of learning is totally undermined.

3. "Depleted Credential"

Another of the exclusionary and dispossessing strategies urban and disadvantaged young people have to speak back to are processes that deflect them into educational cul-de-sacs. Tuck and colleagues' notion of a "depleted credential" (Tuck, Allen, Bacha, Morales, Quinter, & Thompson, 2008, p. 53) is a useful category with which to start thinking about what it is that urban and disadvantaged students are being offered. Tuck et al. (2008) argue that in the case of the U.S., the GED (general educational development) credential, which is the alternative to high school graduation, is used as "a disguise for pushing out unwanted students in New York City high schools" (p. 52). As they put it, a depleted credential is one that "lies less in it being a gateway to higher education and employment and more in being a get-away from inhospitable high schools" (p. 53) for students. In other words, the government-mandated press on schools to be seen to perform highly on tests and the forms of image and impression management these bring to consumerist notions of school choice, puts "pressure on schools to push out students who would not do well on standardized tests" (p. 53)—and in order to save face on this "pushing out," governments have to be seen to be saving face by creating alternative credentials—debased, dumbed-down facsimiles though they may be. What these debauched credentials do is cut students off from access to valued and important knowledge necessary to access higher education and well-paid employment.

At a more general level, the vocationalization of education for urban and disadvantaged students acts as a decoy deflecting working class and students of color into diversionary streams that lead to diminished opportunities for further learning and valuable employment prospects.

Given this partial and synoptic view of the wider conditions shaping and afflicting the educational lives of young people who have been *put at* a disadvantage (notice the deliberate positional inflection here), I want to turn now to Hodges and Welch's (2003) notion of "undoing damage." There are a variety of ways I might have put this, but Tuck et al. (2008) have in my view cut to the chase when they refer to "reclaiming, recovering, and carving out personal/political space" (p. 68). The reason nomenclature like this is so apt here is that it emphasizes the agency young people have in recovering what has been lost or taken from them. Far from being hapless victims they are active agents—which is to say, powerful people.

BRINGING INTO EXISTENCE WHAT CONDITIONS?

The notion of recovering or creating spaces within which to "speak back" is a very useful heuristic with which to conceive of the crafting of any reclamation—or what Anyon (2005) labels 'radical possibilities.' It is after all, out of the ruins, the interstices, the cracks, and the crevices between solidified binaries that new and unimagined options have to be crafted.

The kind of critical democratic engagement that I am speaking to comprises a constellation of three elements with a number of salient features as portrayed in Figure 5.1.

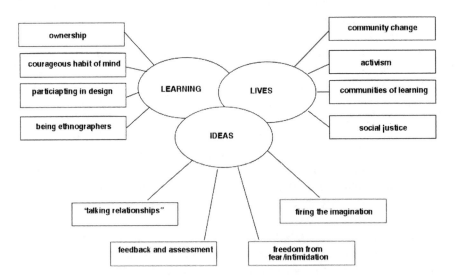

Figure 5.1 Critical democratic engagement around student voice. *Source*: Smyth, 2009.

Drawing from McMahon and Portelli (2004), elsewhere I have summarized what I take critical democratic engagement to mean, in these terms:

> [E]ngagement is located within notions of what it means to be an 'active citizen' rather than compliance as a passive 'spectator'. Engagement occurs in the daily interactions that occur between teachers, students and community members around attempts to produce democratic relationships in schools and between schools and their communities. There is a preparedness to recognize existing inequalities, to challenge authoritative discourses, to confront injustices, and to not accept the status quo. (Smyth et al., 2008, p. 5)

Each of these features seem to me to be deserving of brief discussion in the wider context of student engagement that contests and supplants neoliberal discourses in urban and disadvantaged school contexts. These features, while not masquerading as "standards" or "criteria"—for that would be to become complicit in the whole neoliberal sham of measurement, calibration, and stratification—nevertheless present us a useful set of touchstones around which to "test" the genuineness or authenticity of an alternative.

ON LEARNING

Ownership of Learning

In many respects this is the cornerstone of authentic student engagement—without it, students are less than full stakeholders in their own learning. As long as we fail as adults to fully grasp this and act upon it, then nothing will change and students will continue to do what they are doing in disturbing and growing numbers around the world—exercising active choice by "tuning out," "switching off," and "dropping out" of schooling. In the U.S., they have a name for this—it is called the "silent epidemic" (Bridgeland, Dilulio, & Morison, 2006)—albeit for a very different set of reasons to what I am speaking about here. Young people tell us repeatedly that when they are not accorded a modicum of ownership of their learning, then school is not for them. I will explore some more detail around this issue below in a moment.

Courageous 'Habit of Mind'

What I am alluding to here, and acknowledgement to Cintron (1997) and Gustavson (2007) for arousing my attention here, is Aristotle's notion of *tekhne*—or as Cintron (1997) put it, "a reasoned habit of mind in making something" (p. xii). Following Gustavson's (2007) take on it, having a rea-soned habit of mind means having the disposition to understand that learn-ing occurs when creative spaces are created. My addition of the word "cre-ative" is meant to signify that in the mean times we live in that monologue is preferred over dialogue, it requires extreme courage to speak back to the "tension between idiosyncratic ways of working and the often prescribed and decontextualized ways of working and learning found in many schools" (Gustavson, 2007, p. 4.). Teachers who challenge the dominant viewpoint are at risk of personal and professional damage, but unless they push back into the synthetic reifications, then authentic critical democratic engage-ment by students will not be possible. Having a courageous habit of mind is a quality teachers have to infuse in their students through having them learn "on their own terms"—to borrow from the title of Gustavson's book.

Participating in Design

When we speak about student ownership of learning, this has to involve the full gamut—from inception around what might be worthwhile and rel-evant learning that connects to students' lives, to having a say in shaping the nature of how they will engage with that learning (where, when, and with whom), through to how students will be assessed and judged along the way on their learning (more about this later). If students are drawn into meaningful dialogue around questions of relevance and meaning, and there is a genuine attempt to negotiate a curriculum (even around existing mandated frameworks), then students will experience learning in which they will have a real stake as they experiment and improvise. Issues of stu-dent motivation, discipline, and early school leaving will take on quite a different hue and be seen as they rightfully should, as issues to do with a relevant and engaging learning rather than reasons for castigating, blam-ing, and punishing students.

Being Ethnographers

Acquiring the analytical skills and abilities to be able to reflect on their own learning and to see how it is leading them along pathways towards val-ued educational ends they have devised for themselves (with others), has to be one of the most crucial aspects of becoming engaged learners of the kind being discussed here. I can think of no more appropriate label than one of students-as-ethnographers—by which I mean developing the skills with which to recognize and navigate their way though the policy, practice, and everyday life issues that present as challenges, obstacles, and impediments to their learning and being prepared to name them.

ON IDEAS

"Talking Relationships"

Consistent with what I have been arguing throughout this chapter, in a paper entitled "Marginalization, Identity Formation, and Empowerment," Quijada (2008) argues that in the moral panics that have come to frame young people, "talking relationships" constitute the best available way of capturing "social spaces . . . by individuals who are continually silenced yet demand representation because they afford new possibilities towards social transformation" (p. 209). What Quijada is arguing is that developing relationships by talking with young people is the only real way of challenging stereotypes and understanding marginalization. Providing venues in which such "talking relationships" can be spoken into existence is a crucial venue through which young people can pursue their concerns for social justice.

Feedback and Assessment

This is one of the most contentious educational issues of our times. The entire project of educational assessment and reporting has been completely hijacked by the neoliberal free marketers. They regard ownership of educational measurement and assessment as their inalienable right. Assessment of learning was not devised as a tool of the market economy—as a device for converting citizens into educational consumers with public schools being forced by market forces to shape up or ship out. The challenge is how to reclaim assessment of learning for its rightful purpose—informing students on their learning progress. Students are the only ones who have the real power to demand the return of assessment through having

- a central role in determining the form of assessment (e.g., portfolios)
- direct personal involvement in how information is conveyed to them (e.g., as equal third parties in parent/teacher interviews/conferences)
- full negotiation rights as to the form that assessment will take at the commencement of learning tasks.

These will be controversial matters but unless they are confronted in an activist way then educational experiences will continue to be degraded and diminished. Such actions will need to occur among activist teachers, parents and students in order to restore student's interests to their rightful place. This may be a case for returning to the sage advice of Postman and Weingartner (1969) in their classic *Teaching as a Subversive Activity* and its companion *The Soft Revolution: A Student Handbook* (1971).

Firing the Imagination

One of the features that overwhelmingly characterize the learning of students in urban and disadvantaged contexts is the presumption that they cannot or will not learn. This is ingrained to the point of becoming a mantra and everything else flows from it. The most demeaning and insulting aspect comes in the dumbed-down educational diet on offer to these students—it is uninspiring, deficit-driven, and most of all totally lacking in rigor and variety. In the supposed quest to raise achievement scores in these schools—presumably to enable them to damage themselves even more through school choice and league tables—these schools end up becoming deeply unattractive self-fulfilling ghettoes. They are unattractive to teachers, students are treated in ways that reflect their alleged diminished capacities, and everyone in them responds according to the plan in what Haberman (1991) calls a "pedagogy of poverty".

There is an alternative, and it is patently clear—what Sam Intrator labels teaching that is *Tuned In and Fired Up* (2003). In its sharpest form this is teaching in which teachers "connect, care, conspire with students: they listen, laugh, and love them into learning"—to cite from Rick Jackson on the dustcover. What Intrator (2003) offers us is a window to hope on what is mostly on offer in these schools, where learning is not "ground into the dust," teachers are not "wooden" caricatures, and students' minds are far removed from being "passive and disconnected" (p. 15). The alternative is one in which students are "connected and fired up," "brimming over" (p. 131) with generative thinking, and feel "a connection between the subject under study and their own well-being" (Intrator, 2003, p. 130). Students present as "alive," "engaged," and "provoked," and above all they feel an "emotional attachment" (p. 132) to what they are learning. In part, this means students are being taught to inquire into how things came to be the way they are, and what keeps them that way.

Freedom from Fear/Intimidation

It follows from what I have been arguing that engagement of the kind being suggested needs to occur in an environment free from a culture of blame, where vindictive punishments are not meted out for an inability to progress, and instead, there is a careful cultivation of a supportive climate in which taking risks is encouraged and learning constructively from failure is paramount. This is a long way removed from the current situation in which, to invoke comment of the father of neoliberalism Frederich Hayek's (1976) assertion of social justice being a "mirage," "disadvantaged groups are little more than failures in the marketplace" (Davis, 2008, p. 5).

ON LIVES

Communities of Learning

It almost goes without saying that when young people are asked how they like to learn or what makes learning fun for them, they invariably indicate a desire to learn in the company of one another. Indeed, it is when young people are compelled to learn in isolation, solitude, or without communication with one another that we encounter a further source of "interactive trouble" (Freebody et al., 1995)—as young people make their feelings on this known to the institution of schooling. This is often given expression in the way they liken schools to prisons, containment, and incarceration. It seems that the process of learning for young people almost has hard-wired to it the co-requisite that they need the opportunity to check things out with one another and indeed assist one another in making sense of complexity as well as decisions about their learning. This runs quite counter to the neoliberal project of individualization and the regimes of testing, ranking, comparison, and the attribution of merit—all of which has more to do with the self-edification of adults, schools, systems, or national economies, and very little if anything to do with the inherent needs of young people themselves.

When we inhibit or fail to bring into existence conditions conducive of this kind for young people, what we do is stunt, diminish, and damage their capacity to learn, as they seek recognition from one another in the process of risk-taking, experimentation, and identity formation. Where this often comes to a head is when young people are asked why they "dropped out" of school or terminated their formal learning—and they will often speak quite forcefully about the effect this kind of banishment from their peers has on their self-image. It is an issue they are often prepared to take a strong stand on.

Social Justice

Young people regardless of where they live or come from seem to readily form views about what is fair and just—this can often be around treatment afforded to them personally, but equally it can be in respect of what they consider to be equitable treatment of others. When this occurs in the context of schooling, it is sometimes wrongly interpreted by adults as insolence or insubordination, something to be arrested and which can quickly escalate into a major altercation. This becomes all the more poignant when it is directed back at a teacher or person in authority. It is much rarer for instances of fairness and equity to be seen and acted upon as "teachable moments"—opportunities to be grasped pedagogically for what they offer to work with young people in revealing deeper structural issues of causation. When teachers do seize these nascent opportunities to work with young minds in a safe and receptive way, what occurs is that young people are taught how to examine and analyze the way hidden message systems are made opaque through the workings of power. Socially critical teachers are attuned to capturing and making the most of such opportunities—what Kirshner (2006) calls "sociopolitical problem framing" or the capacity to focus on systemic factors rather than individual pathologies (p. 49).

Activism

In one of the most sobering books on what is being 'done to' American education and young people, in a case study of the New York public education system Salz (2008) makes the point that "protest is not enough: there must be a positive alternative" (p. xix). He makes his point by invoking Wallis (2005): "protest should not be merely the politics of complaint... It should instead show the way for both personal and social transformation. That's what excites people and invites them to give their lives for something larger than themselves" (cited in Salz, 2008, p. xix).

In advancing this perspective, Ginwright, Cammarota & Noguera (2005) provide a most useful five-point entrée into how policies towards young people need to be radically recast, including: (1) jettisoning the current coercive policy trajectory that treats young people as "second-class citizens," effectively amputating them from full democratic participation; (2) a departure from existing conceptual frameworks that are either "problem-driven" (i.e.,see young people as a threat to society) or "possibility-driven" (i.e., view them only as "passive consumers of civic life"); and instead of these, that (3) policies towards young people be conceptualized within the wider political economy and social conditions of their lives, including, most notably, "urban decay, economic deprivation, health care deficiencies, racism, police harassment, and educational demise" (Ginwright et al., 2005, p. 25); and, (4) starting from the political economy of young lives enables an illumination and articulation of "an alternative, social justice framework that emphasizes young people's potential to play a vital role in social and community problem solving" (p. 25); and finally, (5) through social activism conceived in this way, it becomes possible to envisage how young people can act collectively "to change coercive and debilitating public policy" (p. 25).

A framework of this kind has the decided merit of both enabling a focus on the "conditions that impede young people's healthy development" and the institutional failure that inhibits this, while also pointing to "proactive methods" by which young people themselves might replace approaches of "control and containment" (Ginwright et al., 2005, p. 25). While there is not the space to deal with these here, others have provided extensive exemplars—see for instance, Ginwright and James (2002) in their paper entitled "From Assets to Agents of Change: Social Justice, Organizing, and Youth Development." They indicate how young people are increasingly demanding and securing a voice in decisions that affect their lives through making institutions accountable while changing the landscape of communities in which they live.

Community Change

This is a most apposite note on which to transit from the above and bring to a conclusion discussion of my orienting constellation of *critical democratic engagement around student voice*. The essence of what I have been saying variously throughout this chapter is that it is insufficient to have young people"speaking back" simply by raising their voices—this needs to be part of a much wider, deeper, and more strategic process that is sutured into a commitment to social justice, which means learning how to recognize and name inequities and having the courage and being politically savvy and prudent in how they push back into changing the conditions that create inequities in the first place, and that continue to sustain and maintain that state of affairs.

REFERENCES

Anyon, J. (2005). *Radical possibilities: Public policy, urban education and a new social movement.* New York, NY: Routledge.

Bingham, C., & Sidorkin, M. (Eds.). (2004). *No education without relation.* New York, NY: Peter Lang Publishing.

Bridgeland, J., DiIulio, J., & Morison, K. (2006). *The silent epidemic: Perspectives of high school dropouts.* Washington, DC: Civic Enterprises for the Bill and Melinda Gates Foundation.

Cintron, R. (1997). *Angels' town: Chero ways, gang life, and rhetorics of the everyday.* Boston, MA: Beacon Press.

Connell, R. (1996). *Prepare for interesting times: Education in a fractured world.* Inaugural professorial address at the University of Sydney, Australia.

Davis, M. (2008). *Land of plenty.* Melbourne, Victoria: Melbourne University Press.

Fine, M. (1989). Silencing and nurturing voice in an improbable context: Urban adolescents in public school. In H. Giroux & P. McLaren (Eds.), *Critical pedagogy, the state and cultural struggle* (pp. 152–173). Albany, NY: State University of New York Press.

Fine, M. (1991). *Framing dropouts: Notes on the politics of an urban public high school.* Albany, NY: State University of New York Press.

Freebody, P., Ludwig, C., & Gunn, S. (1995). *Everyday literacy practices in and out of schools in low socio-economic urban communities* (Vol. 1). Melbourne, Victoria: Curriculum Corporation.

Ginwright, S., Cammarota, J., & Noguera, P. (2005). Youth, social justice, and communities: Toward a theory of urban youth policy. *Social Justice, 32*(3), 24–40.

Ginwright, S., & James, T. (2002). From assets to agents of change: Social justice and youth development. In B. Kirshner, J. O'Donaghue, & M. McLaughlin (Eds.), *Youth participation: Improving institutions and communities: New directions for youth development 96* (pp. 27–46). San Francisco: Jossey-Bass.

Gustavson, L. (2007). *Youth learning on their own terms: Creative practices and classroom teaching.* London & New York, NY: Routledge.

Haberman, M. (1991). The pedagogy of poverty versus good teaching. *Phi Delta Kappan, 73*(4), 290–294.

Harrison, D. (2009, October 3). Gillard goes Bush. *Sydney Morning Herald.* Retrieved from http://www.smh.com.au/national/gillard-goes-bush-20091002-ggit.html

Hayek, F. A. (1976). *Law, legislation and liberty, Vol. 2: The mirage of social justice.* Chicago, IL: University of Chicago Press.

Hodges, C., & Welch, O. (2003). *Making schools work: Negotiating educational meaning and transforming the margins.* New York, NY: Peter Lang Publishing.

Intrator, S. (2003). *Tuned in and fired up.* New Haven, CT: Yale University Press.

Kirshner, B. (2006). Apprenticeship learning in youth activism. In S. Ginwright, P. Noguera & J. Cammarota (Eds.), *Beyond resistance! Youth activism and community change* (pp. 37–57). New York & London: Routledge.

McMahon, B., & Portelli, J. (2004). Engagement for what? Beyond popular discourses of student engagement. *Leadership and Policy in Schools, 3*(1), 59–76.

Postman, N., & Weingartner, C. (1969). *Teaching as a subversive activity.* Harmondsworth, England: Penguin.

Postman, N., & Weingartner, C. (1971). *The soft revolution: A student handbook for turning schools around.* New York, NY: Delacorte Press.

Quijada, D. (2008). Marginalization, identity formation, and empowerment: Youth's struggles for self and social justice. In N. Dolby & F. Rizvi (Eds.), *Youth moves: Identities and education in global perspectives* (pp. 207–220). New York & London: Routledge.

Salz, A. (2008). What is authentic educational reform? In H. Johnson & A. Salz (Eds.), *What is authentic educational reform? Pushing against the compassionate conservative agenda* (pp. xvii–xxii). Mahwah, NJ: Lawrence Erlbaum.

Sennett, R. (2003). *Respect in a world of inequality.* New York, NY: W. W. Norton.

Shor, I. (1996). *When students have power: Negotiating authority in a critical pedagogy.* Chicago, IL: University of Chicago Press.

Sizer, T., & Sizer, N. (1999). *The students are watching: Schools and the moral contract.* New York, NY: Beacon Press.

Smyth, J. (2006a). Educational leadership that fosters 'student voice.' *International Journal of Leadership in Education, 9*(4), 279–284.

Smyth, J. (2006b). 'When students have power': Student engagement, student voice, and the possibilities for school reform around 'dropping out' of school. *International Journal of Leadership in Education, 9*(4), 285–298.

Smyth, J. (2007). Toward the pedagogically engaged school: Listening to student voice as a positive response to disengagement and 'dropping out.' In D. Thiessen & A. Cook-Sather (Eds.), *International handbook of student experience of elementary and secondary school* (pp. 635–658). Dordrecht, The Netherlands: Springer Science.

Smyth, J. (2008). Listening to student voice in the democratisation of schooling. In E. Samier & Stanley, G, (Eds.), *Political approaches to educational administration and leadership* (pp. 240–251). London & New York, NY: Routledge.

Smyth, J. (2009). Inclusive school leadership strategies in disadvantaged schools based on student and community voice: Implications for Australian education policy. In C. Raffo, A. Dyson, H. Gunter, D. Hall, L. Jones, & A. Kalambouka (Eds.), *Education and poverty in affluent countries: Mapping the terrain and making the links to educational policy.* London & New York, NY: Routledge.

Smyth, J. (2010). The politics of derision, distrust and deficit—The damaging consequences for youth and communities put at a disadvantage. In E. Samier & M. Schmidt (Eds.), *Critical perspectives on trust and betrayal in educational administration and leadership.* London & New York, NY: Routledge.

Smyth, J., Angus, L., Down, B., & McInerney, P. (2008). *Critically engaged learning: Connecting to young lives.* New York, NY: Peter Lang Publishing.

Smyth, J., Angus, L., Down, B., & McInerney, P. (2009). *Activist and socially critical school and community renewal: Social justice in exploitative times.* Rotterdam, The Netherlands: Sense Publishers.

Smyth, J., Down, B., & McInerney, P. (2010). *'Hanging in with kids' in tough times: Engagement in contexts of educational disadvantage in the relational school.* New York, NY: Peter Lang Publishing.

Smyth, J., Hattam, R., Cannon, J., Edwards, J., Wilson, N., & Wurst, S. (2000). *Listen to me, I'm leaving: Early school leaving in South Australian secondary schools.* Adelaide, South Australia: Flinders Institute for the Study of Teaching; Department of Employment, Education and Training; Senior Secondary Assessment Board of South Australia.

Smyth, J., Hattam, R., Cannon, J., Edwards, J., Wilson, N., & Wurst, S. (2004). *'Dropping out,' drifting off, being excluded: Becoming somebody without school.* New York, NY: Peter Lang Publishing.

Smyth, J., & McInerney, P. (2007a). *Teachers in the middle: Reclaiming the wasteland of the adolescent years of schooling.* New York, NY: Peter Lang Publishing.

Smyth, J., & McInerney, P. (2007b). "Living on the edge": A case of school reform working for disadvantaged adolescents. *Teachers College Record, 109*(5), 1123–1170.

Tuck, E., Allen, J., Bacha, M., Morales, A., Quinter, S., & Thompson, J. (2008). PAR praxes for now and future change: The collective of researchers on educational disappointment and desire. In J. Cammarota & M. Fine (Eds.), *Revolutionizing education: Youth participatory action research in motion* (pp. 49–83). New York & London: Routledge.

Warren, M. (2005). Communities and schools: A new view of urban school reform. *Harvard Educational Review, 75*(2), 133–173.

CHAPTER 6

ASPIRATION AND EDUCATION

Toward New Terms of Engagement for Marginalized Students

Sam Sellar and Trevor Gale[1]

ABSTRACT

Aspiration has figured strongly in recent policies around the globe aimed at increasing education participation, particularly for students from low socioeconomic status backgrounds. This emphasis extends from aspiration's prevalence in "third-way" policy strategies over the past two decades, where it has served to uneasily suture together social democratic impulses for broader distribution of resources and neoliberal impulses to stimulate social mobility through individual entrepreneurship in competitive markets. Such an approach has tended to elide the cultural dimensions of aspiration, often representing the desires of those from less powerful communities as deficit in relation to dominant cultural norms. This chapter examines three sets of data: (1) recent aspiration-focused higher education policy from the UK and Australia; (2) analyses of the demographic group often characterized as "aspirational"; and (3) group interviews with teachers working in disadvantaged communities on the urban fringe of an Australian city. Analysis of these data challenges deficit representations and evaluations of the aspirations of mar-

Student Engagement in Urban Schools, pages 91–109

ginalized groups in policy and popular discourse and argues for the need to create dialogic spaces in education, where diverse imaginaries of the future can be heard and valued, and where these groups can speak back to the dominant normative contexts in which they are encouraged to aspire.

Because teenagers are materialistic, I've started talking about what things you want to buy and how do you get to that stage and you can't get to the brand new [car] or a new house or a trip overseas on the dole, you know.

—Sophie, Secondary School Teacher

INTRODUCTION

This strategy, described by a teacher from a school focused on engaging particularly disaffected students, is animated by a key concept for "third way" politics over the past decade—*aspiration.* In the above account, students' engagement is predicated on identifying what they *want* and appreciating how education can enable them to *own or consume* it. Economic aspirations of this kind, here formulated specifically in terms of consumer desire, are considered to be a potent force for stimulating the broader distribution of goods, including the outcomes of education, through market mechanisms. Given the pervasiveness of this neoliberal logic in education policy over recent decades, it is not surprising to see it channelled in this teacher's attempts to engage students by describing how education offers her students a powerful means to economic ends.

Such economic aspirations have been a prominent issue in Australian political debate over the past decade. During the early 2000s, Mark Latham—former leader of the Australian Parliamentary Labor Party—was a prominent exponent of neoliberal-leaning third way politics. Latham's (2003) policies were influenced by his assessment that "within the space of a generation, assumptions about ownership, skills and economic mobility have been transformed" (p. 66), and this change has given rise to a group of aspirational voters that constitute a distinctive fraction of the working class. For Latham, "the workers have had a taste of economic ownership and, not surprisingly, they want more" (p. 67). Writing specifically on education, he suggested that distributive justice policies limit such aspirations, and in response he drew together neoliberal philosophies and social democratic welfare impulses to develop concepts such as "aspirational equality," which he argued better acknowledge "the reality of social mobility, an electorate which wants people to get ahead through their own efforts and enterprise" (Latham, 2001, p. 22). In Latham's account, supporting working-class aspirations for economic assets, as well as helping to create savvy consumers, will help to redress economic inequality by promoting socioeconomic mobility and increased access to its concomitant benefits (Latham, 2003).

More recently, aspiration has emerged as a prominent concept in both Australian and UK higher education (HE) policies; although, it is generally considered to be lacking among low-socioeconomic status (SES) groups, rather than an available resource that is constrained by overly interventionist social justice policies. In both systems, HE policy is placing greater responsibility on universities to conduct outreach programs in schools and the wider community, in an effort to improve student engagement and levels of academic achievement (Bradley, Noonan, Nugent, & Scales, 2008; Commonwealth of Australia, 2009; UK Department for Education & Skills, 2006). In Australia, the most common aim of these programs is to *raise aspirations* for higher education among those from low SES backgrounds (Gale et al., 2010). Raising aspiration is also a primary objective for the UK's national Aimhigher program (Higher Education Funding Council for England, 2009). From this perspective, aspirations for HE appear to be in short supply and in need of stimulus among the same demographic that, in the third way political imaginary, harbor economic aspirations that government must take care not to restrain.

In both instances, discussions of aspiration are characterised by normative evaluation of peoples' attitude towards the future. For example, the apparently "high" economic and material aspirations of a particular working-class element—the "aspirationals"—are judged to provide a desirable and promising impetus for socioeconomic mobility, whereas the apparent lack of aspiration for HE is constructed as a problem that requires intervention at the level of government policy and institutional practice, in order to raise apparently "low" aspirations. Such assessments raise questions about the terms in which people are encouraged to aspire and which are presupposed in their evaluation. We take up these questions in this chapter. The first two sections are diagnostic. They comprise analysis of the discourses of aspiration that are mobilised in discussions of the aspirational working class and in policy texts that describe the need to raise aspiration for HE. In the third and fourth sections we analyze focus group data, in which teachers working in tough schools on the suburban fringe of an Australian capital city explore difficult questions about their students' aspirations and engagement with school. These sections move from a diagnosis of how aspiration is predominantly discussed toward consideration of the importance of engaging with peoples' desires for the future in different terms. We propose that conceptions of aspiration currently prevalent in third way political imaginaries and HE policy contexts stand in contrast to a more ethical conception, which holds the potential to make important contributions to our thinking about socially just forms of student engagement with school and university.

THE ASPIRATIONAL VOTER IN THE THIRD WAY
POLITICAL IMAGINARY

Since the late 1990s, those designated as aspirational voters have figured prominently in Australian and UK politics. Scalmer (2005) argues that, following its usage by Tony Blair, "the language of the 'aspirationals' entered Australian political parlance in 1998... [when] conservative [Labor] strategists... argued that 'aspirational' Sydneysiders would reject strongly redistributive policies" (pp. 5–6). Here, the rhetorical function of aspiration as a rallying point for those pursuing more centrist political visions is already apparent. Courting working-class aspirationals was considered strategically important in the context of reforging Australian Labor Party identity around the conjunction of neoliberal philosophies and more traditional social democratic impulses; a process initiated by Australian Labor governments in the 1980s and early 1990s (Johnson & Tonkiss, 2002). In the Australian context, the language of aspiration came to be strongly associated with Labor politician and one-time party leader Mark Latham. Latham's mobilization of the concept in his arguments concerning economic and education policy provides an instructive case of third way thinking about the aspirational demographic.

The discourse of aspiration developed in Latham's essays and speeches has antecedents in UK politics. Relating an anecdote, in which Tony Blair describes how his awareness of the aspirationals was piqued during an encounter with a self-employed one-time Labor voter, who had switched political preferences due to his perception that Labour policies would prevent him "getting on," Johnson (2004) observes that "one of the strongest Blairite influences on Latham is the key emphasis on attracting aspirational suburban voters" (p. 543). While plenty of ink has been spilled debating the wisdom and merit of electoral strategies premised on winning favor with this group, here we are primarily concerned with how the aspirations of the aspirationals have been represented in Australian political debate, and the role that they played in Latham's thought.

Frequently, discussion of this demographic has positioned them as an upwardly mobile element of the working-class; however, Scalmer (2005) argues that "none of the categories of traditional class analysis adequately describe the 'aspirational' class" (p. 7). Instead, he suggests that this categorisation reflects a familiar pattern of shifting social divisions and apparent mobility producing groups that lie 'in-between' traditional class affiliations. It is difficult to define exactly who the aspirationals are, but this ambivalence increases the political value of the concept: "The very definitional excess that accompanies the term—the incoherent lumping together of consumption, work, attitudes and groupings—is actually an expression of its tactical importance. Like 'the community', 'the people', or 'the battlers', representing the "aspirationals" can be a powerful ideological claim. Political centrality produces discursive abundance" (Scalmer, 2005, p. 6). Indeed, rather than naming any distinctive empirical population, the term perhaps best describes a somewhat ideal "disposition," constituted at the intersection of consumer desire and neoliberal belief in individual enterprise and entrepreneurialism.

Analyzing data collected through the 2005 Australian Survey of Social Attitudes, Goot and Watson (2007) argue similarly that aspirationals are a complex demographic with ambivalent social attitudes and political affiliations. They draw attention to the characteristics of conspicuous consumption and conservative attitudes that are frequently attributed to this group:

> Aspirationals are said to have embraced private consumption ahead of public goods—preferring, for example, private schools and private hospitals. This ties in with their propensity to invest, on the stock exchange or in real estate, and with their places of residence in the outer suburbs, where they gravitate to the new, privatised housing estates.... On a range of social issues—asylum seekers, migrants, law and order—they are thought to embrace conservative positions. (Goot & Watson, 2007, p. 220)

Goot and Watson (2007) consider whether empirical support exists for such perceptions, analysing different 'aspirational' populations based on three separate definitions: the first uses self-employment as the criteria for being 'aspirational', the second expands this definition to include those who aspire to self-employment, and the third is based on 'orientation'. This third definition includes "those strongly oriented to getting ahead financially, or those strongly oriented to getting ahead in career terms" (p. 221). This third group is of particular interest here because it is defined as 'aspirational' based on self-identification of a particular disposition, rather than inferring the 'aspirational' character of the group's members from current or desired employment status.

In comparison with middle-class and non-aspirational working-class respondents, this aspirationally oriented group has a number of distinctive characteristics. For example, they are

- much less likely to have education attainment at the university level (19%) than middle-class respondents (58%), while the non-aspirational working-class have a lower attainment rate again (8%)
- much less likely to own their own home (17%, compared to 40% of both non-aspirational working-class and middle-class respondents)
- more likely to support private schools (28%, compared to 14% of non-aspirational working-class and 19% of middle-class respondents)
- more likely to have bought a plasma television or home entertainments system in recent years (21%, compared to 14% of non-aspira-

tional working-class and 15% of middle-class respondents) (Goot & Watson, 2007)

The differences in levels of educational attainment, as well as attitudes toward education and consumption, are particularly notable. Aspirationals who are focused on "getting ahead" have lower levels of university education than middle-class respondents, but place a greater premium on private education, perhaps signaling a desire to increase their accumulation of educational and cultural goods and their belief in the most effective means for doing so. They also appear to place a greater premium on consumer goods, which may serve as overt markers of relative affluence and economic mobility.

Goot and Watson (2007) suggest that "when it comes to consumption issues—issues of private over public and of 'materialism'—these [aspirational] respondents do appear to be distinctive" (p. 227). This resonates with Latham's argument that the pursuit of economic ownership is a distinguishing characteristic of this group. It is also worth noting that those of aspirational orientation are significantly more inclined to vote Labor. However, this preference is not evident in the aspirational groups defined by self-employment (either broadly or narrowly). Indeed, Goot and Watson conclude that, overall, "neither one sort of aspirational nor the other is particularly distinctive in terms of political attitudes or the way they vote" (p. 236).

On this analysis, there is some empirical basis for the social attitudes imputed to the 'aspirational' demographic, but there is less evidence for their imagined political distinctiveness and electoral importance. Politically, the notion of the aspirational appears to serve a primarily rhetorical function as a 'hinge' concept that enables acknowledgement of social democratic imperatives while promoting neoliberal market logics as the appropriate means for responding to them. This function is evident in Latham's (2003) arguments for the Labor Party adopting policy that

> accepts the basic operating principles of a market economy—entrepreneurship and asset accumulation—while pursuing traditional goals of universal access and equity. Instead of trying to nationalise or regulate the ownership of assets, our objective should be to increase the size of the tent, to bring in new stakeholders. (p. 70)

Johnson (2004) explains that "for Latham the key to unlocking citizen aspirations is economic ownership" (p. 543). In Latham's argument, aspirations for economic ownership are an important source of impetus for achieving social justice objectives. This sentiment is echoed in the student engagement strategy described at the outset of this chapter, where desire for economic and material goods is considered a potential ally in efforts to increase students' access to educational goods. This desire was central to the kind of society Latham sought to foster. His idea was to introduce a 'stakeholder' society, an idea that had been pushed strongly by Tony Blair in the early days of New Labour before being largely dropped, perhaps because it potentially raised ideas of worker or community rights against capital. Latham's conception of stakeholders escapes such dilemmas by constructing them as economic owners in the form of shareholders or investors. (Johnson, 2004, p. 545)

Mobilizing the discourse of aspiration, Latham sought to reconcile the logic of capital with the kinds of economic redistribution more traditionally associated with the Labor Party.

However, it is important to note certain tensions in Latham's argument. In parallel with his discussions of economic policy, he described an approach to educational policy informed by the notion of aspirational equality, which gives emphasis to issues of recognition (Fraser, 1995; Gale & Densmore, 2000; Young, 1990). Latham (2001) proposed that the provision of equal support for people to pursue their diverse aspirations is a more appropriate measure than distributive justice policies that simply aim to bring about equal outcomes. He argued that "a just society is one in which all individuals and institutions are able to fulfil their potential, according to their own values and aspirations' and 'encourages diverse skills and tolerates diverse outcomes, insofar as people seek these things for themselves" (p. 22). However, despite the nominal intention to recognize different values, the economic imperative at the heart of Latham's argument effectively limits this recognition to *diverse economic aspirations*—that is, aspirations informed by a common desire for the accumulation of assets, but to different degrees or in different forms. From this perspective, desires for the future that are expressed in non-economic terms may appear to lack aspiration.

This brief survey indicates that in the third way political imaginary, as by Latham's arguments, *aspiration* is understood in primarily economic terms that reflect the influence of neoliberal market logics. Those elements of the working-class with high aspirations to "get ahead" financially and materially must be encouraged to "realize their potential" without government interference. Interestingly, Latham (2003) argues that the emergence of these aspirationals stems from the education reforms of the Australian Whitlam Labor Government during the 1970s, "which placed tertiary qualifications within reach of working-class families" (p. 66). Increased access to knowledge and skills provided these families with the initial cultural capital that they could convert into economic assets and social mobility. This logic continues to inform current HE policy. However, the problem now appears to be a lack of aspiration for HE and, one can surmise, the economic benefits to which HE provides access. What has caused this apparent shift in levels of aspiration? Or are levels of HE aspiration inconsistent with the levels of more immediately economic aspiration?

RAISING ASPIRATIONS: UNIVERSITIES AND EARLY INTERVENTIONS

Low levels of aspiration for HE among low SES groups are prominently described as a problem for Australian and UK HE policy. The solution is generally considered to involve universities conducting more frequent and sophisticated outreach activities to *raise aspirations* among this cohort. Clearly, a deficit perception of low-SES students and families haunts this logic. As Scalmer (2005) observes, while "aspirationals 'aspire', those who are not 'aspirationals' are (quite offensively) assumed to lack such drive" (p. 6). Those who are not aspirational in the HE context are assumed to lack awareness about, and the desire to access, university. However, closer analysis of the discourse of aspiration in HE policy suggests a relationship between the 'problem' of students' and families' 'low aspirations' and the economic aspirations of the nation.

The prevalence of aspiration as a central issue for HE in our current moment is evident in recent Australian and UK HE reports and policies. For example, the 2008 *Review of Australian Higher Education* sets out the problem in bold terms:

> Improving access and equity in higher education for these groups [low SES, regional/remote, and Indigenous students] is a difficult task and the solutions that will help to resolve this challenge are not immediately obvious. Barriers to access for such students include their previous attainment, *no awareness of the long-term benefits of higher education and, thus, no aspiration to participate* [emphasis added]. (Bradley et al., 2008, p. 27)

Aspiration is also described as a barrier to access in the Australian government's response to this review, which similarly describes the problem as "low awareness of the long-term benefits of higher education resulting in little aspiration to participate" (Commonwealth of Australia, 2009, p. 13). In response, the Australian government has made available substantial funding through schemes that are designed to "create leading practice and competitive pressures to increase the aspirations of low SES students to higher education" and "to provide schools and vocational education and training providers with links to universities, exposing their students to people, places and opportunities beyond the scope of their own experiences, helping teachers raise the aspirations of their students" (Commonwealth of Australia, 2009, p. 14).

A mix of economic and social agendas underscores this emphasis on "aspiration raising," even when this objective is described in terms of broadening students' horizons and spreading the social benefits of further education. Increasing HE participation is considered an important strategy for improving and sustaining the nation's competitiveness in a global knowledge economy. The *Review of Australian Higher Education* (Bradley et al., 2008) argues that "Australia's future will be determined by how well it performs in an economy driven by knowledge-based activities" and that "the higher education system's performance in producing high-quality graduates and research will be crucial to Australia's long-term productivity and growth outcomes" (p. 88). To this end, the Australian government holds an 'ambition' to increase levels of HE attainment, setting a target of 40% of all 25- to 34-year-olds to hold qualifications at the bachelor level or above by 2025. From this perspective, "raising aspiration" effectively means stimulating demand for HE and employment in order support national productivity goals.

At the same time, the government has also set a target for 20% of higher education enrollments at the undergraduate level to be students from low SES backgrounds, reflecting a second "ambition" to more evenly distribute the benefits of HE. While this could be cynically interpreted as an effort to stimulate demand among groups that have not traditionally accessed HE in large numbers, it does signal social democratic impulses to provide more equitable access to HE and, through the provision of such access, to facilitate economic and social mobility for low SES groups. For example, the Australian Government's vision for HE includes the creation of "a fairer Australia... [in which] all Australians will benefit from widespread equitable access to a diverse tertiary sector that allows each individual to develop and reach their potential" (Commonwealth of Australia, 2009, p. 7). Notably, this vision is expressed in language that resonates with Latham's description of "aspirational equality" and its emphasis on ensuring equal opportunities for entrepreneurialism and individual enterprise.

In the UK context, the need for "aspiration raising" is even more prevalent in both policy texts and the logic of intervention programs, and is informed by a similar mix of social and economic imperatives. For example, a primary objective of the Higher Education Funding Council for England (HEFCE, 2009) is "to stimulate and sustain new sources of demand for HE among under-represented communities and to influence supply accordingly" (p. 18). This has involved the provision of "funding to Aimhigher, a national programme to widen participation in HE by raising the aspirations and developing the abilities of people from under-represented groups" (p. 19). Further, the UK Government's (2006) *Widening Participation in Higher Education* policy identifies "raising aspiration" as the second of four strategies for improving access to HE for these groups, and it is replete with references to "developing" aspirations for and promoting the benefits of HE. Even so, the policy calls for further work to address this issue and for feedback regarding what more can be done "to help those [from] disadvantaged backgrounds to raise their aspirations and understand that higher education is achievable and worthwhile" (UK Department for Education &

Skills, 2006, p. 22). As signaled by HEFCE's (2009) commitment "to widening the range and increasing the number of people who take part in HE... for both social justice and *economic competitiveness* [emphasis added]" (p. 19), aiming higher and appreciating the worth of higher education contributes to the nation's economic interests as well as the individual's.

It is interesting to note a passage from HEFCE's (2009) strategic plan, which draws attention to the aspirations of HE institutions (HEIs) and their relationship to national interests: "[A]lthough we [the UK] have a strong and diverse HE system, which is respected across the world, the aspirations and goals of the 130 HEI's... do not necessarily add up to meeting national or even regional interests" (p. 8). In this case, the potential diversity between institutional and national aspirations is constituted as a "problem" that policy must address. Similarly, the Australian government has called for a "new relationship between Government and higher education institutions" (Commonwealth of Australia 2009, p. 47). This relationship will be based on recognizing "the value of institutional autonomy while promoting excellence, supporting growth, and maintaining international competitiveness" (p. 47). To this end, institutions will be required to enter into compacts with the government in order to "facilitate alignment of institutional activity with national priorities" (p. 47). Here, the alignment of aspirations is also a policy issue.

These passages from recent HE policies suggest that the aspirations of particular groups of students and families are not simply a problem in their own right. Rather, it is the *incongruence* of aspirations between the three levels of (1) individual students, (2) institutions, and (3) the nation, which creates cause for concern. For example, central to Latham's argument that distributive justice policies "constrain" the aspirations of working-class families is a perceived incongruence between individual desire for economic advancement and the social democratic ambitions that have traditionally been associated with the Labor Party in Australia. The "low aspirations" of students and families from low SES backgrounds reflect their current incongruence with the economic ambitions of the nation, which involve advancing "the growth of a dynamic knowledge economy" (Commonwealth of Australia, 2009, p. 12), by expanding the HE system. At the same time, the concomitant national ambition to encourage the fairer distribution of educational goods is not necessarily in alignment with the "strategic ambitions" of universities, which may be focused on maintaining the symbolic value and quality of their degrees. Some institutions may consider an influx of low SES students to put their academic status at risk. Table 6.1 provides an example, which is by no means comprehensive, of the different kinds of aspirations that may be evident at the individual, institutional, or national level.

In this sense, evaluation of the relative height of aspiration depends on its congruence with the values that inform the standpoint from which it is

TABLE 6.1 Three Levels of Aspiration

Individual	Institutional	National
Economic (ownership, mobility)	Economic (finance, security)	Economic (growth, competition)
Social-Cultural (learning, agency)	Symbolic (distinction, influence)	Social-Political (social inclusion, widening participation)

evaluated. From a policy perspective, those described as "aspirational" hold economic aspirations that are congruent with national economic policy (or, at least, a particular vision for this policy), while those described as lacking aspiration perhaps have desires for their future that are incongruent with national economic interests. While different kinds of aspirations are present at each level, economic aspirations, and the logic of capital that informs them, are common to all.

APATHY OF ASPIRATION? EXPLAINING THE DIFFICULTY OF ENGAGING STUDENTS IN TOUGH SCHOOLS

We turn now to analysis of data collected during discussions with teachers, who arguably have a relatively immediate sense of their students' thinking about, and preferences for, their futures. The excerpts of teacher discussion analyzed here were collected during a nationally funded research project—*Redesigning Pedagogies in the North*—that was conducted with more than 30 middle-years (upper primary/lower secondary) teachers working in public primary and secondary schools across the outer-suburban fringe of an Australian capital city.[2] The communities served by these schools are located in a region that Thomson (2002) has described as a "rustbelt": an area in which the post-industrial exodus of manufacturing industries during the mid to late twentieth century produced a "combination of a concentration of loss of employment and its long-term effects on particular people" (p. 26). Many of the schools in these communities are renowned for being difficult places to teach and learn.

This discussion took place during one of a series of three reference groups, in which a small group of teachers explored possibilities and challenges for socially just teaching in this particular region. While similar in structure to focus groups, the reference groups differed in that they positioned teachers as "co-theorists" of pedagogy. Through interlocution with each other and the researcher, teachers extended from prompts to analyze their pedagogies and their experience working in these schools. Prompting the particular discussion analyzed in this chapter was the question of what changes had occurred during their time teaching in this region, and what impact these changes, or perhaps broader social changes, may have had on their pedagogies.

After some general conversation—about changing social attitudes, poverty-related issues specific to this area, and the effect of both on classroom dynamics—one of the teachers, Sophie,[3] raised the question of what causes the significant levels of student disengagement evident in these schools: Is it apathy or *is it that the students are not aspirational?* This initiated some discussion about whether it is one or the other, or a combination of both. Sophie then continued her line of inquiry, suggesting that one cause for low aspirations is multigenerational unemployment and the fewer experiences that many families have with post-school educational and occupational pathways as a result. While this is certainly an issue in this region, Megan, who teaches primary school, argues that her students *are* aspirational. However, she notes that low levels of academic achievement significantly reduce the likelihood of these aspirations being realized:

> I still have them while they're young so they still have these . . . *they are aspirational* [emphasis added]. One of my girls, to one of my more disruptive boys, turned around and she said, "Well you're the loser because I'm smart and I'm going to be rich, and you're just going to sit around annoying people for the rest of your life" . . . but the issue is that they say to me "I want to be a lawyer, I want to be a doctor, I want to be a vet," and you just look at their literacy and you go, "This is not going to happen for you." . . . So now I talk about, I don't talk about "What do you want to be?", I say "What sort of thing are you thinking of doing, like working with animals, working with kids, building with your hands?" (Megan)

It is worth noting how the student in this account describes her aspirations in terms of economic advancement—becoming "rich"—in contrast to the lack of mobility implied in "sitting around for the rest of your life." Further, Megan describes a range of professions to which her students aspire, all of which require HE. Contrary to representations of these students as lacking aspiration, she describes how they hold relatively high aspirations, although they are not yet able to articulate the role of HE in attaining them. Yet, in Megan's assessment, these aspirations often appear "unrealistic." She explains how she counsels students to consider occupations in their field of interest that may be more "realistic," effectively mediating their aspirations toward lower horizons. For example, one could work with animals as a veterinary nurse rather than as a veterinarian, thereby circumventing the need for a university qualification.

This "mediational" strategy appears to harbor a form of deficit thinking, which Megan quickly moves to counter:

I might just want to backtrack and qualify, when I was saying they want to be all these professions and you look at their literacy and you say "It can't happen," I mean it can't happen for them in the immediate future. It may be that they go back and do it as mature age students, et cetera, but it's that, um, you know, that's always possible, but at some stage they're going to have a realization, and then the danger is they say then "Oh well I'm just giving up." (Megan)

Rather than simply lowering her students' aspirations in a straightforward manner, Megan describes how she attempts to negotiate a difficult ethical tension. Given that many students in these schools experience educational disadvantage, she must decide between providing naive support for her students high aspirations, thereby creating the conditions for disengagement if these prove unobtainable, or encouraging students to lower their aspirations to occupations that may enable them to work in their area of interest, although perhaps in roles that attract lower status and remuneration.

Later in the discussion, Sophie reiterates this risk of students "giving up" if they realize that school won't provide them with access to their preferred future: "What we've got is lots of kids who are outside [the cohort of students who successfully navigate formal education] looking in, saying 'I want to get there, but I don't know how so I'm going to give up.'" In response, Megan pursues a different explanation for why these students disengage with school, which departs from her previous emphasis on low levels of academic achievement:

Maybe some of them don't want to.... Maybe that's the issue, maybe what's happening is that because we are such middle-class people, and the way that we measure success is materialistic, you know, you've got a nice big house, you drive a fancy car, you've got a massive mortgage, "Well you're doing really well there!" Maybe it's just that, and maybe it's not, but that they're choosing that that's not how they want to be measured, and that's not as important to them as it is to us. Maybe we are just saying "This is what's important because that's how we live," but it's not how they feel they need to live. (Megan)

This raises another difficult question about whether aspirations can be normatively evaluated according to values that may be specific to a particular class. Can we talk about "high" and "low" aspirations in universal terms—as much current policy appears to do—if this assessment is always made from a particular class and cultural standpoint?

BEYOND ECONOMIC DISCOURSES OF ASPIRATION?

This introduces a new dimension into the discussion: the possibility that aspirations are inherently related to culturally specific values, and that these values demand a complex *politics of recognition* rather than normative evaluations that prioritize questions of redistribution (e.g., Latham's emphasis on economic ownership). Of course, this is not to say that people living in poverty do not aspire to more dignified and secure material conditions, or to the various freedoms that economic security affords. Rather, we must consider whether economic security should be made to depend on subscription to a particular set of middle-class values and strategies.

Reflecting on ethnographic work with the poor in Mumbai, Appadurai argues for this approach to conceiving of aspiration as a *cultural capacity*. For Appadurai (2004), the concept of aspiration denotes a cultural relationship to the future that is generally obscured by the language of economics, which he argues has become the default "science of the future" (p. 60). Indeed, discussion of aspiration in the policies analyzed here is almost exclusively framed in economic terms: growth, ownership, productivity, competitiveness, human capital. In the context of neoliberalism, this economic view emphasizes the wants and choices of individuals. However, contrary to this assumption, Appadurai proposes that "aspirations form parts of wider ethical and metaphysical ideas which derive from larger cultural norms" (p. 67). Further, he argues that:

> Poverty is partly a matter of operating with extremely weak resources where the terms of recognition are concerned.... [T]he poor are frequently in a position where they are encouraged to subscribe to norms whose social effect is to further diminish their dignity, exacerbate their inequality, and deepen their lack of access to material goods and services. (Appadurai, 2004, p. 66)

Perhaps most obvious among these norms, at least in the context of the present analysis, is the neoliberal belief in economic growth and consumer desire as the key to increasing wealth and reducing poverty. This belief does not, however, account for the increasing disparity between capital and labour, and between rich and poor, that capitalist economic growth has generally produced (Gale, 2005; Wallerstein, 1998). As Bauman (2005) suggests, "while the poor get poorer, the very rich—those paragons of consumer virtues—get richer still" (p. 41). He continues: "the poorer the poor, the higher and more whimsical are the patterns of life set in front of their eyes to adore, covet and wish to emulate" (p. 41). The plasma television, which 21% of aspirationals (compared to 14% of the non-aspirational working class and 15% of middle-class respondents) have recently purchased (Goot & Watson, 2007), is perhaps a potent symbol of the influence that consumer values have on aspirations and perceptions of social status.

Indeed, another teacher, Brad, continued to explore the difficult question of how to understand the aspirations of others across class differences. In Brad's case, this difference has arisen due his socioeconomic mobility as a result of becoming a teacher. Brad has lived in this particular outer-suburban region for much of his life, and has worked in low-pay, low-status jobs prior to entering the teaching profession. He recalls his wife explaining to him that his improved economic position potentially undermines his ability to relate with the experiences and values of some students in his class. Most notably, the signifier of his newly acquired middle-class status is a plasma television:

> "Yah, yah, Brad, you've played the hard life and you've done this and you've done that, and you think you're going to be at one with the kids," she said, "but you come home and you still watch a *plasma telly*." . . . I don't want to call myself middle-class, but by definition I have to be, and I still haven't got the grind, I know for every fortnight, and this is terrible, I'm going to get paid, and bloody well. . . . They're still seeing me as a teacher that's, you know, all these holidays, I'm well-off, you know . . . but do I really know what it's like to be living there? (Brad)

While the difficulty of understanding the cultural values according to which the aspirations of others are formed and pursued is reiterated here, it is important not to overstate this cultural difference, or to draw lines between "cultures" that are too neat (Benhabib, 2002). As Appadurai (2004) cautions, "there may not be anything which can usefully be called a 'culture of poverty' (anthropologists have rightly ceased to use this conceptualization), but the poor certainly have understandings of themselves and the world that have cultural dimensions and expressions" (p. 65). While it is entirely inappropriate to suggest that those from less affluent backgrounds should not aspire to improved economic and material circumstances, it is important to consider whether conceiving of aspiration in predominantly economic terms, characterized in our current times by neoliberal ideologies and consumer values, establishes a normative context, underpinned by the logic of capital, in which the objects of "high" aspiration are only ever available to the relatively few. As Bauman (2005) explains, poverty is not just a material condition—it also "means being excluded from whatever passes for a 'normal life' . . . [and] in a consumer society, a 'normal life' is the life of consumers" (p. 38). The question is whether high aspirations, conceived in these terms, actually undermine the possibilities for creating more just social and economic conditions.

The pervasiveness of consumer logic as the framework in which aspirations are currently formed is exemplified in a statement that concluded this passage of teacher discussion, and which prefaces this chapter. Referring to Megan's strategy of mediating aspirations by discussing what students "want to do," in contrast to "what they want to be," Sophie proposes a different strategy, which involves discussion of what students wish to *buy*:

> You talk about what things you want to do, rather than what you want to be. I've started talking about, because teenagers are materialistic, I've started talking about what things do you want to buy... and how do you get to that stage, and you can't to the brand new [car] or a new house, or a trip overseas, on the dole, you know you can't get to that... and we started talking about in terms [of] materialis[m]. (Sophie)

In response, Megan observes that "it's a bit of a scary thing if you have to inspire them with materialistic observations." At the very least, it reinforces cultural norms that narrow the possibilities of what it might mean to aspire and, in doing so, create the conditions for some to be excluded from a "normal" life. While not wishing to undermine the intent of Sophie's pedagogical experiment, which is driven chiefly by the desire to engage students, we must consider what injustice is done when high aspirations are premised on levels of consumption and economic ownership that can only ever be available to a few.

CONCLUSION

A feature common to each of the contexts examined here is the *representation* of others' aspirations. In each instance those whose aspirations are the object of scrutiny—aspirational voters, students who lack aspiration, or those whose aspirations potentially diverge from middle-class values—are absent from the discussion. Indeed, it seems likely that most people would not describe themselves as having "low" aspirations. Rather, this evaluation is more likely to be attributed to people by others with incongruent values and desires. Of course, whether or not this is the case is a matter for empirical research, which we argue offers strong possibilities for extending thinking about aspiration beyond economic frameworks (and the neoliberal logic that currently animates them) and beyond a discourse that represents and evaluates the aspirations of others in dominant terms.

Appadurai (2006) argues that research, when understood as "the capacity to systematically increase the horizons of one's current knowledge, in relation to some task, goal or aspiration" (p. 176), plays a fundamental role in peoples' pursuit of their preferred futures, and therefore that "without systematic tools for gaining relevant new knowledge, aspiration degenerates into fantasy or despair" (pp. 176–177). This is the dilemma that Megan raised when she described her attempts to mediate between these two undesirable outcomes. Following Appadurai's argument, research into aspirations is perhaps best conducted by aspirants themselves or, at the very least, with these aspirants. In school contexts, this research could be pursued through curriculum units in which aspirations, and the rich networks of cultural values and norms that influence them, constitute topics for inquiry and dialogue. Work of this kind would enable teachers to explore, *with their students*, the role that class and cultural values play in the development and pursuit of their aspirations, while also engaging in sustained and critical curriculum conversations about the dominant norms to which the less powerful are encouraged to subscribe. While this is not the place, and we are without space, to provide more detailed consideration of exactly what form such curricular inquiry into aspirations might take, we suggest that the work of Moll, Gonzalez. and colleagues (Gonzalez, Moll, & Amanti, 2005; Moll, Amanti, Neffe, & Gonzalez, 1992) provides instructive examples of how to research the cultural knowledge embedded in students' homes and community lives in order to draw on this knowledge as a resource for curriculum design and classroom conversation.

Those who are variously described as either aspirational or lacking aspiration, while not homogenous by any means, generally occupy less powerful social and economic positions. However, they have at times exerted substantial political agency. As Scalmer (2005) explains, "those who dwell 'in-between' [traditional class divisions] have often contributed to radical political change. Perhaps, if those dubbed the 'aspirationals' are ever allowed to find their own voices, this may happen once more" (p. 9). This is our hope in proposing critical curriculum work that engages students in researching and representing their own desires for the future and the cultural contexts that shape them.

NOTES

1. National Centre for Student Equity in Higher Education, University of South Australia, GPO Box 2471, Adelaide, SA, 5001, Australia.
2. Led by a research team from the Centre for Studies in Literacy, Policy and Learning Cultures (University of South Australia), RPiN was funded by the Australian Research Council (LP0454869) as a linkage project with industry partners: the Northern Adelaide State Secondary Principals Network, the Australian Education Union (SA Branch), and the South Australian Social Inclusion Unit. Chief Investigators included Robert Hattam, Phillip Cormack, Barbara Comber, Marie Brennan, Lew Zipin, Alan Reid, Kathy Paige, David Lloyd, Helen Nixon, Bill Lucas, John Walsh, Faye McCallum and Brenton Prosser, with assistance from Kathy Brady, Philippa Milroy and Sam Sellar.
3. Teachers in the study have been assigned a pseudonym.

REFERENCES

Appadurai, A. (2006). The right to research. *Globalisation, Societies and Education, 4*(2), 167–177.

Appadurai, A. (2004). The capacity to aspire: Culture and the terms of recognition. In V. Rao & M. Walton (Eds.), *Culture and Public Action* (pp. 59–84). Stanford, CT: Stanford University Press.

Bauman, Z. (2005). *Work, consumerism and the new poor* (2nd ed). Berkshire, UK: Open University Press.

Benhabib, S. (2002). *The claims of culture: Equality and diversity in the global era.* Princeton, NJ: Princeton University Press.

Bradley, D., Noonan, P., Nugent, H., & Scales, B. (2008). *Review of Australian higher education: Final report.* Canberra, ACT: Commonwealth of Australia, Department of Education, Employment and Workplace Relations (DEEWR).

Commonwealth of Australia, DEEWR. (2009). *Transforming Australia's higher education system.* Canberra, ACT: Author. Retrieved from http://www.deewr.gov.au/HigherEducation/Documents/PDF/Additional%20Report%20-%20Transforming%20Aus%20Higher%20ED_webaw.pdf

Fraser, N. (1995). From redistribution to recognition: Dilemmas of justice in a 'post-socialist' age. *New Left Review, 212,* 68–93.

Gale, T. (2005). *Rough justice: Young people in the shadows.* New York, NY: Peter Lang Publishing.

Gale, T., & Densmore, K. (2000). *Just schooling: Explorations in the cultural politics of teaching.* Buckingham, UK: Open University Press.

Gale, T., Hattam, R., Comber, B., Tranter, D., Bills, D., Sellar, S., & Parker, S. (2010). *Interventions early in school as a means to improve higher education outcomes for disadvantaged (particularly low SES) students.* Canberra, ACT: Commonwealth of Australia, DEEWR. Retrieved from http://www.deewr.gov.au/HigherEducation/Publications/Pages/InterventionsEarlyInSchool.aspx

Gonzalez, N., Moll, L. C., & Amanti, C. (Eds.). (2005). *Funds of knowledge: Theorizing practices in households, communities and classrooms.* Mahwah, NJ: Lawrence Erlbaum Associates.

Goot, M. & Watson, I. (2007). Are 'aspirationals' different? In D. Denemark, G. Meagher, S. Wilson, M. Western & T. Phillips (Eds), *Australian social attitudes 2: Citizenship, work and aspirations* (pp. 217–240). Sydney: UNSW Press.

Higher Education Funding Council for England (HEFCE). (2009). *Strategic plan 2006–2011.* Bristol, UK: Author. Retrieved from http://www.hefce.ac.uk/pubs/hefce/2009/09_21/09_21.pdf

Johnson, C. (2004). Mark Latham and the ideology of the ALP. *Australian Journal of Political Science, 39*(3), 535–551.

Johnson, C., & Tonkiss, F. (2002). The third influence: The Blair government and Australian labor. *Policy & Politics, 30*(1), 5–18.

Latham, M. (2001). *What did you learn today?* Crows Nest, Australia: Allen & Unwin.

Latham, M. (2003). *From the suburbs: Building a nation from our neighbours.* Annandale, Australia: Pluto Press.

Moll, L., Amanti, C., Neffe, C., & Gonzalez, N. (1992). Funds of knowledge for teaching: Using a qualitative approach to connect homes and classrooms. *Theory into Practice, 32*(2), 132–141.

Scalmer, S. (2005). Searching for the aspirationals. *Overland, 180,* 5–9.

Thomson, P. (2002). *Schooling the rustbelt kids: Making the difference in changing times.* Crows Nest, NSW: Allen & Unwin.

United Kingdom, Department for Education and Skills. (2006). *Widening participation in higher education.* Retrieved from http://www.dcsf.gov.uk/hegateway/uploads/6820-DfES-WideningParticipation2.pdf

Wallerstein, I. (1998). *Utopistics or, historical choices of the twenty-first century.* New York, NY: The New Press.

Young, I. (1990). *Justice and the politics of difference.* Princeton, NJ: Princeton University Press.

CHAPTER 7

TRANSFORMATIVE STUDENT ENGAGEMENT—AN EMPOWERING PEDAGOGY

An Australian Experience in the Classroom[1]

David Zyngier

ABSTRACT

This chapter re-examines student engagement especially in disadvantaged communities and explores possibilities for transformative education beyond compensation through an exemplary program, ruMAD (Are You Making a Difference). The complexity of issues relating to student engagement (and early school leaving) cannot be fitted neatly into decontextualized accounts of youth experience, school interaction, and socio-environmental factors that in the first instance create student disempowerment and disengagement with school. An engaging pedagogy ensures that what teachers and students do is based on pedagogical reciprocity through what I have termed CORE (Connecting, Owning, Responding, and Empowering) pedagogy. In order to enhance student engagement we need to be linking curriculum, pedagogy,

Student Engagement in Urban Schools, pages 111–131

and assessment to identity, politics, and social justice where teachers become "elegantly subversive" and promote a student engagement that is empowering, developing a sense of entitlement, belonging and identification, so that teachers create pedagogical practices that engage students providing them with ways of knowing that enhance their capacity to live fully and deeply.

INTRODUCTION

No arbitrary obstacles should prevent people from achieving those positions for which their talents fit them and which their values lead them to seek. Not birth, nationality, colour, religion, sex, nor any other irrelevant characteristic should determine the opportunities that are open to a person—only his [or her] abilities.
—Friedman & Friedman, 1980, p. 132

It has been suggested that the success of public (government or state run) schools in Western democracies may well be part of the reason that at least in Australia they are faced with many seemingly overwhelming difficulties (Bonner & Caro, 2007). These schools, designed to create a "stable educated and prosperous economy and society" (Bonner & Caro, 2007, p. 159) have been portrayed as the "zenith of democracy," but can we remain a functioning democracy without a strong public education system? A former Director of Education for the Organization of Economic Cooperation and Development (OECD) concluded that the school system in Australia does little to address inherited inequality, instead reproducing existing social arrangements, "conferring privilege where it already exists and denying it where it does not" (Bonner & Caro, 2007, p. 164). McGraw concludes, "Educational inequity in the sense considered here involves a relatively strong relationship between educational outcomes and social background, with the implication that the education system is consistently conferring privilege on those who already have it and denying it to those who do not" (McGraw, 2006, p. 18).

Australia has witnessed a growing trend to mass secondary education in the past 50 years. In 1940 only 1 in 10 students completed 12 years of school. In the 1970s this rose to 1 in 3 and then 3 of 4 in the 1990s. There has been a corresponding flow on into higher education with 1 in 4 attending university in 2000s. While this could be seen as a harmonic view of education and economy, it, however, "represents a goal rather than an achievement" (Teese, 2007, p. 39). Comforting as these high rates might be, in the Australian context it rests not on higher aspirations conditioned on industrial change but on a collapsing full-time labor market that effectively trapped people in schooling.

Teese (2007) has argued that the expanding education system, driven by neoliberal choice policies has resulted in an increase in social inequalities and economic segregation rather than its narrowing, as those parents with the economic and cultural capital have (re)moved their children from the local government-funded high and elementary schools to the better resourced, high fee-paying private school system. This has resulted in what Teese has termed "residualized" or "sink schools" (Teese, 2000, 2007). Social divisions between schools split resources distributing these unevenly including the unequal distribution of "negative resources" (relative liabilities)—poor students in urban schools are poor in many ways—as a result of the groups they come from—minorities, disabled, poor, migrant, refugees, broken homes, itinerant workers, rejected from other schools. Public schools are now increasingly being liberated from both geography and government administration—the last 20 years has witnessed an increasing push towards self-management and devolution (Teese, 2007, p. 17).

STAKING A CLAIM FOR THEIR CHILD'S ADVANTAGE— AT WHAT POINT TO MOST PUBLIC SCHOOLS SIMPLY BECOME SINKS OF DISADVANTAGE?

The three major neoliberal economic reforms—marketiztion, privatization, and rationalization—based on the so-called free-market ideology of Friedmanism, Thatcherism, and Reaganomics pushed for a reduction in government responsibility including education. The result of these three policies created a deregulated and heavily subsidised market of private schools, designed to shift enrolments away from the public sector. Talking up the language of choice and competition, various federal and state minsters of education introduced reforms in response to what they described as observed deficiencies in the system.

This continues today with the calls for increased public private partnerships (PPPs) and corporate support of public schooling. The effects on education (and elsewhere) are profound. Marketization led to the reorganization of schools around market principles (Whitty, Power, & Halpin, 1998); privatization has seen increasing levels of public funding shift to private providers—public funding of private effort (the free market goal of ensuring diversity and choice); and rationalization resulted in the restructuring of schools through closures or amalgamations, particularly of smaller schools on grounds of efficiency, of curriculum provision and depth, and a resultant redundancy of thousands of experienced teachers. During this same period of time the Federal conservative (Liberal-National Coalition) government led a campaign that was increasingly strident in its accusation that comprehensive public schooling was responsible for a perceived and claimed fall in teaching and learning standards (Leigh & Ryan, 2006,

2008). The result of these interventions has seen an increase in economic and social divisions in and between schools in Australia.

Many schools started to lose their middle-class families and "accumulate the deficits created by this loss" (Bonner & Caro, 2007, p. 41) further making it difficult to cater to all students. Schools in poorer areas have become residualized repositories of failure or *sink schools*, denuded of numbers and cultural capital resources (Teese & Lamb, 2007).

> The question everyone in the political class is tiptoeing around is this. At what point do most public schools simply become sinks of disadvantage, places where the residue of kids with average or below average IQs and more than their fair share of other problems confound everyone's efforts to teach them life's basic skills? You could reformulate the question by asking: at what stage does the abandonment of public-sector education by what used to be called the lower middle-classes reach its tipping point? (Pearson, 2007)

While families with social power use education to "stake a claim" for their child's advantage, families without such cultural and social capital rely on governments to assert those claims. While the process of marginalisation has been difficult to prevent, continuing to "follow [this] path ... has elements of despair, racism, cover up, official avoidance [resulting in] a paralysis of public initiatives" (Bonner & Caro, 2007, p. 112). If serious competition drove school reform, then the winners were schools serving wealthy suburbs. These reforms have led to low SES schools in Australia being drained of the most capable students, resulting in higher concentrations of students from the most disadvantaged communities (Lamb, 2007). If competition drove school reform then the winners were schools serving wealthy suburbs— reforms have led to low SES schools being drained of most capable students—higher concentrations of students from most disadvantaged communities (Lamb, 2007).

AN EDUCATION REVOLUTION—OR IS IT JUST MORE OF THE SAME?

With the election of a new Labor government in November 2007 came a proposed "education revolution." The newly elected Prime Minister said that he

> cannot understand why public institutions such as schools should not be accountable to the community that funds their salaries and their running costs. Right now, we do not have accurate, comprehensive information to allow rigorous analysis of what schools and students are achieving.

This must change. That is why today I announce that we will be making agreement on individual school performance reporting a condition of the new national education agreement to come into effect from 1 January 2009. (Kevin Rudd, Address to the National Press Club on August 27, 2008)

Once again, the teachers who are responsible for the excellent achievements of Australian students (in comparison to other OECD countries) are being blamed for their supposed failures (Tomazin, 2008). Yet Prime Minister Rudd and his Deputy and Minister for Education, Gillard, together with their counterparts in Labor Victoria, are now proposing to copy the much-critiqued (Boyd, Grossman, Lankford, Loeb, & Wyckoff, 2006; Darling-Hammond, Holtzman, Gatlin, & Heilig, 2005; Laczko-Kerr & Berliner, 2002) New York model of individual school performance reporting and public comparison of so-called *like schools* as determined by students' entry scores and scores on standardized tests, parental income, ethnic composition, and other data as well as the educationally bankrupt policies of *Teach for America* (Decker, Mayer, & Glazerman, 2004).

And the solution proposed? Encourage so-called disengaged teachers to leave the profession (Pike, 2008), give top education graduates and top teachers financial incentives to work in so-called failing schools, and publish league tables that would rank schools' performance to make them more accountable (Dinham, Ingvarson, & Kleinhenz, 2008).

Despite the neoliberal agenda taking a firm hold in schools across Australia, there are some schools that are finding cracks in and spaces amid the commercial status quo to do amazing things especially for children from culturally, linguistically, and economically diverse (CLED) communities. Broadly speaking, the strategies fall into the following three areas: new pedagogies and curricula, social support and well being, and community participation. It is the new pedagogies and curricula that I believe hold the greatest potential for what I have called the elegant subversion of the current dominant paradigm of division and disadvantage.

Key strategies adopted in programs emphasizing new pedagogies and curricula are:

- connectedness between subject areas, and between classroom activities and the real world
- intellectual challenge in key curriculum areas, valuing of diversity, building positive relationships, and communication

The chosen strategies align well with the features of engaging schools (Murray, Mitchell, Gale, Edwards, & Zyngier, 2004). Most of the programs described have been initiated, developed, or modified in context-specific ways, and in so doing reflect the important point that there is no single recipe for program development (Smith et al., 2001a, 2001b). Those programs, drawing on particular pedagogical frameworks, have done so in order to meet the specific needs of groups of students. The pedagogical frameworks are invariably modified to suit particular classes, curriculum requirements, and curriculum content. In those cases in which there is systemic funding, the emphasis is on using funds to sponsor cluster and school-based initiatives that are responsive to the needs of schools, their students and teachers, and the local community (Murray et al., 2004).

The rest of this chapter reviews a school program that is *elegantly subversive* in that it is achieving high levels of authentic and productive student engagement together with the required results by doing school differently, especially for children from CLED communities. In doing so, I highlight the achievements of one particular project (out of many) that has had enormous transformative impact on the participants and their communities.

RUMAD (ARE YOU MAKING A DIFFERENCE)

The ruMAD program (see http://www.rumad.org.au/) began as a pilot project of The Education Foundation in 2001 (Zyngier & Bruner, 2002) and currently in 2010 has over 230 schools throughout Australian participating. From its beginnings, the ruMAD program recognized that

> In our current society, inequity exists, with people coming from places of privilege and disadvantage. Local community networks are where people first learn about inclusive and representative processes. Real and lasting improvement in many areas of social need can only be achieved through structural change. Band-aid or quick-fix solutions will not necessarily address the underlying issues. (Shor, 1992, p. 7)

It has the following aims:

- The active participation of young people in the community through action research projects
- To provide young people with opportunities for engaging, independent, student-centred learning
- To model engaging, student-centered learning for teachers
- To enable young people to make a difference in their school or community
- Supporting student leadership
- Creating the conditions for identifying core values
- Building social competencies such as self-esteem and confidence
- Building the skills and knowledge to solve real-world problems. (Shor, 1992)

The ruMAD program claims that "students who participate...will be empowered to positively transform situations where they see disadvantage or unfairness in their own and others' lives" while involvement seeks to "empower students to inquire, act and reflect on the issues that are of real concern to them, and promote active citizenship" (Shor, 1992, p. 10). It is an inquiry-based pedagogical framework that (1) accords with state and federal policy emphasis on the incorporation of values education into school curricula; and (2) encourages, educates, and empowers young people to enact and facilitate social change and make a difference within their school and community. Predicated on the belief that everyone is able to improve and help change the communities in which they live, the program provides participants with opportunities for experiential civic engagement in areas of their own interest and choice; environmental issues like recycling and land degradation, homelessness, poverty and bullying and harassment at school. These program aims are based on

> a commitment to the values of equity—seeking a fair and just distribution of economic resources and political power; of access—providing fair and equal access to public services which is essential to achieving and maintaining a decent lifestyle; creating the opportunity for participation in social and political life and in the decisions which affect people's lives; and equality—ensuring opportunity and the capacity to achieve according to everyone's potential and to live without discrimination [emphases in original]. (Shor, 1992, pp. 10)

The ruMAD program has also been described as "a unique way of promoting...innovative learning...firmly based on the belief that we are all able to improve and make a difference within the communities in which we live and that everyone has the ability to work towards changing the circumstances of...people in the community" (Bell, Shrimpton, & Leger, 2004, p. 6).

Over 1000 Australian schools have participated in ruMAD since its inception. In 2008 some 35,000 students in 2008 alone were spoken to about ruMAD. This, however, does not reflect the actual number of students who then went on to participate in projects.

Four main educational objectives underpin ruMAD:

- to engage young people in issues of social justice
- to engage young people with a high level of authenticity
- to promote student-led classrooms, thereby challenging teacher practice
- to create real community change (Westheimer & Kahne, 2004)

It presents the concept of engaged and facilitated learning through Roger Hart's Ladder of Youth Participation[2] as a fluid continuum. A number of elements of the ruMAD program and philosophy were identified as holding particular attraction and relevance for schools as they provided students and teachers with the following:

- opportunities for real community engagement (both within and beyond school grounds)
- opportunities for engagement with real issues
- opportunities for transformative citizenship going beyond responsible citizenship or thin democracy to participation in thick democracy (Carr, 2008; Gandin & Apple, 2005)
- *opportunities for effecting and sustaining change (so that the change perpetuates)*
- opportunities for independent learning
- opportunities for changed teacher practice (Stokes & Turnbull, 2008)

RuMAD has at its core the philosophy that students need to be involved in curricula and pedagogy that

- come from the kids' own ideas about what is possible, inspiring enthusiasm among all those involved
- create real and lasting change by tackling the main causes of the problem
- acknowledge and build on previous successes, big or small
- get kids involved in the community to tackle issues of social justice, responsibility, tolerance, and cultural diversity
- create awareness and understanding of the needs of others through personal action
- allow everyone involved in the project to take greater responsibility for their own lives
- share the results with others, inspiring them to take further action
- consider the effects on the environment, society and economy (both positive and negative)
- help kids to express their views, become critical thinkers and learn how to put problem solving skills into action in order to create the world they wish to live in (Zyngier & Brunner, 2002, p. 42)

The ruMAD organization provides schools with curriculum materials and resources that enable students to design, implement, and evaluate action projects within their community that will make a difference. Examples of projects developed in primary schools include building links between the school and a local nursing home, anti-bullying strategies; supports for homeless people, support for children with cancer, and environmental degradation and restoration projects.

WHAT DOES A TYPICAL MAD PROJECT LOOK LIKE?

"Jessie's Creek" School: Whitfield District Primary School

Whitfield is an agricultural township in the King River valley 170 kilometers northeast of Melbourne. The primary (elementary) school has around 20 students from kindergarten to grade 6 (ages 5–12).[3] Jessie's Creek runs through the town and behind the school and the river was cloaked in a blanket of weeds that had accumulated over the years aided by dumping of green garden waste (weeds, grass clippings, etc.) as well as miscellaneous rubbish. Despite the creek being the town's main water supply, there was also a lot of rubbish scattered about. Creepers, ivy, blackberry, and Lucerne covered the creek that looked like a botanical garden; however, nothing was indigenous (National Resource Management, 2008).

The adults in the town decided to have a meeting to clean up the creek, but after three hours no decision could be reached. The students at the primary school took on a ruMAD project to carry out a biodiversity study of the creek and aimed to clean it up. The biodiversity study enabled the students to understand that invasive and often noxious plants, many of which were the result of inappropriate farming and land-management practices, had overwhelmed the creek's indigenous flora. From the outset, the ruMAD students of Whitfield PS have been at the center of the campaign to save Jessie's Creek, mustering community support by producing brochures, conducting surveys, and sending letters to government bodies linked with management of the creek.

After carrying out the biodiversity study, and after only one afternoon of attempting to clean up the creek, the students decided that there must be a better approach to making a difference to the creek as they now understood that the problem was greater than just a localized pollution issue. They looked at how they could influence other people and organizations to come on board and partner with them in making a difference to Jessie's Creek. Thomas (grade 6 boy, Whitfield District Primary) explains, "We quickly realized hand weeding wasn't going to do the trick, so we used an excavator to remove the big weeds." The students wrote to environmental organizations like the Wilderness Society, Greening Australia, and the Rural City of Wangaratta (the local shire) and shared their findings. They developed a survey for the local community, produced a brochure to publicize their ideas, and prepared presentations so they could speak to environmental groups like Landcare, the North East Catchment Management Authority, and the School Principals of the Goulburn North East Region of Education.

After the weeding and excavating, the locals could not believe the difference it made to the appearance of the entire town. They explained they had not seen the creek for 50 years (National Resource Management, 2008). A grade 6 girl from Whitfield District Primary commented, "You have to believe in what you are doing and make a fuss to get things moving. People were surprised that kids could do this stuff." With a greater awareness of what was required for long-lasting change, the students studied local native vegetation before planting hundreds of trees and shrubs along the creek together with a variety of grasses and sedges that were placed in flood-prone areas to prevent further erosion.

From their presentations, representation, and letters, the students attracted funding and support from the Commonwealth Environmental Fund, from the activist environmental group Australian Geographic, and the Victorian Government as well as in-kind contributions from the North East Catchment Management Authority (CMA). Students were able to raise funds totaling more than Au$40,000, which they used to mobilize local action for the environment.

Students and teachers from surrounding areas were also affected by the project and pitched in with assistance with weeding and planting. Many of these schools have now started their own ruMAD projects. A neighboring school, Myrhee Primary School in another rural township with around 30 students from grades 1 to 6, started to research the problem of litter in the regional center of Wangaratta. Their survey found the most common form of litter was the plastic bag, but the community was ignorant of the size of the problem at that time. So the students set out to educate the community through a series of surveys and then direct action. They found that 10,000 bags were used weekly. At first, the students made their own calico bags with environmental slogans but could not keep up with demand. Therefore, they tried to source a manufacturer—only to find that all such items were imported from China, which they realized was not an environmental solution. As a result of further research, they found a supplier prepared to manufacture onshore. The story ran in local papers and was picked up by national news, which raised widespread community awareness of the impact of the plastic bag pollution. By the end of that project, Myhree Primary students had reduced the use of shopping bags in wider Wangaratta by 55% and began sending out information to other schools in the state. By moving beyond the symptoms and tackling the actual cause of the problem, by the end of 2009 the students had forced the Victorian government to legislate against the free distribution of plastic shopping bags. Today (2010), people throughout Australia have rejected the use of plastic bags and use recycled, reusable "green bags" or pay for the privilege of plastic at their checkout. Federal legislation is currently being promoted in Parliament to ban completely the use of plastic bags.

Their focus for the children has moved now to understanding the impact of inappropriate farming practices that have disturbed the ecological balance in the fragile ecology of the area. They therefore have moved from mere moving weed regrowth to planting more native trees and shrubs along the creek. Work also began on a section of neglected public land between the school and town center. The longer-term focus will be on tackling weeds in the state forest and creating a wildlife habitat corridor to the state forest in the west to fully restore the flora and fauna indigenous to the area denuded by years of malpractice by farmers, developers, and logging companies.

An evaluation of the ruMAD project (Bell & Shrimpton, 2004) concluded as follows:

- students developed organizational and leadership skills, greater community awareness and sense of responsibility, and self-confidence
- schools developed partnerships with the local community
- the projects brought about real community change that students could see and feel a part

Their evaluation noted that enabling factors associated with implantation of ruMAD in the school include a high degree of student ownership, congruence between school philosophy and ruMAD aims, broad-based participation by students and teachers, and key people in the school (teachers/leaders) being committed to the program. Future directions for the program include exploring ways in which ruMAD projects can be integrated into the school curriculum.

The ruMAD project described here inspired the young people to make real and lasting change in their world. It assumes that young people have the power and potential to make a difference by working and learning together and gives them the tools to shape their own destiny and take action on issues about which they care. Thus ruMAD enabled the students to lead change within their communities through becoming justice-oriented citizens (Westheimer & Kahne, 2004). RuMAD is values-focused and student-led, and at the very core starts from student-identified values and visions.

DISCUSSION: WHAT ARE THE POSSIBILITIES FOR TRANSFORMATIVE ENGAGEMENT OF ALL STUDENTS?

What this chapter has demonstrated is that the re-examination of education provision in so-called disadvantaged communities can foster the transformative engagement of students in empowering and collaborative experiences that link the three message systems of education (curriculum, pedagogy, and assessment) to identity, politics, and social justice. Teachers and schools can become elegantly subversive through a strong sense of collective effort that may initially be built on isolated individual projects as happened in the example of Jessie's Creek.

Programs like ruMAD are based on both redistributive and significantly recognitive social justice (Gale & Densmore, 2000). They are school-focused, student-centered, and antibureaucratic, giving prominence to teacher and student agency. Such discursive positioning of teachers and students together and reciprocally as solution makers not as problems highlights the importance of teacher and student agency (Hargreaves, 1994; Schlechty, 1997; Woods, Jeffrey, Troman, & Boyle, 1997).

The success of the program described here provides evidence that productive student outcomes for CLED children will be successful if non-government organizations (NGOs), teachers, and academics work together, deconstructing the binary of hands-on versus heads-on learning and teaching. The program described here has achieved this by redressing the lack of attention to family and neighborhood literacies and funds of knowledge (New London Group, 1994). At the same time, they fully appreciate the need to reverse the debilitating and counter-educative practices of high-stakes academic testing, artificial streaming or setting of students, and subject choice underpinning the competitive academic curriculum. Instead they reward professional development for teachers that includes learning about and promoting change (Thompson, 2007).

CONCLUSION: CORE PEDAGOGY THROUGH PEDAGOGICAL RECIPROCITY

Important work is currently being undertaken in Australia (and elsewhere) on the kinds of pedagogies that improve outcomes for all students (Lingard, Ladwig, Mills, Bahr, Chant, & Warry, 2001a, 2001b), but in particular those variously labeled as "at risk" of early school leaving, disadvantaged, or from low socioeconomic backgrounds.

Many students do not believe their school experience has much bearing on their future and do not feel that they are accepted by their classmates and teachers (Zyngier, 2007); they gradually feel disaffected and withdraw from school life. Some become disruptive and exert a negative influence on other students (Willms, 2003). As one former student noted, "when you are standing outside the classroom all day, it is very difficult to learn" (Brown et al., 2001, p. 105). Exemplary programs like ruMAD are further evidence that an engaging pedagogy should ensure that what teachers and students do together is based on what I have termed CORE Pedagogy.

In order to create a more inclusive and empowering education system, one that engages with and responds to marginalised youth, we need to ensure that all students, not just the mainstream majority, feel that they belong and identify. In order to do this, schools "need to tap into the cultural knowledge of parents, guardians and community workers—this means that we value the different perspectives and knowledges that all people from all places have and can bring into the school system" (Dei, 2003, pp. 250–251).

Research with disadvantaged (McFadden & Munns, 2002) and marginalized (Slade & Trent, 2000) middle-years students (Brown et al., 2001) suggest that it is the students themselves who will be able to tell us that they are engaged, and will say whether their education is working for them in a culturally sensitive and relevant way (Education Foundation, 2002). It is the students who will say whether the offers that education purports to provide are real or illusionary. It is also at the messy point (McFadden & Munns, 2000) of teachers and students responding to each other in pedagogical reciprocity in relation to classroom pedagogical practices where we are truly going to see whether or not students feel that school is for them (Alexander, 2000). Rogoff, Turkanis, and Bartlett (2001) use the term *community of learners* to describe a pedagogy of adults and children engaging in learning activities together and collaboratively. It is within this space that education can provide a chance that is not illusionary (McFadden & Munns, 2000) and that can indeed be engaging and lead to purposeful, relevant, and productive educational outcomes.

This pedagogical reciprocity "disconfirms unilateral authority [and] by accepting student discipline, a power-sharing teacher then becomes *democratically* (not *institutionally*) authorised to make higher demands on the students because students have been authorised to make higher demands on the teacher" (Shor, 1996, p. 125). My research (McMahon & Zyngier, 2009; Zyngier, 2005, 2007a, 2007b, 2008) has suggested that the complexity of issues relating to student engagement (and early school leaving) cannot be fitted neatly into decontextualized accounts of youth experience, school interaction, and socio-environmental factors that in the first instance create student disempowerment and disengagement with school. A transformative student engagement was found to be an empowering one, developing a sense of entitlement, belonging, and identification, where teachers "create pedagogical practices that engage students providing them with ways of knowing that enhance their capacity to live fully and deeply" (hooks, 1994, p. 22).

Critically, if students are to successfully engage in doing thick democracy (Gandin & Apple, 2005) in school and their knowledge systems, then these systems must connect to and engage with the students' cultural knowledge while also "affirming the different strengths that knowledge forms bring to classroom pedagogy" (Dei, 2003, p. 252). This pedagogical reciprocity is critical if those most at risk are to find themselves in schools, so that their knowledges, histories, and experiences are validated and accounted for. Otherwise students are doing time, not doing education (Dei, 2003, p.251).

A critical perspective rejects an understanding that student engagement is something that is done *to* students by teachers. While "rapidly changing social, cultural, and technological conditions insist that [teachers] rethink" (Latham, Blaise, Dole, Faulkner, Lang, & Malone, 2006, p. 1) of themselves as teachers and learners, students too are subjectively different as a result of their relationship to new times (Green & Bigum, 1993). I refer to this new relationship between teachers and students as pedagogical reciprocity.

Through pedagogical reciprocity, what the teachers and students do together is termed CORE pedagogy and involves the following:

- *connecting* to and engaging with the students' cultural knowledge
- *ownership* by the students so that all students were able to see themselves as represented in the work as "ownership in their education reduces the conditions that produce their alienation" (Shor, 1992, p. 51)
- *responding* to students' lived experiences and, actively and consciously, critically commenting on that experience
- *empowering* students with a belief that what they do will make a difference to their lives and the opportunity to voice and discover their own authentic and authoritative life.

The teachers involved in the ruMAD program described here located their pedagogical practices in socio-constructivist and transformative pedagogies and were able to authentically engage their students, moving from being personally responsible through participatory action to becoming justice-oriented citizens (Westheimer & Kahne, 2004) involved in thick democratic (Carr, 2008; Gandin & Apple, 2005) work. This was also the view of both their students and their teaching colleagues.

My research (Zyngier, 2005, 2007a, 2007b, 2008) indicates that not all conceptions of engagement equally promote academic success for marginalized students. The instrumentalist and socio-constructivist conceptions of pedagogy portray engagement as "politically and educationally neutral" (McMahon & Portelli, 2004, p. 72). Where these conceptions dominate the field, these conceptions use engagement to advantage in the competition for legitimacy and authority in the pedagogical field (Bourdieu & Wacquant, 1992). Many programs designed to *re-engage students*, (un)wittingly reinforce the status quo, reproducing a pedagogy of poverty (Haberman, 1991) within their classrooms, even when this is not their aim. Transformative engagement, as employed by the ruMAD Program was not pedagogy *for* students or pedagogy *to* students, but pedagogy *with* the students, as an outcome of their pedagogical reciprocity. However, "participation is a means, not an end...for empowering education" (Shor, 1992, p. 51). In the transformative classrooms, CORE pedagogical reciprocity made "students [feel] validated for the powers they possess, but have not been taught to use" (Shor, 1987, p. 107). In this situation, the students exhibited a "sense of power and the clarity" about themselves and show evidence of a restoration of self-confidence "eroded through years of depressant schooling" (Shor, 1987, p. 107).

This research indicates that, for students who do not come from 'main-stream' culture (the 'gold' standard of school success), it is necessary (but not sufficient) to privilege student backgrounds in classroom pedagogy. Where this occurs under conditions of pedagogical reciprocity, the students have developed a strong sense of identity and begin to learn the 'rules' of the dominator culture (hooks, 1994; Sarra & Australian College of Educators, 2003) empowering the students actively to contend with and resist the claims of the dominant stance (Bourdieu & Wacquant, 1992).

It is possible, through pedagogical reciprocity, for teachers to reconceive student engagement "where difference is accorded respect and all voices are deemed worthy. [This] can make the classroom a place where students come out of shame . . . to experience their vulnerability among a community of learners who will dare to hold them up should they falter or fail" (hooks, 2003, p. 103).

By making strange the familiar concepts of risk, connectedness, and engagement, this research highlights teachers' pedagogical practices that affect the extent to which they practice pedagogical reciprocity and CORE pedagogy. The extraordinary disruption of familiar order empowers students and converts them from manipulated objects into active and critical subjects with critical agency (Shor, 1987). The role of teachers in this transformation is to become the "architect of the undoing and redoing" (Shor, 1987, p. 97). It is then not surprising that this is "an inspiring and awesome situation for teachers, who so often feel trapped in the slough of despond. So much gained or lost" (Shor, 1987, p. 97). My research confirms Haberman's hypothesis that "The whole school faculty and school community—not the individual teacher—must be the unit of change: and there must be patience and persistence of application, since students can be expected to resist changes to a system they can predict and know how to control" (Haberman, 1991, p. 292).

A CORE pedagogy, founded on pedagogical reciprocity is an opportunity "for activating individual enhancement as well as social critique, community and social change; school-parent-community collaboration will strengthen adolescents' commitment to schooling" (Fine, 1995, p. 86).

In order to solve such problems, we need to be linking curriculum, pedagogy, assessment to identity, politics, and social justice, where teachers take a historical and sociological perspective beyond the classroom and the school—becoming elegantly subversive through a strong sense of collective effort that may be built on what otherwise might be considered isolated individual projects. This research has highlighted the pedagogical possibilities for teachers to make a difference for their students' futures through CORE pedagogical reciprocity which conceives students' engagement as being generatively connected to students' lived experiences. Whether teachers will decide on the path of least resistance, continue to try to change their students, or try to change what they do remains to be seen. Elegantly subversive programs like ruMAD challenge the dominant hegemonic retributive and redistributive (Gale, 2000) views that assert that, since school works for middle-class students, then working-class students "must deserve the blame" (Howe & Moses, 1999, p. 39).

QUESTIONS FOR REFLECTION

1. What is happening in your school or school system to promote greater student engagement and connectedness with the real world? What issues stand in the way or prevent such promotion?
2. Use the principals and philosophy of ruMAD to understand and critique a service learning school-community program that you are familiar with. Do the same analysis using Westheimer and Kahne's (2004) four principles. How might you alter this service learning to make it more closely aligned with these perspectives and pricniples?
3. If you are a teacher how does your teaching reflect CORE pedagogical reciprocity? What would you have to do to make it more so?
4. If you are (or were) a student does your experience of school reflect CORE pedagogical reciprocity? What would have made it more so?

NOTES

1. An earlier version of this chapter was presented at *the Learning Democracy by Doing: Alternative Practices in Citizenship Learning and Participatory Democracy* conference held at the Ontario Institute for Studies in Education, Transformative Learning Centre at the University of Toronto in 2008 and subsequently published; see Zyngier (2009).
2. The Ladder of Youth Participation is a conceptual model created and developed by UNICEF sociologist Roger Hart. Based on a study of a youth involvement in a hundred international environmental organizations, the Ladder was first featured in Hart's *Children's Participation: From Tokenism to Citizenship* (1992). It comprises eight "rungs" or ways in which organizations involve young people, from "manipulation," "decoration," or "tokenism" through "assigned but informed," "consulted and informed," "adult-initiated, shared decisions with young people" to "young people-initiated and directed" and

"young people-initiated, shared decisions with adults." See Holdsworth, Stokes, Blanchard, & Mohamed (2007).
3. See the website of the National Resource Management department of the Australian federal government for maps and more details at http://www.nrm. gov.au/projects/vic/nev/2006-02.html.

REFERENCES

Alexander, R. J. (2000). *Culture and pedagogy: International comparisons in primary education.* Oxford, UK: Blackwell.

Bell, C., Shrimpton, B., & Leger, P. S. (2004). *Making a difference in schools and the community: Evaluation of ruMAD? (Are you making a difference?) Program in Victorian Schools.* Melbourne, Victoria: Centre for Program Evaluation, The University of Melbourne.

Bonner, C., & Caro, J. (2007). *The stupid country: How Australia is dismantling its public education system.* Sydney, NSW: University of New South Wales Press.

Bourdieu, P., & Wacquant, L. J. D. (1992). *An invitation to reflexive sociology.* Chicago, IL: University of Chicago Press.

Boyd, D., Grossman, P., Lankford, H., Loeb, S., & Wyckoff, J. (2006). How changes in entry requirements alter the teacher workforce and affect student achievement. *Education Finance and Policy, 1*(2), 176–216.

Brown, J., Mukherjee, D., Stokes, H., Tyler, D., Hebron, H., Stafford, J., … Dwyer, P. (2001). *Building relationships—making education work: A report on the perspectives of young people.* Canberra, ACT: Australian Centre for Equity through Education, Australian Youth Research Centre (Melbourne University), Commonwealth Department of Education, Training and Youth Affairs.

Carr, P. (2008). Educators and education for democracy: Moving beyond "thin" democracy. *Interamerican Journal for Education for Democracy, 1*(2), 147–165.

Darling-Hammond, L., Holtzman, D., Gatlin, S. J., & Heilig, J. V. (2005). Does teacher preparation matter? Evidence about teacher certification, Teach for America, and teacher effectiveness. *Education Policy Analysis Archives, 13*(42), 1–51.

Decker, P. T., Mayer, D. P., & Glazerman, S. (2004). *The effects of teach for America on students: Findings from a national evaluation.* Princeton, NJ: Mathematica.

Dei, G. J. (2003). Schooling and the dilemma of youth disengagement. *McGill Journal of Education, 38*(2), 241.

Dinham, S. E., Ingvarson, L., & Kleinhenz, E. (2008). Investing in teacher quality: Doing what matters most. In *Teaching talent: The best teachers for Australia's classrooms* (pp. 6–56). Melbourne, Victoria: Business Council of Australia.

Education Foundation (Producer). (2002). *What school kids want* [VHS]. Australia: Author.

Fine, M. (1995). The politics of who's "at risk." In B. B. Swadener & S. Lubeck (Eds.), *Children and families "at promise": Deconstructing the discourse of risk* (pp. 76–97). Albany, NY: State University of New York Press.

Friedman, M., & Friedman, R. (1980). *Free to choose: A personal statement* (1st ed.). New York, NY: Harcourt Brace Jovanovich.

Gale, T. (2000). Rethinking social justice in schools: How will we recognize it when we see it? *International Journal of Inclusive Education, 4*(3), 253–269.

Gandin, L. A., & Apple, M. (2005). Thin versus thick democracy in education: Porto Alegre and the creation of alternatives to neo-liberalism. *International Studies in Sociology of Education, 12*(2), 99–116.

Green, B., & Bigum, C. (1993). Aliens in the classroom. *Australian Journal of Education, 37*(2), 119–141.

Haberman, M. (1991). The pedagogy of poverty versus good teaching. *Phi Delta Kappan, 73*(4), 290.

Hargreaves, A. (1994). *Changing teachers, changing times: Teachers' work and culture in the postmodern age.* London, UK: Cassell.

Hart, R. (1992). *Children's participation: From tokenism to citizenship.* Innocenti Essays No. 4. Florence, Italy: UNICEF, International Child Development Centre.

Holdsworth, R., Stokes, H., Blanchard, M., & Mohamed, N. (2006). *Civic engagement and young people in the city of Melbourne.* Melbourne, Victoria: Australian Youth Research Centre, University of Melbourne.

hooks, b. (1994). *Teaching to transgress: Education as the practice of freedom.* New York, NY: Routledge.

hooks, b. (2003). *Teaching community: A pedagogy of hope.* New York, NY: Routledge.

Howe, K. R., & Moses, M. M. (1999). Ethics in educational research. *Review of Research in Education, 24,* 21–59.

Laczko-Kerr, I., & Berliner, D. (2002). The effectiveness of "teach for America" and other under-certified teachers on student academic achievement: A case of harmful public policy. *Education Policy Analysis Archives, 10*(37).

Lamb, S. (2007). School reform and inequality in urban Australia: A case of residualising the poor. In R. Teese, S. Lamb, M. Duru-Bellat & S. Helme (Eds.), *International studies in educational inequality, theory and policy* (vol. 3, pp. 1–38). Dordrecht, The Netherlands: Springer.

Latham, G., Blaise, M., Dole, S., Faulkner, J., Lang, J., & Malone, K. (2006). *Learning to teach: New times, new practices.* South Melbourne, Victoria: Oxford University Press.

Leigh, A., & Ryan, C. (2006). *How and why has teacher quality changed in Australia?* Canberra, ACT: Research School of Social Sciences Centre for Economic Policy Research, Australian National University.

Leigh, A., & Ryan, C. (2008). *How has school productivity changed in Australia?* Canberra, ACT: Research School of Social Sciences Centre for Economic Policy Research, Australian National University.

Lingard, R., Ladwig, J., Mills, M., Bahr, M., Chant, D., & Warry, M. (2001a). *Queensland school reform longitudinal study: Final report* (Vol. 1). Brisbane, Queensland: Report prepared for Education Queensland by the School of Education, The University of Queensland.

Lingard, R., Ladwig, J., Mills, M., Bahr, M., Chant, D., & Warry, M. (2001b). Queensland School Reform Longitudinal Study: Supplementary Materials (Vol. 2). Brisbane, Queensland: Report prepared for Education Queensland by the School of Education, The University of Queensland.

McFadden, M., & Munns, G. (2000, December). *Chance, illusion and engagement.* Paper presented at the Australian Association for Research in Education Annual Conference, Sydney.

McFadden, M., & Munns, G. (2002). Student engagement and the social relations of pedagogy. *British Journal of Sociology of Education, 23*(3), 357–366.

McGraw, B. (2006). *Achieving quality and equity education.* Paper presented at the VASSP Annual Leadership Conference, Melbourne. Retrieved from http://www.aspa.asn.au/images/conferences/state/vassp2006/mcgawppt.pdf

McMahon, B., & Portelli, J. P. (2004). Engagement for What? Beyond Popular Discourses of Student Engagement. *Leadership and Policy in Schools, 3*(1), 59–76.

McMahon, B., & Zyngier, D. (2009). Student engagement: Contested concepts in two continents. *Research in Comparative and International Education Symposium Journals, 4*(2), 164–181.

Murray, S., Mitchell, J., Gale, T., Edwards, J., & Zyngier, D. (2004). *Student disengagement from primary schooling: A review of research and practice.* Clayton, Australia: CASS Foundation & Centre for Childhood Studies, Faculty of Education, Monash University.

National Resource Management. (2008). *Students save Whitfield waterway.* Australian Government. Retrieved from http://www.nrm.gov.au/projects/vic/nev/2006-02.html

New London Group (1995). *A pedagogy of multiliteracies: Designing social futures.* Haymarket, Australia: NLLIA Centre for Workplace Communication and Culture

Pearson, C. (2007, March 3–4). Our forsaken schools. *Weekend Australian.* Retrieved from http://www.theaustralian.com.au/news/opinion/christopher-pearson-our-forsaken-schools/story-e6frg6zo-1111113088523

Pike, B. (2008). *Blueprint for early childhood development and school reform: School reform discussion paper.* Melbourne, Victoria: Victorian Government. Retrieved from http://www.education.vic.gov.au/about/directions/blueprint2008/papers.htm

Rogoff, B., Turkanis, C. G., & Bartlett, L. (2001). *Learning together: Children and adults in a school community.* New York, NY: Oxford University Press.

Rudd, K., & Gillard, J. (2008). *Quality Education: The case for an education revolution in our schools.* Australian Government, Department of Education, Employment and Workplace Relations. Retrieved from http://www.deewr.gov.au/Schooling/Programs/Pages/QualityEducation-ThecaseforanEducationRevolutioninourSchools.aspx

Sarra, C., & Australian College of Educators. (2003). *Young and black and deadly: Strategies for improving outcomes for indigenous students.* Deakin West, ACT: Australian College of Educators.

Schlechty, P. (1997). *Inventing better schools: An action plan for education reform: The Jossey-Bass education series.* San Fransisco, CA: Jossey-Bass.

Shor, I. (1987). *Critical teaching and everyday life.* Chicago: University of Chicago Press.

Shor, I. (1992). *Empowering education: Critical teaching for social change.* Chicago: University of Chicago Press.

Shor, I. (1996). *When students have power: Negotiating authority in a critical pedagogy.* Chicago, IL: University of Chicago Press.

Slade, M., & Trent, F. (2000). What the boys are saying: An examination of the views of boys about declining rates of achievement and retention. *International Education Journal, 11*(3), 221–227.

Smith W., Butler-Kisber, L., LaRoque, L., Portelli, J., Shields, C., Sparkes, C., & Vibert, A. (2001a). *Student engagement in learning and school life: Case reports from project schools* (Vol. 2). Montreal, Quebec: Office of Research on Educational Policy, McGill University.

Smith, W., Butler-Kisber, L., LaRoque, L., Portelli, J., Shields, C., Sparkes, C., & Vibert, A. (2001b). *Student engagement in learning and school life: National project report* (Vol. 1). Montreal, Quebec: Office of Research on Educational Policy, McGill University.

Stokes, H., & Turnbull, M. (2008). *Real engagement with real issues: An evaluation of the ruMAD? Program, final report.* Melbourne, Victoria: Education Foundation Australia & Australian Youth Research Centre, University of Melbourne

Teese, R. (2007). Structural inequality in australian education: Vertical and later-stratification of opportunity. In R. Teese, S. Lamb, M. Duru-Bellat, & S. Helme (Eds.), *International studies in educational inequality, theory and policy* (vol. 3, pp. 36–91). Dordrecht, The Netherlands: Springer.

Teese, R., & Lamb, S. (2007). School reform and inequality in urban Australia. A case of residualising the poor. In R. Teese, S. Lamb, M. Duru-Bellat & S. Helme (Eds.), *International studies in educational inequality, theory and policy* (vol. 1). Dordrecht, The Netherlands: Springer.

Thompson, P. (2007). Making education more equitable: What can policy makers learn from the Australian Disadvantaged Schools Programme? In R. Teese, S. Lamb, M. Duru-Bellat, & S. Helme (Eds.), *International studies in educational inequality, theory and policy* (vol. 3, pp. 239–256). Dordrecht, The Netherlands: Springer.

Tomazin, F. (2008, April 7). Shake-up to hit bored teachers. *The Age.* Retrieved from http://www.theage.com.au/news/national/shakeup-targets-bored-teachers/2008/04/06/1207420202545.html

Westheimer, J., & Kahne, J. (2004). What kind of citizen? The politics of educating for democracy. *American Educational Research Journal, 41*(2), 237–269.

Whitty, G., Halpin, D., & Power, S. (1998). *Devolution and choice in education: The school, the state, and the market.* Buckingham, UK: Open University Press.

Willms, J. D. (2003). *Student engagement at school: A sense of belonging and participation: Results from PISA 2000.* Organization for Economic Co-Operation and Development. Retrieved from http://www.sourceoecd.org/9264018921

Woods, P. (1997). *Restructuring schools, reconstructing teachers: Responding to change in the primary school.* Buckingham, UK: Open University Press.

Zyngier, D. (2005). Advancing student engagement through changed teaching practices. *The International Journal of Learning, 12*(1), 1–11.

Zyngier, D. (2007a). The challenge of student engagement—What the students say they want —Putting young people at the centre of the conversation. *LEARNing Landscapes, 1,* 93–116.

Zyngier, D. (2007b). Listening to teachers—Listening to students: Substantive conversations about resistance, empowerment and engagement. *Teachers and Teaching Theory and Practice Journal, 13*(4), 327–347.

Zyngier, D. (2008). (Re)Conceptualising student engagement: Doing education not doing time. *Teaching and Teacher Education, 24*(7), 1765–1776.

Zyngier, D. (2009). Education, democracy and social justice: The Australian experience— doing thick democracy in the classroom. In K. Daly, D. Schugarensky, & K. Lopes (Eds.), *Learning democracy by doing: Alternative practices in citizenship education and participatory democracy* (pp. 248-263). Toronto, Canada: Transformative Learning Centre, Ontario Institute for Studies in Education, University of Toronto.

Zyngier, D., & Brunner, C. (2002). *The r.u.MAD? Program. Kids making a difference in the community with MAD projects* (Vol. 1). Melbourne, Victoria: Education Foundation.

CHAPTER 8

THINKING THE UNTHINKABLE

Teachers Who Engage Students in Poverty
"In this class you can imagine..."

Geoff Munns

ABSTRACT

This chapter draws on research into student engagement in low SES communities in Australia. The research has been designed to give hope to poor urban and rural communities that they might "think the unthinkable": that there are teachers who can strongly contribute to the improvement of the educational and life circumstances of their children and so positively contribute to their community's well-being. Drawing on research frameworks around student engagement developed in the Fair Go Project (Munns, 2007), the current study undertakes intensive case study research into the classroom pedagogies of 30 teachers, exploring the causal impact of their work on the social and academic outcomes of their students. The classroom stories of two teachers will be told in this chapter. Against a theoretical backdrop that shows how students are positioned within discourses of power, it will provide a clearer picture of how teachers might engage students in poverty and so help them negotiate hitherto tenuous pathways towards educational success.

Student Engagement in Urban Schools, pages 133–149
Copyright © 2012 by Information Age Publishing
All rights of reproduction in any form reserved.

133

"My teacher says that in this class you can imagine." The Year 6 girl had been talking about her teacher during a focus group interview. The words, and her conviction in saying them, stayed with me for a long time. I was just finishing a week in her classroom conducting research into student engagement in low socioeconomic status (SES) communities in the Fair Go Project (Fair Go Team, 2006). The focus group was to explore students' views of their classroom and consider these against classroom observations and teacher interviews. What happened in this interview arrested me on a number of levels. First, all the other students in the interview shared the girl's sentiments. They talked about how their learning was fun and exciting, explained the ways their teacher gave them a positive attitude and helped them have friends, shared that "the work is like entertainment and joyful." Put plainly, the students "got" what their teacher was doing with them in the classroom and felt he was different than other teachers. Second, the girl's words reminded me of the song lyrics I had borrowed a couple of years earlier as a metaphor for the classroom changes the Fair Go Project (FGP) had been implementing with teachers to engage their low SES students (Munns, 2007):

> Didn't I come to bring you a sense of wonder
> Didn't I come to lift your fiery vision bright
> Didn't I come to bring you a sense of wonder in the flame.
> (Van Morrison, 1985, track 12)

The "sense of wonder" imagery captured the direction and force of these pedagogical changes. "Wonder" has meanings as both a phenomenon and an intellectual action. That is, it can carry ideas of marvel and surprise, but can also point to reflective processes. The FGP research had shown that when teachers work on engaging pedagogies, students in low SES schools can become positively surprised by learning experiences in their classrooms. They can also be involved in vital imaginings and reflections about their learning that can draw them as insiders into classroom discourse communities. Taken together, the surprise and the imaginings become the classroom ingredients for student engagement. It is these ideas and their illustration that will be taken up in this chapter

There are three sections that follow. The first describes research frameworks around student engagement developed in the FGP. The second introduces two teachers and tells their classroom stories, highlighting the relationship between their pedagogy and student engagement. The third utilises the student engagement framework to provide a clearer picture of how teachers might engage students in poverty and so help them negotiate hitherto tenuous pathways towards educational success.

THE FAIR GO PROJECT'S STUDENT ENGAGEMENT FRAMEWORK

The FGP is a joint undertaking between a team of researchers from the University of Western Sydney (School of Education) and Priority Schools Programs[1] (NSW Department of Education and Training). It has had two research phases. The first phase was action research employing a co-researching ethnographic methodology, and it brought together university researchers, teachers, and school students. The student engagement framework was developed in this phase. In the second phase, the research involves intensive case study research into the classroom pedagogies of 30 "exemplary" teachers of students in poverty. These teachers are recognized for the ways they engage their students, and the case studies explore the causal impact of their work on the social and academic outcomes of their students. The student engagement framework is both a methodological and analytical tool for this phase.

The student engagement framework was reached in two ways. The first was through utilizing ideas from within the sociology of pedagogy, and the second was inductively from the research. Both the literature review and the action research were simultaneous processes. A more detailed discussion of the project and its theoretical framing can be found in Munns (2007). The framework describes two levels of student engagement: small "e" engagement (engagement) and big "E" engagement (Engagement). The first is substantive classroom engagement, a multifaceted interplay of the cognitive, affective, and operative processes and experiences at high levels. Put simply, this is when students are thinking hard, feeling good, and working well. This view of engagement is consistent with the research literature (Fredricks, Blumenfeld, & Paris, 2004). The second, Engagement, is that longer and more enduring relationship with schooling and education that is rejected in large numbers by students living in poor communities (Abowitz, 2000). Big "E" Engagement is a commitment to school as a place and education as a resource: the belief that "school is for me" (McFadden & Munns, 2002).

The FGP theorizes that these two levels of student engagement are embedded, and their interplay is influenced by the messages that students receive in classrooms. Bernstein (1996) argued that classrooms deliver powerful messages to students through their curriculum, pedagogy, and assessment practices. These messages helped shape individuals' perceptions of what they might do now and in the future, and what they might become when they leave school. In this way schools and classrooms operate to structure the consciousness of students. The research of the FGP is based on the idea that classroom messages can be engaging as much as they are disengaging. The research literature has highlighted the kinds of disengaging messages

TABLE 8.1 Discourses of Power and Disengaging Messages for Low SES Students

knowledge	"Why are we doing this?"—restricted access to powerful knowledge
ability	"I can't do this"—feelings of not being able to achieve and a spiral of low expectations and aspirations
control	"I'm not doing that"—struggles over classroom time and space and debilitating consequences of resistance and compliance
place	"I'm just a kid from"—devalued as individual and learner
voice	"Teacher tells us"—no say over learning with teacher as sole controller and judge

that low SES students have historically received (Comber & Thomson, 2001; Hayes, 2003; Mills & Gale, 2002). In the FGP framework, these messages are generalized and categorized within "discourses of power" (knowledge, ability, control, place, and voice) and summarized in Table 8.1.

Many students in poor communities daily experience conservative and controlling classroom pedagogies (see, for example, Haberman's [1991] "pedagogy of poverty") that deliver low levels of decontextualized learning. Students soon learn in these classrooms that they are lacking in ability, have no voice, are not valued, and are compelled either to accept or to struggle over the classroom spaces. In order to interrupt these discourses of power, an alternate pedagogy is promoted in the Fair Go Project (Figure 8.1).

It is a pedagogy that directly targets the five discourses (knowledge, ability, control, place, and voice) through both the nature of the classroom learning

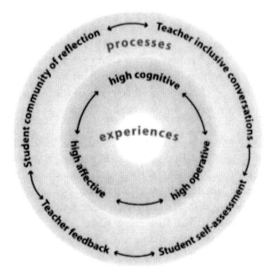

Figure 8.1 The Fair Go pedagogy.

experiences (inner circle) and the classroom processes (outer circle). The experiences are directly related to the definitions of engagement. The figure shows that these experiences need to be developed, so there is a balanced interplay between high cognitive, affective, and operative learning experiences and processes. Within this balanced interplay, developing high cognitive activities might deploy elements from the intellectual quality dimension of productive pedagogies (Hayes, Mills, Christie, & Lingard, 2006). The high operative component would pay careful attention to developing students as competent and empowered learners across their entire classroom experience. "High affective" assumes that the teacher and students are involved in pedagogical conversations that strongly negotiate learning situations that will bring about mutually stimulating and enjoyable emotions associated with classroom work. The classroom processes aim to build a reflective and supportive learning community. The research suggests that this dual approach builds classrooms in which students are challenged and motivated and are given opportunities to become more successful learners. They feel valued within an atmosphere of sharing and reflection where their voice as learners is encouraged and respected.[2] The messages are engaging (Table 8.2).

The next section of this chapter introduces the classroom pedagogies of two exemplary teachers in the current research phase and the impact of these on student responses to the curriculum.

INTRODUCING TWO TEACHERS WHO ENGAGE THEIR STUDENTS

Dan and Chantal teach in urban schools located in low SES communities. Dan is a new career teacher, in his third year of teaching. By contrast, Chantal is a teaching principal who has taught for 20 years. There are marked

TABLE 8.2 Discourses of Power and Engaging Messages for Low SES Students

knowledge	"We can see the connection and the meaning"—reflectively constructed access to contextualised and powerful knowledge
ability	"I am capable"—feelings of being able to achieve and a spiral of high expectations and aspirations
control	"We do this together"—sharing of classroom time and space: interdependence, mutuality and power with
place	"It's great to be a kid from"—valued as individual and learner and feelings of belonging and ownership over learning
voice	"We share"—environment of discussion and reflection about learning with students and teachers playing reciprocal meaningful roles

differences in their approaches to teaching, but much in common at the heart of what engages their students.

Dan (Year 6[3])

Dan teaches in a large inner suburban primary school (800 students) in Sydney, Australia. The student cohort represents over 40 cultural-linguistic groups, with the majority being Muslim and Arabic-speaking Australians. Almost 100% of the students come from multilingual backgrounds (language backgrounds other than English). The school is a very supportive learning community, with a stated purpose "to strive for excellence and equity." Importantly for a teacher like Dan, the school's leadership encourages him to take risks and be innovative in his pedagogy, within a context of strong support, professional dialogue, and high expectations.

Dan's classroom is characterized by active, constructivist, and negotiated learning. All students, regardless of academic level, are constantly involved with big ideas, important themes, and high intellectual quality. Students perceive learning as fun due to Dan's capacity to initiate activities using surprise, unexpected props, or actions. Learning experiences are authentic and regularly extended outside the classroom and connected with the local community. He sustains a sense of excitement in learning by involving students in problem-solving and guiding them with questions that develop ownership, respect, and autonomy. Dan's pedagogy has changed students' attitudes. They now realize that they can be accountable for learning. Individual contribution, effort, and risk-taking are valued. Planning, process, and engaging messages are features of Dan's teaching. Quality teaching is the focus over behavior. Here is how Dan describes his approach to teaching:

> The challenge I face at the beginning of each term is to ensure every student will be an insider, totally engaged in what they do at school. While this challenge is sometimes only measured with small successes, I always try to reflect on how I might improve my planning and pedagogy for better engagement. . . . As a teacher, my worst days are always those in which I chose to focus on managing the behavior of my students above the quality of my planning and pedagogy. Satisfaction is going home at the end of a day knowing the classroom was buzzing all day with self-motivated learning as a result of careful planning, informed pedagogy, and deep critical reflection. . . . I believe my students relate to my classroom with positive emotions. I avoid using teacher power to regulate behavior.

Analysis of Dan's pedagogy after classroom observations revealed the following features that the research believes work towards high levels of student engagement:

- There is a high rotation of challenging, rich tasks. The pedagogy features hard work for both the students and their teacher. There are no back-outs or compromises, and the pedagogy needs perseverance for all involved.
- Students are critical learners, continually being asked to think and solve authentic, hands-on challenges for themselves with the teacher as co-learner.
- The classroom is a multi-modal environment: Students are skilled users of technology and are expected to be able to use it autonomously.
- Students make decisions. Dan sees them as "guardians of knowledge." All learners are included in the design of the task.
- Minor discipline issues are handled dispassionately and explicitly. Discipline issues are regarded as "works in progress . . . these kids are a great project."
- Strong teaching and learning attention are provided for lower-level students. In other situations, low ability students might have received a nagging behavior focus rather than a teacher who shares their thinking, assists them as a co-learner, and expects success with differentiated tasks and assessment.
- Very few students get punished during any day, and no one influences the planned pedagogy. Dan believes he can "control" the students but chooses rather to share the pedagogical spaces.
- The pedagogy works towards high ideals of learning, and this is maintained without worrying about what others might think. Dan is true to his own pedagogical beliefs and tries not to falter in these.

It is acknowledged at this stage that such a snapshot of a teacher's work cannot fully capture the complexities of a classroom, particularly as it daily plays out as a discursive community. That is beyond the scope of this chapter. Nonetheless, it can start to offer a picture of the relationship between a teacher's pedagogy and student engagement within a theoretical framework. With respect to the FGP engagement framework detailed above, it seems reasonable to suggest that Dan's pedagogies offer high cognitive, high affective, and high operative learning experiences for all learners (inner circle) and actively work towards building a reflective and supportive learning community (outer circle). This will be discussed further in the final section. Student engagement is difficult to measure (see Fredricks et al., 2004), a point that this research fully accepts. Even so, intensive and sustained classroom observations in this classroom revealed that a potentially challenging group of students showed strong involvement with and acceptance of their learning experiences. They were often "in task" (Fair Go Team, 2006). As the students put it: "We do learning and it's fun at the same time...exciting...experiments and projects....Fun, exciting...the teacher helps us with the hard work. In other classes we just wrote stuff from the board and learnt nothing." Perhaps these comments are measure enough of student engagement.

Chantal (Teaching Principal)

Chantal is principal of a small primary school (180 students) in an inner suburban community in Sydney. Not dissimilar to Dan's school, it has a large population of students living in multilingual families (80%), and Arabic is the largest language group. When Chantal was appointed to the school as principal (2006), it had fewer students and she was both a teacher and a principal. This was a deliberate choice, as she wanted to be a teacher and a leader. The school has since grown to the point where she no longer needs to teach, but she maintains active teaching roles in the school. As a teaching principal, Chantal continued her recognition of the importance of high expectations and the need to increase student participation in learning rather than accepting student passivity.

For our research, we observed Chantal teaching a number of different primary-aged groups (approximately 9- to 12-year-old students). As mentioned above, Chantal has a different approach to teaching than Dan. She has an explicit approach and is more strongly foregrounded in classrooms, while still allowing students' choices in the design of activities. Her teaching encourages students to be active and reflective in their learning. Continual reflections refocus tasks, processes, and learning quality. Cooperative learning is frequently employed to cater to the needs and abilities of multi-staged, academically mixed, and culturally diverse groups of students. Students perceive learning as fun and exciting due to Chantal's capacity for humor and her ability to focus on conversations about learning, higher-order thinking, and challenging work. Learning experiences are invariably authentic and problem-based, promoting responsibility and shared decision making about the school. Empathy, respect, and ownership are encouraged. As with Dan, Chantal values quality pedagogy over behavior, though she does keep a tighter "principal's rein" over her students. Chantal's commitment is obvious and infectious. "My whole belief, my philosophy, my passion is out there—it's on my sleeve." She goes on to outline her philosophy:

> Explicit teaching of literacy and numeracy underpins my teaching programs. These programs are focused on deep understanding and are significant for both teachers and students. Lessons engage students in meaningful classroom practice and provide a quality learning environment where learning about the real world is an active, collaborative process built on high expectations and a commitment to improving practice and enhancing students' learning.

Following is an analysis of the key elements of Chantal's engaging pedagogies:

- There is an overarching focus on meta-cognition and the use of technical language.
- All classroom work is challenging, with continual reflections about learning refocusing the task, processes, and learning.
- Risk-taking and self-regulation are encouraged throughout. Feedback targets risk-taking and autonomy. There are frequent opportunities for students to be decision-makers.
- A consistent use of narrative links learning activities and builds relationships.
- Discourse is consistently conversational, often personalized and related to Chantal's and the students' worlds.
- Students remain very industrious and receptive for the most part of each lesson—there are strong signs of engagement throughout all lessons. Students are expected to "get into it" and do so.
- Lessons move on and students are expected students to be "on the game"—to remain focused and follow the learning processes.
- There is a calm but firm focus characterized by humor and positivity, but always on learning. Distracted students are quickly brought back to task without emotion. Students not on task are not appreciated and they know it. This brings an unhurried, learning-focused environment with time to think.

The FGP realizes there are many different ways towards student engagement, and these are invariably linked with contextual issues, student responses and teacher-preferred style. So while Chantal's classrooms look, feel and sound different to Dan's, her pedagogy resonates strongly with the FGP student engagement framework. There are high cognitive, high affective and high operative learning experiences for all learners (inner circle), her students are actively involved in reflective and supportive learning communities (outer circle). As with Dan, her students understand and appreciate what she is doing for them:

> She helps us imagine, use stories, ask questions, mix up words, read between the lines to get meaning.... When explaining and we work, she asks us to wait, absorb, wait, so that we understand.... She makes us feel confident and happy by walking around, smiling when we are doing something hard.... She is always positive.... She talks about learning a lot, tells us some of her tricks, tells funny stories, uses humor.... She gives reasons for changing behavior, uses a polite, calm voice, then they understand.... She talks about learning and being a safe, respectful learner.

These two snapshots of classrooms are offered as exemplars for engaging teaching within the framing of the FGP. Of course, this is not to suggest that these are the only pedagogical ways that students can become engaged. However, they do offer a picture of classrooms where there is a strong suggestion that the teachers' approaches to learning have encouraged student engagement. Important questions can then be explored about what is common and engaging in their pedagogies. This chapter now turns again to the FGP student engagement framework to propose a response to those questions.

ENGAGING STUDENTS IN POVERTY

The FGP student engagement framework was earlier introduced and described as both a methodological and analytical tool. In this section the pedagogy and the engaging messages are deployed in an attempt to provide a more detailed theoretical explanation about what Dan and Chantal do in common to engage their students.

The Pedagogy

Figure 8.1 suggests that for pedagogy to be engaging, both the planned learning experiences (inner circle) and the classroom processes (outer circle) are important and need to work together. The experiences target the definition of student engagement.

What follows are the some of the key features of Dan's and Chantal's teaching as analyzed through the pedagogical features of the frame. The nature of the learning experiences are first summarized (inner circle).

High cognitive leaning experiences (how students are encouraged to think hard)

- Classroom rewards are intrinsic and linked to learning.
- Learning processes are valued as much as learning products.
- There is a high rotation of high intellectual quality tasks across all subject areas.
- Higher-order thinking is encouraged through well-designed and prepared tasks.
- Key vocabulary, concepts, and responses are continually explored, explained, and personalized through teacher–student and student–student discourse.
- Students are guided to provide reasons for their analytical responses and encouraged to question their conclusions.

- Knowledge is often accessed through shared discovery.
- Critical literacy operates in whole-class, group, and individual work.
- There is strong integration among key content areas and processes—barriers between subjects are minimized.
- Frequent opportunities for reflective meta-cognition are encouraged.

High affective learning experiences (how students are encouraged to feel good)

- Learning is linked with real-life contexts, the students' world, school issues, and the local area.
- Deliberate choices are made not to reveal the activities of the day ahead of time and to capitalize on surprise and positive connotation with each learning sequence.
- Opportunities are provided for students to share their work with families and other class audiences.
- Hands-on learning and a variety of resources are used to arouse student curiosity.
- Joint task construction and inclusivity are encouraged.
- Humor and narrative are regular features.
- Important themes and subtexts are presented to students through literary and visual texts that evoked emotion and opportunity for students to identify, understand, and empathize with big ideas.
- Students are challenged to achieve and use imagination.
- Many different ways to learn are employed—classrooms operate in many different ways.
- The classrooms do not operate through control and punishment.

High operative (how students are encouraged to become better learners)

- Learning activities are frequently collaborative.
- Discourses encourage students to cooperate and support each other.
- Students are encouraged to be reflective, to be critical, and to test things out for themselves—their opinions and ideas are valued.
- Teaching tasks allowed for student experimentation and different and collaborative approaches to learning are encouraged.
- Movement around the classroom is part of task design.
- Priority is given to learning processes and activities, peer modeling, and presentation of final learning products and outcomes, rather than "showcasing" learning through a collection of artefacts.

- Students are helped to be competent independent users of technology.
- Classroom discourses are dominated by talk about learning rather than behavior.
- Students are regularly endorsed as potential and actual learners.
- Effort in performing task to the highest level is valued.

The learning processes (outer circle) have the following common features. Analysis shows that there are very strong connections and overlaps between the inner and outer circles. This is entirely expected.

Student community of reflection (conscious environment of cooperative sharing of ideas and processes about learning), focuses on substantive conversations encouraging student control and voice, movement away from compliance as a way of students responding to task completion, and evaluation and towards shared ownership over all aspects of the learning experiences)

- Teacher's oral and written scaffolds provided orientation and parameters for learning activities and group work.
- Group roles and responsibilities facilitated the balance between student direction and teacher guidance of learning, while providing a strong structure for students' self-regulation—groups are regularly "shuffled" so that students get used to working with each other.
- Individuals and groups are all involved regardless of academic level and their ideas and opinions are valued and validated—all students have access to all learning experiences,
- Scaffolding often operates with a dual purpose—the teacher assisted the lower stage or ability learning group and this in turn provided a scaffold for the rest of the class who are self-directed and working independently (individually and in groups).
- There is a strong reinforcement of the school and the classroom as a community with student input to decision making.
- Classroom discourses habitually reinforce and build the community: "it's about shared responsibility...if you're not about participating...what you put in is what you get out."

Teacher inclusive conversations. Emphasis is on sharing power with students with a visibility that encourages sharing of classroom culture, promotion of thinking and opportunities for students to interact and share processes of learning. The focus is on learning, not behavior, moving towards conversations about learning that are shared, mutual, and reciprocal.

- Tasks require students to convey understanding with each other and the teacher in substantive oral and written communications

- Students are invited to be learners through teacher discourses and reflective conversations about learning.
- Teacher talk focuses on learning over behavior, aided by thoughtfully designed learning activities.

Student self-assessment offers continuous opportunities for students to think about and express ideas about the processes of their learning. The focus is on cognitive, affective, and operative aspects of learning and towards deeper levels of reflection, moving away from teacher as sole judge and towards students taking more responsibility for evaluation of learning.

- Criteria are negotiated for learning tasks, and students are expected to check and interpret their performance.
- Questioning techniques promote student discussion, an examination of each other's ideas, and guided students' acceptance of a variety of responses.
- Students are encouraged to consider multiple perspectives and recognize that choices exist in ways they construct and assess knowledge.

Teacher feedback fosters an awareness of the power of written, oral, and symbolic feedback on students' self-concept as learners and moves towards feedback tied to investing more effort, more attention, or more confidence into the task being undertaken.

- Feedback is specific to learning and positive participation
- Positive responses to students and demonstrated high expectations builds confidence that they could achieve.
- Reflective, meta-cognitive discussions are used to deepen and consolidate knowledge.

The common features of Dan's and Chantal's pedagogies highlight a particular approach to teaching that the FGP proposes are likely to encourage enhanced levels of student engagement. The FGP framing also suggests that these kinds of learning experiences and processes will send engaging messages to the students. The final part of this section draws on research data to show these messages in action in both these classrooms.

The Messages

Table 8.2 showed how these messages play out across five discourses of power. The argument here is that discourses of power connect classroom discourses with the wider dimensions of social power (Munns, 2007). Research data gathered in both Dan's and Chantal's classrooms indicated that messages played out in the following engaging ways for their students.

Knowledge

- Students are positioned as joint constructors of knowledge: predictors, interpreters, evaluators, and reflectors.
- Deep knowledge and understanding are reached without capitulation to busy, low-order tasks that occupy and obtain silent compliance.
- Meaning and knowledge are reached by connecting students' own contexts with the wider world and relating their leaning to different audiences and specific purposes.
- Choices, suggestions, and responses are valued by the teacher and often by each other.

Ability

- All students are involved in work of high academic standard regardless of academic level.
- There are high expectations for all students that they are capable of completing tasks, and there is support to cater to different academic levels.
- Students understand the different participation dynamics of different individuals and groups, and all accept their designated amount of collaboration according to their membership.
- Individual confidence in their abilities is built by supported opportunities to reflect on their work.

Control

- Behavior issues are rephrased around learning, not compliance
- Teacher power is not exercised—reason and doing the "right thing" centralize classroom relationships.
- There is a dominant teacher rationale that no student is to be criticized negatively nor have self-concepts lowered.
- Teacher has the capacity to clarify and be explicit, to remain calm and exercise patience, and to be humorous.

Place

- There is a genuine teacher validation of and affection for the positive aspects of the local community.

- Authentic learning tasks are linked with the students' world.
- Parents and community members are welcomed into the learning community.

Voice

- Learning design generates choices in learning options.
- Open-ended and kinaesthetic activities give students continuous and multiple opportunities to make decisions within their learning.
- All students have frequent occasions to exercise voice; maintain learning decisions; share learning time, attention, and space; and reflect on learning.

In summary, research data gathered and analyzed from these two classrooms present a pedagogy that the FGP believes is likely to encourage and maintain enhanced levels of student engagement. It is a pedagogy that resonates strongly with Newmann's "authentic instruction" (1996) and Haberman's "good teaching" (1991), approaches to teaching and learning shown to improve social and academic outcomes for all students, and especially those living in poverty. In presenting classroom stories about two teachers recognized for the engagement of their students, there is an illustration of how the design of learning experiences and the crafting of classroom processes can send positive, engaging messages to students who might otherwise find school a less rewarding and satisfying environment. This is the premise on which the FGP was founded.

THINKING THE UNTHINKABLE

This chapter draws on research designed to give hope to poor urban and rural communities that they might "think the unthinkable": that there are teachers who can strongly contribute to the improvement of the educational and life circumstances of their children and so positively contribute to their community's well-being. Against a theoretical backdrop that shows how students are positioned within discourses of power, it has attempted to provide a clearer picture of how teachers might engage students in poverty and so help them negotiate hitherto tenuous pathways towards educational success. In these classrooms, students know that they can imagine.

ACKNOWLEDGMENT

I would like to acknowledge a number of educators committed to improved educational experiences and outcomes for low SES students who have contributed to the ideas explored in this chapter. First, I would like to recognize Dan Sprange (Hampden Park Public School) and Chantal Mamo (Granville South Public School), who opened up their classrooms and their teaching for the research and contributed strongly to the analysis of their pedagogies. Second, Caroline Hatton contributed perceptive research observations. Finally, I acknowledge the University of Western Sydney Fair Go Team, whose classroom research and critical participation brought forward the student engagement framework discussed in this chapter.

NOTES

1. Priority Schools Programs (PSP) are aimed at improving educational outcomes for students living in the poorest communities in NSW. It was previously known as the Priority Schools Funding Program (PSFP) and the Disadvantaged Schools Program (DSP).
2. Again, this description only provides an outline of the framing. More detail about all aspects of the FGP engagement framework and data from the research can be found in Fair Go Team (2006) and Munns (2007).
3. Year 6 is the final year of primary (elementary) schooling in New South Wales (Australia). Students in Year 6 are usually 11 and 12 years old.

REFERENCES

Abowitz, K. (2000). A pragmatic revisioning of resistance theory. *American Educational Research Journal, 37*, 877–907.

Bernstein, B. (1996) *Pedagogy, symbolic control and identity: Theory, research, critique.* London: Taylor & Francis.

Comber, B., & Thomson, P. (2001, June/July). *Just new learning environments: New metaphors and practices for learners and teachers in disadvantaged schools.* Paper presented at the Department for Education and Skills, "Experiencing Change, Exchanging Experience" Virtual Conference.

Fair Go Team. (2006). *School is for me: Pathways to student engagement.* Sydney, NSW: Priority Schools Funding Program, NSW Department of Education and Training.

Fredricks, J.A., Blumenfield, P.C. & Paris, A.H. (2004). School engagement: Potential of the concept state of the evidence. *Review of Educational Research, 76*(1), 59–109.

Haberman, M. (1991) The pedagogy of poverty versus good teaching, *Phi Delta Kappan, 73*(4), 290–294.

Hayes, D. (2003). Making learning an effect of schooling: Aligning curriculum, assessment and pedagogy. *Discourse: Studies in the Cultural Politics of Education, 24*(2), 225–245.

Hayes, D., Mills, M., Christie, P., & Lingard, B. (2006). *Teachers and schooling making a difference.* Crows Nest, Australia: Allen and Unwin.

McFadden, M., & Munns, G. (2002). Student engagement and the social relations of pedagogy. *British Journal of Sociology of Education, 23*(3), 357–366.

Mills, C., & Gale, T. (2002). Schooling and the production of social inequalities: What can and should we be doing? *Melbourne Studies in Education, 43*(1), 107–125.

Morrison, V. (1985). A Sense of Wonder. On *A Sense of Wonder* [CD]. Kensington London: Polydor.

Munns, G. (2007). A sense of wonder: Student engagement in low SES school communities. *International Journal of Inclusive Education, 11*, 301–315.

Newmann, F., & Associates. (1996). *Authentic achievement: Restructuring schools for intellectual quality.* San Francisco, CA: Jossey-Bass.

CHAPTER 9

RECONSIDERING THE RHETORIC OF ENGAGEMENT

I and Thou in the Classroom

Deborah L. Seltzer-Kelly

ABSTRACT

All too often, neoliberal educational rhetoric demands that students engage
curricula that are remote from their own experiences and immediate needs
to support national priorities focused upon global economic competition. Essential knowledge and skills are defined by standards, dispensed by teachers,
and assessed by standardized tests in a model Paolo Freire characterized as
"banking" education. Nearly a century ago, John Dewey opposed this model of
education, arguing that if any genuinely educative process is to take place, curricula must meaningfully engage the knowledge and proficiencies of students
and their communities. Dewey's perspective, then, casts the teacher as the mediator between the student and the curriculum, engaged with the student in
"conjoint" inquiry. As I will argue here, implicit in this construction is a notion of reciprocity that requires that the teacher–student relationship be one
of "empathic engagement," or what Martin Buber termed the I/Thou relationship. Incorporation of the works of Gregory Bateson and Mary Catherine
Bateson deepens our understanding of the complexity of this teaching and

Student Engagement in Urban Schools, pages 151–169
Copyright © 2012 by Information Age Publishing
151

learning process, and moves us to consider deficiency in terms of the interaction, rather than assigning pathology to the student. Critically, discomfort with discussions of the spiritual aspects of teaching, as well as fear that this might equate to the imposition of religion in the realm of public education, may hinder robust considerations of teacher-student interactions. It is vital, however, that teacher educators take up these complex and difficult issues if we are to prepare teachers for work in the challenging arena of public education.

As I write, I am in my fifth year of teaching a course that involves mentoring preservice teaching interns (aka: student teachers) through an action research study in their internship classrooms. I have now taught versions of this course at two universities in two widely separated and vastly different geographic regions, spanning urban, suburban, and rural school districts. The interns themselves have also been marvelously varied: they have come from elementary and secondary licensure programs, and have completed majors in content areas including core subjects, fine arts, and physical education. They range in age from 21-year-old undergraduate education majors to mature professionals who have returned to seek a graduate teaching degree as part of a midlife career change.

I find, though, that the processes and the results that I see in this course are remarkably consistent. As they begin data collection, my students increasingly engage *their* students' knowledge and learning processes—or fail to. They encounter the real-life results of their teaching practice and have to figure out how they can use this information to teach the learners who struggle. For many, the action research cycle helps them to conceive of teaching as a new and intriguing form of puzzle-solving; they will delightedly share the surprising things their students say in class, while at the same time they wonder over the things that are obvious to them, but that their students seem unable to grasp. From some interns, though, I instead hear an unending litany of the failures and deficiencies of their students: the neglect of homework and reading assignments; the indifference to low grades; the seeming inability to come to class prepared, to pay attention, to engage "meaningfully," "substantively," or "deeply." Often, these complaints culminate in a diagnosis that is applied to individual children and/or to communities as a whole: "lack of work ethic."

It's hardly surprising, really, that many preservice and in-service teachers would argue that it is not the fault of the teacher that the student is not learning. After all, teachers in general education classrooms are confronted every day with students who struggle with basic literacy, let alone the prerequisite knowledge assumed in core content areas at each grade level. It hasn't been terribly long since I also taught in a public school classroom, since I had to find ways to work past the despair I experienced when I truly realized the depth and breadth of these challenges (Seltzer-Kelly, 2009). From the psychological perspective, blaming the students for their learning difficulties can represent one "out" for a beleaguered educator, since "students' educational deficits [may] pose a threat to teachers' sense of themselves as competent educators. If they can externalize the deficits and make it the students' fault, then it's not a reflection on their teaching abilities" (S. Gurland, personal communication, September 14, 2009).

Still, however much I can understand the source of this either/or thinking, where the only choices are to take on the blame or to pathologize the student, I also see it as a vital diagnostic indicator. It signals, in my view, a cluster of attitudes and/or a lack of maturity, knowledge, and skills that will effectively inhibit genuine teaching and learning in all settings, but that is particularly devastating in urban and at-risk environments. If I am to be a part of the wider community working for change, I must be able to deploy a systems-based understanding of the problems, combined with robust methods for individual and classroom-based approaches—and I must find ways to help the teachers I work with to do this also. This is particularly urgent because many of the preservice teacher educators I work with will go on to teach in East Saint Louis and Chicago, as well as in notoriously poverty-stricken rural areas such as Cairo, Illinois. They will be hired by schools designated "at-risk," where individuals who are members of racial and ethnic minorities are disproportionately represented.

Preparing preserving teachers for effective teaching in these challenging environments is a complex issue, and I increasingly believe that it must be done with a commitment to fostering engagement by the teachers, rather than pathologizing students and their communities for lack of engagement. I approach this through a mix of critical, pragmatist, and postmodern perspectives, considering the implications of recent philosophical and empirical work in curriculum studies and teacher education. I draw particularly upon the scholarship of William E. Doll, Jr. (1993, 1999, 2002) in doing so. It was he who first directed my attention to the work of John Dewey and its implications for teaching method some years ago, and more recently I am indebted to him for the connection to complexity theory and the work of Gregory Bateson. I emphasize that what follows is not an empirical research report. Rather, working qualitatively and integrating autoethnography with philosophical and empirical educational thought, what I undertake is to formulate a descriptive analysis for future consideration and empirical evaluation.

POWER, AUTHORITY, EFFICIENCY, AND THE CURRICULUM

As Mary Catherine Bateson (2005) has observed on the cultural level, the usual direction of teaching authority has been transformed across many spheres: Parents have come to rely upon their children's expertise with electronic devices, relations between employers and employees have become collaborative rather than directive in many workplaces, and educators at all levels are—at least nominally—expected to listen to and respect the knowledge of diverse students and communities. At the same time, though, as Bateson (2005) notes, there has been a backlash—the move to reassert traditional notions of authority and control that is reflected in the implementation of high-stakes testing to privilege the "time-tested certainties" (p. 10) that are enshrined in standardized curricula. It may also be seen as just one aspect of the larger postmodern competition among claims offered by differing cultures and knowledge structures that Toulmin (1972) sees as an attempt to clearly establish "what concepts have a genuine intellectual authority over us, or any serious right to our attention" (p. 50).

Doll (2002) has argued that contemporary constructions of curriculum in the public system of education to a remarkable degree still bear the imprint of the Enlightenment ordering of knowledge proposed by Peter Ramus. In Doll's view, U.S. curriculum scholars such as Franklin Bobbitt and Ralph Tyler were preoccupied by efforts to discover the most efficient methods by which the ideal curriculum could be transmitted to learners in a classroom, revealing the influence of Frederick Taylor's industrial efficiency model. It also reflects the conception that the knowledge to be transmitted consists of inert matter to be conveyed identically to every learner, rather than being the product of active and idiosyncratic engagement by the learner. This is the model that Paolo Freire (1970/2001) characterized as "banking" education and critiqued for its inhibition of genuine learning as well as its domesticating effects upon individuals who might otherwise become critical.

The basic idea that to really learn—to "engage" the curriculum—students need to be able to make connections between it and their own lives and experiences is hardly controversial. The National Association of Secondary School Principals (NASSP, 1996, 2004, 2006), for example, has issued a series of *Breaking Ranks* reports that emphasize this point, and these were supported by other mainstream organizations including the Carnegie Institute and the College Board. However, the degree to which the curriculum itself is malleable, as well as how much control over this is exercised by the teacher, is still the subject of considerably more debate.

In *The Child and the Curriculum*, John Dewey (1902/1976) proposed that the teacher must be understood as a classroom mediator between the learner and the material that was to be learned. He described the process of planning for instruction as akin to the creation of a map "as a guide to future experience; it gives direction; it facilitates control; it economizes effort, preventing useless wandering, and pointing out the paths which lead most quickly and most certainly to a desired result" (p. 284). This process-based and adaptive approach to learning is well-aligned to understandings of evolutionary epistemology as the underlying model for advances in scientific knowledge (Seltzer-Kelly, 2008). It also clearly renders the curriculum "teacher-dependent not teacher-proof" since "the teacher's planning and pedagogy...must be done in a reflective, interactive way" (Doll, 1993, p. 15). Clearly, then, in this model teachers require a deep understanding of the content to be able to envision multiple approaches to it. Further, they must possess the personal flexibility and the interest in the direction their students' learning is taking needed to manage this process.

Like Doll, Aoki (1992/2005) was concerned with the industrialized and efficiency-based mode of approach that has permeated educational thought, "wherein teachers are mere facilitators to teaching built into programmed learning packages.... a technological understanding of teaching whose logical outcome is the robotization of teaching: schools in the image of Japanese automobile factories—heaven forbid!" (p. 189). Critically, Aoki tells us, "the essence of teaching still eludes our grasp" (p. 190). He suggests that we must begin by exploring a notion of pedagogy where teaching is understood as "a tactful leading that knows and follows the pedagogic good in a caring situation" (p. 191).

Elsewhere, Aoki (1987/2005) explicitly connected conceptions of curriculum as inert knowledge with the construction of the student as inert—less than human. He wrote that when we fail to understand these issues, when we get "caught up unconsciously in a technological ethos that...tend[s] toward a machine view of children as well as a machine view of the teacher... [we are] understanding people, teachers, and children not as *beings* who are *human* but rather as *thing beings* [emphasis in original]" (p. 358). It is this pattern, in his view, that has transformed North American educational settings into sites of diminishment and alienation.

It is also useful to examine this dynamic from the philosophical perspective, in which an encounter with the Levinasian Other poses a threat to the fabric of our own identity. As Todd (2009) explains, the tendency is to either attempt to absorb the other party into our frame of reference, or, if they resist that treatment, to Otherize them: to demonize and make of them another whose being is unacceptable. According to Todd, this interaction with another who is genuinely an Other is a problem that our society has really not yet come to terms with, and for which we lack even a vocabulary; we tend, rather, to assume that the difference will become dissolved by understanding. Doll (1999), similarly, considers the violence inherent in these encounters as "a dark underside" to the purity and reason that is claimed for the modernist approach to knowledge and that is embodied in the current proliferation of neoliberal notions of education and teaching. The alternative, the antidote to alienation, that I will explore here is that teaching must instead be understood "not only as a mode of doing but also as a mode of being-with-others" (Aoki, 1987/2005, p. 359).

THE MESSY CATEGORY OF TEACHER "DISPOSITIONS"

Frustratingly, as I see every year among my action research students, the same preservice educators who struggle to connect with the Levinasian Other in the person of the students are often also the ones who are the most truly passionate about their content areas. Frequently, they are the highest achievers in their coursework, in and out of our department. They have gone into teaching to share their deep and abiding love of literature, their joy in the wonders of biological systems, their endless fascination with the formation and historical development of the United States, or the pleasures of mathematical complexity. Often, in other words, they appear initially to be exactly the kinds of educated and dedicated individuals whom we would most want to see in the teaching profession; they are the best "performers" in the department, committed and conscientious in everything they do.

Unfortunately, some of these bright and successful individuals make the very worst teachers; they turn out to be quite inflexible in thinking about and dealing with their students' educational struggles: the low reading and math skills, the lack of interest in and engagement with the curriculum, the inappropriate behaviors. Most devastatingly, from a critical pedagogical perspective, they are completely unable to see the knowledge their students *do* possess—to recognize the insights and achievements in any student work that does not fit neatly into their vision of what students are *supposed* to have learned from the particular lesson.

Given that "joylessness" and "lack of imagination" are not descriptors on any of my rubrics, it can be remarkably difficult to assess these interns in ways that will reveal how very poor their classroom engagement is. These qualities are traditionally considered to be "attitudes," and have generally been rather messily subsumed by the category of "dispositions," which does not ordinarily play any part in grading. At the same time as we hesitate to use these characteristics for any purpose other than counseling, widespread attention to them has gained the attention of the largest accreditation body in the United States, the National Council for Accreditation of Teacher Education, or NCATE (2006), as they note: "institutions often identify dispositions that encourage pre-service educators to be caring teachers" (p. 4). However, the degree of difficulty programs in teacher education confront in assessing for dispositions is also clear: "NCATE expects institutions to assess teacher candidate dispositions based on observable behavior in the classroom. NCATE does not recommend that attitudes be evaluated" (NCATE, 2006, p. 10). The problem is not only of how we will define the personal characteristics that adequately equip preservice teachers for the classroom, but how we will assess their presence or absence in the classroom.

In an editorial introduction to an entire issue of *The Journal of Teacher Education* dedicated to a discussion of dispositions, Borko, Liston, and

Whitcomb (2007) conclude that we are in the realm of trying to discuss, not just the "quibbles over apples and oranges," but "rather over apples and fishes" (p. 360), given that one side is arguing for values, the other is making claims based upon empirical systems of measurement, and neither side is really addressing arguments made by the other. Advocates of assessment of dispositions define them as "an individual's tendencies to act in a particular manner" (p. 361) and argue that it is vital to consider these since particular skills—especially those that are on display and assessed for during internship—may or may not persist after the intensive observations of the internship. Opponents of dispositions assessment argue that there is no clear definition of dispositions, let alone criteria for their assessment.

THE ETHIC OF CARE AND THE PROBLEM OF OBJECTIFICATION

The notion that good teaching goes far beyond content knowledge and a "toolbox" of pedagogical strategies is hardly new; the discussions over dispositions are just the latest in a long series of attempts to capture the qualities that excellence in teaching demands. One aspect of this, the idea that caring teachers can play a vital role in student learning, is increasingly well-established empirically. In a series of four studies she has conducted related to "expectancy effect," Gurland (Gurland, 2004; Gurland & Evangelista, 2009; Gurland & Grolnick, 2003, 2008) has demonstrated that students' performance and achievement are influenced by how much (or how little) they believe their teachers like them.

Working from the philosophical realm, Nel Noddings (1995) has famously been at the forefront of advocating for an "ethic of care" as a matter of social welfare, as well as for the sake of classroom learning: "We should want more from our educational efforts than adequate academic achievement, but we will not achieve even that unless our children believe they themselves are cared for and learn to care for others" (p. 116). Provocatively, though, from my perspective, Noddings concludes this discussion by saying, "caring is not just a warm, fuzzy feeling that makes people kind and likable. Caring implies a continuous search for competence. We want to do our very best for the *objects* [emphasis added] of our care" (p. 116). This casting of the student as the object of the teacher's care, rather than as a partner (if one of junior status) in a reciprocal relationship seems deeply troubling from a variety of perspectives.

Feminist philosophers have found Noddings's construction of unidirectional "one-caring" deeply troubling. Houston (1990) believes that even as "Noddings insistently reminds us that attention is a moral act" (p. 115), her relegation of ethical scrutiny to a subsidiary role can give rise to a danger of exploitation. This, among other problems, can reify the historic role of the woman as infinitely self-sacrificing nurturer, perpetuating a system in which women may be subjected to abuse, while still obligated to believe the best of the abuser. Hoagland (1990), similarly, points out that the one-care model is the very social pattern that accustoms the young male to unidirectional caring, rather than to reciprocal relations. She is further troubled by the lack of ethical critique assumed by Noddings's model, and the absence of acknowledgement of "a self that is both related and separate" as well as "a vision of, if not a program for, change" (p.111).

While caring behavior in Noddings's sense does clearly constitute nurturing for the person of the student, my point here is that it is a mistaken mode of approach for the purpose of nurturing learners across the range of purposes envisioned for education, including acquisition of knowledge and preparation for the democratic interaction and reciprocity envisioned in what Dewey (1916/1980) termed "social relations." In addition, as signaled by the articulation of the student as the *object* of the teacher's care, Noddings's one-care model fails to incorporate any particular level of engagement by the teacher with the thoughts and ideas of the student. Noddings's conception, in effect, reifies the objectification of the student; it merely puts a new—and surface—gloss of caring upon the longstanding and deeply flawed perspective that constructs the teacher as the dispenser and the child as the recipient for the range of transactions that occur in the classroom.

TEACHING "AS A MODE OF BEING-WITH-OTHERS"

I vividly remember the day during my own internship when I truly understood how much more my students knew than I had realized, when I first "got" how compelling a guide for my pedagogy my students' insights might be—as opposed to my own. I had spent a day in the computer lab with the 34 high school sophomores in my second period history class, as my students explored a web page called "'The White Man's Burden' and Its Critics." (This resource, created by American Studies scholar Jim Zwick on his BoondocksNet site, sadly no longer exists.) The website included Kipling's poem and the astonishing outburst of reaction to it in the U.S., including editorials, poems satirizing Kipling's work, and cartoons by critics of American imperialism. While some of my students were fascinated, many more had difficulty understanding the messages it contained, or especially the larger dialog.

The next day, as we discussed what they had learned about U.S. imperial ambitions in the early 20th century, one student said something like, "Well, that's just like how the Native Americans were treated." The discussion took off from there to examine paternalistic assumptions and the ways that these had informed all kinds of international and internal relations. The same students who had been unable to grapple with the meanings of the cartoons and editorials they had seen on the day before could suddenly understand them and make broader connections. Through no effort or insight of my own, I had been landed right in the middle of a "teachable moment," an opportunity for deep and authentic educational exchange.

In the moment, I felt the fervent wish that I had the freedom to seize this opportunity and move on to consider the history of U.S. engagement with the American Indian nations next. Unfortunately, it was a world history course, and we had examined U.S. imperialism more or less in passing as a part of the larger phenomenon among Western nations. We were scheduled to move on to World War I next, and then to return to imperialism some time later when we considered the decolonization process—and its legacy—in Africa and Asia. Thus, I had to content myself with affirming the depth of my students' insights, and hoping that they could continue to apply these ideas to the theme of European colonization.

As I have looked back at this experience through the intervening years, the other significant feature of this experience was the fact that my lead teacher had labeled this young man as "just an ordinary kid—not very motivated." My own experiences with him prior to this had tended to confirm that impression; he had stood out neither as a good student nor as a terribly difficult one, although he was quite social and popular. My further conversations with him over the following weeks revealed that my initial thought—that he himself was of American Indian ancestry—was incorrect. His family was Eastern European in origin, and he had no personal friends whose experiences had informed this idea; it had just come to him. To the degree that he was able to make connections between the experiences of the Philippine population and his own experiences, I suppose it was because, as a teenager, he resented his own lack of intellectual and personal autonomy and thus was able to empathize with the plight of the colonized.

In the years that followed, as I taught among populations of other "very ordinary" kids, this pattern repeated itself: many students who were labeled as top achievers performed reliably, but didn't necessarily think creatively or suggest novel connections. It was often the students who were not generally considered to be successful who surprised me with the depth and originality of their insights, and who were able to synthesize broadly. These tended to be students who appeared to be disengaged from the classroom much of the time, indifferent to educational achievement, but who would check in briefly, deliver devastatingly insightful comments, then retreat again.

Part of the challenge for me in luring these students into active engagement with me and with the curriculum was that they perceived much of high school content as completely irrelevant to themselves and their lives.

I knew this because they told me so, clearly and repeatedly. And they were right. Despite the aforementioned consensus as to the importance of helping students to make connections between their own lives and experiences and educational materials that may be strange and distant, the curricular materials available to teachers in their classrooms do not facilitate this, nor does typical preservice teacher preparation.

The very nature of the textbooks commonly in use points to the static and enshrined nature of knowledge as it is commonly conceived. As a beginning teacher, for example, I was struck by the paradox embodied by the list of "correct" responses to the so-called "Critical Thinking" questions in the teachers' editions of my textbooks. And as a friend pointed out to me, the ribbons sewn into those teachers' editions invoke visions of massive Bibles mounted on church pulpits for public proclamation of divinely given knowledge. All of this seems designed to prohibit change or innovation in teaching these materials, and to encourage teachers to engage with the official curricula, rather than with their students. And how, if we are to discard this rigid formulation and challenge this air of sanctitude attached to traditional curricula, do we prepare our preservice teachers to facilitate critical thinking, and to become critical thinkers themselves?

This question is, as noted earlier, only partially addressed by discussions of "dispositions." Schertz (2007) has argued that in order for children to learn to engage one another in cooperative terms rather than competitive, an atmosphere of reciprocity must be maintained in the classroom to support the development of empathy and intersubjectivity. As Schertz (2007) sees, this is stymied by "the structures and practices of traditional schools, which are as a rule ridden with hierarchical, authoritarian power relationships from the classroom to the principals' office . . . and characterized by chronic 'class struggle' between teachers and students" (p. 176). A part of this class struggle, as I argue, is the imbalance created by unidirectional relationships—including those that involve caring as well as those embedded in traditional constructions of curriculum—that inevitably construct the teacher as superior and the student as the inferior recipient. The alternative to this is that we "adopt values related to change and adaptability, listening and responsiveness" (M.C. Bateson, 2005, p. 12).

Gere, Hoshmand, and Reinkraut (2002) have characterized the essential quality of engagement for teachers in terms of empathy, "the capacity for full engagement with the personal reality of others," and aesthetic regard, "a deep appreciation for the uniqueness and value of each individual" (p. 155). These are the prerequisites for the intersubjectivity combined with deep reflexivity required for what the authors term "empathic engagement" (p. 159). In order for effective educational processes to occur, this quality must be accompanied by discernment: the professional judgment that allows the teacher to assess the students' knowledge and comprehension and provide appropriate learning opportunities. The key, in their view, is "to ensure that discernment is compatible with practicing empathic connection and aesthetic regard in teaching—to preserve the sacred nature of transformative encounters" (Gere et al., 2002, p. 175). They invoke the thought of Martin Buber to theorize sacred space in the classroom.

Buber (1923/1937) himself vividly described what happens when another is experienced as the inhuman *It*, rather than the personal and intimate *Thou*; it "has no part in the experience. It permits itself to be experienced, but it has no concern in the matter. For it does nothing to the experience, and experience does nothing to it" (p. 5). For too many teachers, in my view, the teaching experience tends to reside entirely within their own experience; it seems to escape their notice that there is another genuine being on the other end of the transaction. In freezing their sense of a student in terms of their assessment of the student's achievement in the class, or on the basis of a set of interactions, this teacher has, in Buber's sense, reduced the student to "a specific point in space and time . . . a loose bundle of named qualities" (Buber, 1923/1937, p. 8). In this way, "he [sic] ceases to be *Thou* and instead is reduced to an *It*" (p. 9).

Buber (1923/1937) supposed that "through each process of becoming that is present to us, we look out toward the fringe of the eternal Thou" (p. 101), arguing that our interactions reach toward a greater reality than can be encompassed purely in terms of the teacher and student. This would seem to land us in problematically religious territory. However, as Rexroth (1959) noted, religious writings can have symbolic value for social systems, which is why Buber's *I and Thou* has had at least as much influence on, and application to, interpersonal psychology as upon religious thought. Buber's work is "a philosophy of joy, lived in a world full of others" (Rexroth, 1959, p. 10) where "the reciprocal response I and Thou is the only mode of realization of the fullest potential of each party. The one realizes itself by realizing the other" (p. 34).

As Rexroth and others have argued, ideas that have roots in religion and spirituality do not necessarily have to be pursued in that way; we can view them phenomenologically and existentially. Cunningham (2010) weaves together classical thought on the role of the *daimon*—variously conceived as one's internal higher self, and as an external sort of "guardian angel"—with Dewey's understanding of the role of dramatic rehearsal for the future to advocate for an understanding of a phenomenological view of "coauthoring of selves," where the realization of the unique potential of every individual is recognized and embraced as a vital role of the school. Clearly, as he sees, this requires a very different preparation for preservice teachers, including the need to ensure that they are prepared to experience and to model self-actualization as an ongoing life process.

APPROACHING TEACHER PREPARATION FOR
ENGAGEMENT THROUGH COMPLEXITY THEORY

Despite arguments to the contrary in the realm of dispositions, I believe that many or most of these qualities may be describable and measurable for teacher educators. To approach the observable and measurable, we must draw from the realm of psychology and integrate some constructions of reflexivity. In other words, it may be time to draw the discussion over dispositions back into less ephemeral discussions of teacher preparation.

My first glimpse into this very different approach, and especially into ways that this mode of teacher engagement with students might be clearly described and observed, came when, at Bill Doll's invitation, I attended a meeting of the Chaos & Complexity special interest group (SIG) at the 2009 American Educational Research Association (AERA) conference. Nora Bateson (2009) presented her uncut version of her documentary film "An Ecology of Mind," a biography of noted anthropologist and psychologist (and her father) Gregory Bateson, whose work has attracted remarkably little notice among educators. In one scene, the viewer sees Mary Catherine Bateson reflecting upon a videotaped family counseling session that she has watched repeatedly as part of her professional supervision of the counselor. The nominal patient is the child, who has behavioral problems. Bateson describes the ways that, over repeated viewings of the session, her perspective as to the actual source of the problem shifted several times. She began by seeing the child as the problem in and of himself. She then has moved toward considering the mother as the precipitating factor, then the father, and finally after many viewings of the interactions in the session, has begun to wonder whether the therapist is fomenting dysfunction. Finally, she comes to understand the situation in terms of Gregory Bateson's thought: to see dysfunction as a product of the interaction of systems, rather than as residing in any individual locus.

The ability to engage in repeated metacognitive iterations, and especially to rethink one's own earlier assumptions and to explore alternatively explanations and causations, suggests that there is a degree of emotional and/or cognitive maturity that is needed. Encouragingly, I have found that there are several existing rubrics for reflective thinking among preservice teachers that seem to render these qualities as observable characteristics—as opposed to trying to assess attitude or "dispositions." Some recent measures assess specifically for preservice teachers' ability to NOT simply affix blame, but to consider complex causation, and to incorporate the experience of the other as well as one's own experience.

El-Dib's (2007) Inventory of Reflective Thinking via Action Research (IRTAR) is a measure for depth and complexity of reflection in early writing assignments. He found that over half of his Egyptian preservice teachers had difficulty thinking deeply about the causes of their students' learning and behavioral difficulty and tended to focus upon simplistic formulations rather than examining the complex dynamics that interact in the classroom. Similarly, Fund, Court,and Kramarski's (2002) WRITT Evaluative Tool measures students' levels of progression from the simple level of descriptive writing to what they call "complex bridging," where students become able to make connections among their observations in the classroom, their own ideas and beliefs, and the assigned course readings. Ward and McCotter's (2004) instrument offers a robust assessment for preservice teachers' ability to move from self-focused accounts of classroom interactions, through a dialogic posture, and into a "transformative" mode that allows complex connections to be made among the concerns and priorities of educational institutions and students' and teachers' needs and interactions. Watts and Lawson (2009) expanded the use of this rubric by adding explicit meta-analytic activities to their instruction and assessment that incorporated a focus upon teaching as immersion in a community of practice.

The issue of reflexivity also returns us to a consideration of the process of self-actualization, as conceived by Cunningham (2010). As he suggests, if the teacher is to facilitate self-actualization, this supposes that she or he personally has some experience with the process. In what are popularly supposed to be the words of Malcolm X (although I have been unable to locate the reference), "We can't teach what we don't know, and we can't lead where we won't go" (as cited in Howard, 1999, p. 4). This also re-enlivens the question of religion and faith; after all, for many individuals, their own mode of being-with-others in the classroom and in the larger world is grounded in an explicitly spiritual/religious outlook. This suggests that somewhere in the teacher preparation process we must attend to supporting our preservice teachings in understanding their own sense of teaching as a mode of personal connections with others, including any explicitly religious elements.

Doll (1993) believes that

> teacher attitudes…reflecting fundamental world-view [are] critical. Often these assumptions are not evident, for they lie deep within our cosmological being and are known to us only in a tacit and murky manner. Bringing these private visions, these 'ises' of our being-in-the-world, into the light of public scrutiny is an important part of both self-discovery and the development of communal "oughts." (p. 159)

While Sleeter (2005), among others, has advocated for the importance of teachers becoming aware of their own constructions of knowledge, and Howard (1999) incorporates some mention of the role of religion in both dominance and in healing from the legacy of hate and discrimination, explicit exploration of one's own religious and spiritual identity and the roles that these have played in the development of one's identity as a teacher is quite rare. Parker Palmer (1980), for example, considers teaching explicitly in spiritual terms, as a matter of vocation. However, reading and discussion of his and similar works has, in my experience, been largely confined to religious institutions and small special interest groups (SIGs) at conferences, rather than forming a part of preparation for a career in public education.

In *A Common Faith*, Dewey (1934/1986) suggests that we can think about ideals that have effect upon the transpersonal level without having to become grounded in any specific construction of religion. While he began as an outspoken critic of religion, later in life Dewey returned to the topic to try to separate the problems that he saw associated with specific, organized religions from the possibilities that a religious outlook can offer. As he observed, "Any activity pursued in behalf of an ideal and against obstacles and in spite of the threats of personal loss because of conviction of its general and enduring value is religious in quality" (Dewey, 1934/1986, p. 27). It is, in this view, when we make the attempt to dissociate these ideals from their grounding in any particular religion and to attach them to a common endeavor, that genuine progress in the human condition can be achieved.

Conversely, I would argue that when we prohibit individuals (either explicitly or implicitly) from engaging in conversations that bring these shared ideals together for examination and consideration, we very effectively prevent advancement. The challenge is to find a way to have conversations that admit multiple modes of understanding and engagement without privileging any particular model. This seems especially problematic in an era in which there have been repeated and highly polarizing political controversies over such topics as displays of the Ten Commandments in courthouses, moments of silence as a form of disguised prayer in public schools, and the removal of the words "under God" from the Pledge of Allegiance. As an opponent of the first two and an advocate of the last, I find it rather ironic that I am now advocating for far more openness on the subject of religion in public education. My advocacy is aligned most strongly with Dewey's proposition: that we must allow space for exploration of principles that for many arise from religion. I would argue that this is vital both so that preservice and in-service teachers can gain their own clarity and self-actualization in order to mentor these processes in their students, and also so that those that have instrumental value for public life can become a part of the shared public endeavor.

COMPLEX SYSTEMS AND RESISTANCE TO CHANGE

Like Doll, I have, somewhat paradoxically, come to my interest in complexity and relationship with the Other in the classroom context through my commitment to an evolutionary understanding of scientific method, especially as it applies to education (Seltzer-Kelly, 2008). This is a postmodern move, as Doll (1999) explains, and derives from following the thought of Stephen Toulmin and rejecting the scientistic metanarrative that has infused modernist constructions of science, with its algorithmic formulations of knowledge and discovery, and its claims for science as rational and objective, standing apart from (and over) culture. This is replaced by a Deweyan perspective "of science as practical doing, always problematic, always accepting the contingency of its own specific procedures—dealing at best not with truth and certainty but with 'warranted assertability'" (Doll, 1999, p. 85). This Deweyan perspective, steeped in particularity and multiplicity, naturally encompasses the postcolonial and postmodern concerns with decentering whiteness in the curriculum and creating space for counternarratives.

This move also draws us into a postmodern sense of self and other, where we reject the metanarrative construction and the tendency to colonize the Other, in favor of accepting and coming into relationship with incommensurability. This, as Doll (1999) sees clearly, is a deeply radical move. Drawing from Bernstein, he says:

> Wow! Oh Wow! Developing an on-going "self-conscious sensitivity of the need always to do justice to 'the Other's' *singularity*!" What does this do to our concepts of ethics and education? Both ethics and education, imbued strongly with modernist Reason, have assumed the rightness of "us," with the Other being either a barbarian or misguided. When the Other is not be persuaded by reason as to the rightness of "our" position, we use force to solidify not just our position but its rightness. Now, in our post, and global, age, we are asking for a new consciousness, one that deals with responsibility not in terms we usually know—responsibility *of, for, to* (terms tacitly expressing our rightness)—but in terms of *as*. Responsibility *as*, as a part of our being human (and Latour would add of our being nonhuman, too), requires us to honor the singularity of all. (p. 89)

Preparing our preservice teachers as they make this move—away from viewing their students as barbarians or misguided, and toward honoring the singularity of all—is, of course, a complex task. It challenges a great many old and familiar ways of doing things, and for many who are steeped in traditional views of education and educators, it challenges/threatens notions of self and of authority. Thus, it also meets with substantial resistance from across a range of perspectives.

THE (DIS)COMFORT OF (UN)CERTAINTY

The construction of curriculum and teaching methods as objective, authoritative and universal—accompanied by the marginializing and pathologizing of the students and communities who do not achieve well in this environment—is a part of the current neoliberal environment that encourages and reinforces this kind of labeling. As Michael Apple (2001) has argued, the complex hegemony that supports neoliberalism incorporates groups that range from those with financial interests in the current system—the corporations that create and distribute standards-based texts and testing programs—to social and religious conservatives. Significantly, across all of these groups, there is benefit to pathologizing the students and communities who fail to achieve on these standardized measures. The alternative would require that there be a comprehensive re-examination of the complex of social, economic, and educational changes that would be needed to truly enable all children to achieve their fullest potential in education and in life.

As Bateson (1972/2000) saw, false epistemologies can be remarkably resistant to change, even in the face of their clear unworkabiilty: "There is an ecology of bad ideas, just as there is an ecology of weeds, and it is characteristic of the system that basic error propagates itself" (p. 492). Earlier, he had explored reasons for this:

> [P]eople are self-corrective ... against disturbance, and if the obvious is not of a kind that they can easily assimilate without internal disturbance, their self-corrective mechanisms work to sidetrack it, to hide it, even to the extent of shutting the eyes if necessary, or shutting off various parts of the process of perception. Disturbing information can be framed like a pearl so that it doesn't make a nuisance of itself. (Bateson, 1968/2000, p. 435)

This resistance to change plays out, through "theories of control and to theories of power. In that universe, if you do not get what you want, you will blame somebody and establish either a jail or a mental hospital, according to taste, and you will pop them in it if you can identify them" (Bateson, 1972/2000, p. 494).

What is gained from all of these efforts to pathologize learners for failing to learn, then, is the comfort of certainty. The alternative—the solution, from the perspectives that I present here, is to "adopt values related to change and adaptability, listening and responsiveness" (M.C. Batreson, 2005, p. 12). It is also vital that in the field of teacher preparation we engage this concretely and with explicit consideration for classroom practice, given the disillusionment that the theory-praxis gap embodied in critical pedagogical approaches brought to many educators (Wardekker & Miedema, 1997).

Further, we must robustly engage institutional and governmental dialogs over how the concepts of science and rigor are applied to the area of accountability, rather than merely critiquing and then evading these practices. Qualitative researchers have experienced loss of legitimacy and governmental funding through the current ideological backlash, a part of a pattern of "cultural, political, and economic discourses that constrain how we can think and act—who and what is excluded in constructing the rational, the progressive, and the good—and who and what are excluded from possibility of thought and action, policy, and conclusions" (Bloch, 2004, p. 107). If we are to present an alternative to the narrowly focused definition of science and legitimate research—what Lather (2004) has termed "bad science for bad politics...a partisan tool" (p. 17) in the hands of those wishing to strengthen and preserve authoritarian systems of knowledge—we must be prepared to offer possibilities grounded in a complex and dynamic view of science, rather than simplistic scientism.

REFERENCES

Aoki, T.T. (2005). Inspiriting the curriculum [1987]. In W.F. Pinar & R.L. Irwin (Eds.) *Curriculum in a new key: The collected works of Ted T. Aoki* (pp. 357–365). Mahwah, NJ: Lawrence Erlbaum Associates.

Aoki, T.T. (2005). Layered voices of teaching: The uncannily correct and the elusively true [1992]. In W.F. Pinar & R.L. Irwin (Eds.) *Curriculum in a new key: The collected works of Ted T. Aoki* (pp. 187–197). Mahwah, NJ: Lawrence Erlbaum Associates.

Apple, M. (2001). *Educating the "right" way: Markets, standards, God and inequality.* New York, NY: RoutledgeFalmer.

Bateson, G. (2000). Conscious purpose versus nature. In *Steps to an ecology of mind.* Chicago: The University of Chicago Press. (Original work published 1968).

Bateson, G. (2000). Pathologies of epistemology. In *Steps to an ecology of mind.* Chicago: The University of Chicago Press. (Original work published 1972).

Bateson, M.C. (2005, August 28). Learning to teach, teaching to learn. *The Philadelphia Inquirer.* Retrieved from http://mcatherinebateson.blogspot.com/2005/09/learning-to-teach-teaching-to-learn.html

Bateson, N. (Producer & Director). (2009). *An ecology of mind.* [Film – Unedited version]. Bellingham, WA: Author.

Bloch, M. (2004). A discourse that disciplines, governs and regulates: The National Research Council's report on scientific research in education. *Qualititative Inquiry, 10*(1), 96–110.

Borko, H., Liston, D., & Whitcomb, J.A. (2007). Apples and fishes: The debate over dispositions in teacher education. *Journal of Teacher Education, 58*(5), 359–364.

Buber, M. (1937). I and Thou. (R.G. Smith, Trans.). New York, NY: Charles Scribner's Sons. (Original work published 1923).

Cunningham, C. (2010, April/May). *How would a focus on unique potential transform schools?* Paper presentation at the American Education Research Association (AERA) Annual Meeting and Conference, Denver, CO.

Dewey, J. (1976) The Child and the curriculum. In J.A. Boydston (Ed.), *John Dewey: The middle works, 1899–1924* (Vol. 2, pp. 272–291). Carbondale, IL: Southern Illinois University Press. (Original work published 1902)

Dewey, J. (1980). Democracy and education. In J.A. Boydston (Ed.) *John Dewey: The middle works, 1899–1924* (Vol. 9, pp. 1–370). Carbondale: Southern Illinois University Press. (Original work published 1916).

Dewey, J. (1986). A common faith. In J.A. Boydston (Ed.), *John Dewey: The later works, 1925–1953* (Vol. 9, pp. 1–58). Carbondale: Southern Illinois University Press. (Original work published 1934).

Doll, W. E., Jr. (1993). *A post-modern perspective on curriculum.* New York, NY: Teachers College Press.

Doll, W.E., Jr. (1999). Conversing with the other. *Journal of Curriculum Theorizing, 15*(3), 83–90.

Doll, W.E., Jr. (2002). Beyond methods? Teaching as an aesthetic and spirit-ful quest. In E. Mirochnik & D.C. Sherman (Eds.), *Passion and pedagogy: Relation, creation, and transformation in teaching* (pp. 127–151). New York, NY: Peter Lang.

El-Dib, M.A.B. (2007). Levels of reflection in action research: An overview and an assessment tool. *Teaching and Teacher Education, 23*(1), 24–35.

Freire, P. (2001). *Pedagogy of the oppressed* (30th Anniversary Ed.). New York, NY: Continuum. (Original work published 1970)

Fund, Z., Court. D., & Kramarski, B. (2002). Construction and application of an evaluative tool to assess reflection in teacher-training courses. *Assessment & Evaluation in Higher Education, 27*(6), 485–499.

Gere, S.H., Hoshmand, L.T. & Reinkraut, R. (2002). Constructing the sacred: Empathic engagement, aesthetic regard, and discernment in clinical teaching. In E. Mirochnik & D.C. Sherman (Eds.), *Passion and pedagogy: Relation, creation, and transformation in teaching* (pp. 153–176). New York, NY: Peter Lang.

Gurland, S. T. (2004). *Adult styles of interaction and children's expectancies: Implications for clinical rapport.* Unpublished doctoral dissertation, Clark University, Worcester, MA.

Gurland, S. T., & Evangelista, J. (2009, April). *Teacher–student relationship quality over time: A social-cognitive perspective.* Paper presented at the biennial meeting of the Society for Research in Child Development, Denver, CO.

Gurland, S. T., & Grolnick, W. S. (2003). Children's expectancies and perceptions of adults: Effects on rapport. *Child Development, 74,* 1212–1224.

Gurland, S. T., & Grolnick, W. S. (2008). Building rapport with children: Effects of adults' expected, actual, and perceived behavior. *Journal of Social & Clinical Psychology, 27*(3), 226–253.

Hoagland, S. L. (1990). Some concerns about Nel Noddings' *Caring. Hypatia, 5*(1), 109–114.

Houston, B. (1990). Caring and exploitation. *Hypatia, 5*(1), 115–119.

Howard, G.R. (1999). *We can't teach what we don't know: White teachers, multiracial schools.* New York, NY: Teachers College Press.

Lather, P. (2004). Scientific research in education: A critical perspective. *Journal of Curriculum and Supervision, 20*(1), 14–30.

National Association of Secondary School Principals (NASSP). (1996). *Breaking ranks: Changing an American institution.* Reston, VA: Author.

National Association of Secondary School Principals (NASSP). (2004). *Breaking ranks II: Strategies for leading high school reform.* Reston, VA: Author.

National Association of Secondary School Principals (NASSP). (2006). *Breaking ranks in the middle: Strategies for leading middle level reform.* Reston, VA: Author.

National Council for Accreditation of Teacher Education (NCATE). (2006). *A statement from NCATE on professional dispositions.* Washington, DC: Author. Retrieved from http://www.ncate.org/public/0616_MessageAWise.asp?ch=150

Noddings, N. (1995). Teaching themes of caring. *Education Digest, 61*(3), 24–28.

Palmer, P. J. (1980). *To know as we are known: Education as a spiritual journey.* San Francisco, CA: HarperOne.

Rexroth, K. (1959). *The Hasidism of Martin Buber.* Bureau of Public Secrets: Kenneth Rexroth Archive. Retrieved from http://www.bopsecrets.org/rexroth/buber.htm

Schertz, M.V. (2007). Empathy as intersubjectivity: Resolving Hume and Smith's divide. *Studies in Philosophy and Education, 26,* 165–178.

Seltzer-Kelly, D. (2008). Deweyan Darwinism for the 21st century: Toward an educational method for critical democratic engagement in the era of the Institute of Education Sciences. *Educational Theory, 58*(3), 289–304.

Seltzer-Kelly, D. (2009). Adventures in critical pedagogy: A lesson in U.S. history. *Teacher Education Quarterly, 36*(1), 149–162.

Sleeter, C.E. (2005). *Un-standardizing curriculum: Multicultural teaching in the standards-based classroom.* New York, NY: Teachers College Press.

Todd, S. (2009, March). *Can there be pluralism without conflict? Ingesting the indigestible in democratic education.* Plenary address at the Philosophy of Education Society Annual Meeting and Conference, Montreal, Canada.

Toulmin, S. (1972). *Human understanding, Volume I: The collective use and evolution of concepts.* Princeton, NJ: Princeton University Press.

Ward, J.R., & McCotter, S.S. (2004). Reflection as a visible outcome for preservice teachers. *Teaching and Teacher Education, 20*(3), 243–257.

Wardekker, W. L., & Miedema, S. (1997). Critical pedagogy: An evaluation and a direction for reformulation. *Curriculum Inquiry, 27*(1), 45–61.

Watts, M., & Lawson, M. (2009). Using a meta-analysis activity to make critical reflection explicit in teacher education. *Teaching and Teacher Education, 25*(5), 609–616.

CHAPTER 10

TEACHING CONTROVERSIAL ISSUES

An Educational Imperative

Amanda Cooper and John P. Portelli

ABSTRACT

This chapter arises out of a qualitative study investigating how the views of student leaders (and some of their staff advisors) illuminate the discussion in the broader literature around issues of student leadership, conflict, diversity, and social justice in secondary schools. Dealing with controversial issues (CIs) permeated the dialogue about conflict, diversity and social justice in secondary schools and, accordingly, is at the core of equity issues within our increasingly pluralistic societal context. We argue that addressing CIs in schools is an educational imperative for meaningful student engagement and for the development of a critical democracy which, in turn, should be founded on a relentless pursuit of equity.

Controversy is the basis of change and, hopefully, improvement. Its lack signifies the presence of complacency, the authoritarian limitation of viewpoint expression, or the absence of realistic alternatives to the existing circumstances. An articulate

Student Engagement in Urban Schools, pages 171–195
Copyright © 2012 by Information Age Publishing
All rights of reproduction in any form reserved.

presentation of a point of view on a controversial matter breathes new life into abiding human and social concerns. Controversy prompts re-examination and, perhaps, renewal. Education is controversial.
—Noll, 1989, p. i

Conflict is the gadfly of thought. It stirs us to observation and memory. It instigates to invention. It shocks us out of sheep-like passivity, and sets us at noting and contriving . . . conflict is a "sine qua non" of reflection and ingenuity.
—Dewey, 1922, p. 300

This chapter arises out of a qualitative study investigating how the views of student leaders (and some of their staff advisors) illuminate the discussion in the broader literature around issues of student leadership, conflict, diversity, and social justice in secondary schools (Cooper, 2008). Dealing with controversial issues (CIs) permeated the dialogue about conflict, diversity, and social justice in secondary schools and, accordingly, is at the core of equity issues within our increasingly pluralistic societal context. We argue that addressing controversial issues in schools is an educational imperative for meaningful student engagement, especially given the growing neoliberal context that privileges facts over values, narrow rationality and limited accountability over emotions and moral responsibility, and one-size-fits-all and standardization rather than differences and alternate ways of fulfilling basic educational needs.

SETTING THE CONTEXT

Social diversity is ubiquitous in modern society. Schools are microcosms of our larger pluralistic society and, as such, they too are comprised of many different groups who hold many different values, beliefs, and perceptions about the world and the nature of education. Issues pertaining to social diversity—religion, gender, sexual orientation, ethnicity, race, socioeconomic status, and (dis) ability—are often labeled "controversial" (Adams, Bell, & Griffin, 2007; Hicks & Holden, 2007; McLauglin, 2003, 2005; Oulton, Day, Dillon, & Grace, 2004; Soley, 1996). Deeming a topic "controversial" often has negative connotations within traditional conceptions of education, where controversial issues are often associated with negative conflict. Because of this negative conceptualization, there is a tendency to avoid discussing topics in schools that are deemed controversial due to fear (on the part of teachers, administrators, or district leaders) of inciting conflict or offending different groups of stakeholders (Hess, 2004, 2005). Avoiding the discussion of controversial issues is problematic for a number of reasons (that will be outlined throughout the chapter), most of which have to do with the pursuit of democratic education and equity as well as engaging students in a curriculum that is relevant to their lived experiences (Goodson, 2008; Portelli & Vibert, 2001, 2002). Controversial issues are often connected to issues of power, dominance, and oppression between privileged and marginalized groups; hence, avoiding these discussions often results in the propagation of the status quo to the detriment of the many groups outside the dominant group.

We propose a different conception of controversial issues, highlighting that disagreement is not synonymous with negativity (and conflict); rather, we argue that addressing these issues creates opportunities for meaningful learning and pursuing equity and democratic transformation in schools. It is our contention that we cannot shy away from acknowledging and discussing controversial issues due to that fact that they are inevitable. Our argument is anchored in the unequivocal view that students have a constitutionally protected right to participation and citizenship within their own education (Canada, 1982; Deuchar, 2008; Ryan, 2006) and to be treated as individuals with the capacity to make a significant contribution through engaging critically with real-life issues. As educators it is our professional obligation to address these issues and engage in meaningful and substantive dialogue about these important issues with our students. In fact, democratic education requires it. Education at its core is about preparing students to become responsible citizens in an increasingly global society (Adams et al., 2007; Deuchar, 2008; Hess, 2004, 2005; Hicks & Holden, 2007; McLauglin, 2003; Oulton et al., 2004). In the end, every student will unavoidably interact with others different from themselves and have to deal with controversial issues. Divergent views can be brought together in the spirit of inquiry and a critical discourse in schools that have the potential to become an expression of critical democracy.

ORGANIZATION OF PAPER AND SUMMARY OF ARGUMENTS

The first section of this chapter briefly explores the various definitions and conceptions of controversial issues, specifically outlining the differences between mere disagreements, controversy, controversial issues, and offence. We argue, using perspectives from participants in conjunction with the broader literature, that addressing controversial issues in schools is necessary for student engagement. Namely that:

1. CIs are inevitable and mirror important societal issues. Sheltering students from these issues is not only irresponsible, but also insulting to students, as it implies deficit thinking surrounding their capability

to think critically about and to make a substantive contribution to important societal issues.

2. CIs are crucial for the development of a critical democracy which, in turn, should be founded on a relentless pursuit of equity:
    i. students have the constitutionally protected right to engage in these issues and take an active role in their own education
    ii. a major purpose of education is to prepare students for democratic citizenship which, in turn, requires an active role in trying to change society for the better. Ultimately, responsible citizenship, in the current societal context, requires advocating for equity among different groups. In order to effectively achieve this aim, students must be aware of these issues and also learn how to navigate disagreement in a productive and mutually beneficial manner.
3. Discussing CIs has many benefits for students:
    i. Developing critical thinking skills and dispositions, and increasing political involvement after graduation
    ii. Student engagement with a curriculum of life

Cumulatively, the reasons outlined provide a morally sound argument for dealing with controversial issues.

The final section of this chapter uses a concrete example from the study—a discussion of equity in relation to recognizing difference—to explore the benefits and potential learning associated with substantive dialogue around controversial issues. We conclude by outlining the implications of the issues discussed throughout the chapter for educators and schools.

One further note on the format of this chapter is that we have chosen against traditional methods of reporting research organized to depict a step-by-step linear process through which research occurs (methods, followed by data collection, followed by data analysis). Many social scientists would agree that this cleaned, anesthetized, logical write-up bears almost no resemblance to the way in which research *actually* occurs! The literature on reconstructed logic versus logic-in-use (originally proposed by Kaplan in 1964) highlights the nonlinear nature of the social world and human interaction: "Reconstructed logic refers to the rational explication of the methodology of a field, more or less as it would exist in the ideal. Logic in use is the way science is actually played out" (Sechrest & Sidani, 1995, p. 78). This decision is an attempt to convey our conception of educational research within real-life contexts as a complex, iterative process between ourselves, the participants, their individual contexts, and the literature from the field that perpetually informs and shapes the study and our interpretations of its findings.

AN OVERVIEW OF THE STUDY

This research was conducted at Canadian Student Leadership Conference (CSLC) held September, 2007, in London, Ontario. CSLC is an annual event held by the Canadian Association of Student Activity Advisors (CASAA), hosted by different provinces and territories, bringing together and training student leaders and teachers from all over Canada. In 2007, 663 teachers and students from all ten provinces attended (the territories were not represented; see Figure 10.1).

The theme (LEAD ON: Lead with Enthusiasm, Acceptance, Diversity and Optimism Now) focused specifically on training student leaders to deal with equity issues locally and internationally in the face of increasing diversity, in order to develop citizens who have the capacity to cope with the complex challenges arising from rapid globalization.

Data were collected from multiple sources including (1) 18 one-hour, semi-structured interviews conducted with 12 student leaders and six teachers (two of whom were administrators) from six provinces across Canada (Ontario, Alberta, British Columbia, Prince Edward Island, New Brunswick, and Newfoundland); (2) documents from CSLC and the CASAA website (www.casaaleadership.ca); and (3) participant observation throughout the duration of the conference (including videotaped key note speaker presentations, attending training sessions for teachers and student leaders, and informal interaction with participants). Data were triangulated and ana-

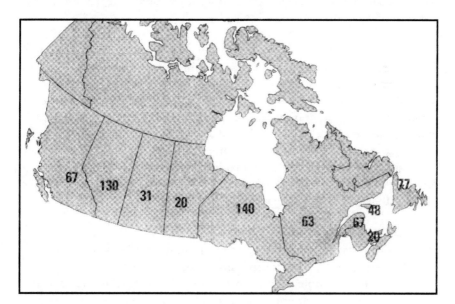

Figure 10.1   CSLC 2007 National representation by province.

lyzed to determine commonalities and differences among the values, ways of thinking, beliefs, and practices of teachers and students in relation to diversity and social justice within secondary schools across Canada.

DEFINING THE "CONTROVERSIAL"

A wide body of literature examines the nature of controversy and what constitutes a controversial issue (Hess, 2004, 2005; Holden, 2007; Malikow, 2006; McLauglin, 2003; Oulton et al., 2004; Soley, 1996; Stradling, 1985; Stradling, Noctor, & Baines, 1984). McLauglin (2005) outlines three general categories in relation to dictionary definitions of controversy: "(i) 'argument,' 'debate,' (ii) 'disagreement,' 'dispute,' 'contention,' 'contradiction,' 'opposition,' and (iii) 'prolonged,' 'involving many people,' 'arousing strong views,' 'on a matter of opinion which is open to serious disagreement'" (p. 62). He also argues that we must move beyond these simplistic and tautological definitions. Controversial issues are more than mere disagreements. For example, if two teachers were to disagree on whether classes should start at 8:55 a.m. or at 9:00 a.m., it is merely a disagreement, not a controversial issue. However, the issue of standardized testing itself might be a controversial issue due to the widespread recognition and evidence that it privileges the dominant majority at the expense of other groups due to inequitable levels of social capital, while at the same time it is also seen as necessary by certain policy makers.

Crick (1998) highlights controversy as "an issue about which there is no one fixed or universally held point of view. Such issues are those which commonly divide society and for which significant groups offer conflicting explanations and solutions" (p. 56). The idea of issues that are divisive to societal groups is helpful, in that it speaks to the nature of these issues. Stradling's (1985) definition adds that these conflicting explanations and solutions are based on "alternative values" (p. 9). Because different viewpoints on matters of controversy are often value-based, it becomes virtually impossible to reach consensus on many of these issues. Oulton, Dillon, and Grace (2004) maintain that teaching about controversial issues must explicitly take their nature into account, emphasizing in particular that:

1. Groups within society hold differing views about them.
2. Groups base their views on either different sets of information or interpreting the same information in different ways.
3. The interpretations may occur because of the different ways that individuals or groups understand or "see" the world (i.e., their worldview).

4. Differing worldviews can occur because the individuals adhere to different value systems.
5. Controversial issues cannot always be resolved by recourse to reason, logic, or experiment.
6. Controversial issues may be resolved as more information becomes available. (p. 412)

Understanding that consensus may not be possible is crucial in the process of addressing controversial issues. In fact, McLauglin (2005) maintains that questions surrounding controversial issues are exacerbated "by [the] realisation of the point that what actually *is* a controversial issue is itself controversial" (p. 63). An example of what is not controversial might be helpful in defining what is.

The KKK propagating hatred and violence against Blacks and the global majority[1] (GM) might at first glance be considered controversial as it clearly relates to racism (an often cited controversial issue); however, there is only one stance—against discrimination, violence, and hatred according to our constitution and the inalienable rights of every citizen—that is defensible. Therefore, the issue in itself is not controversial; rather, it is an offense. Malikow (2006) explains "a controversy exists when both a strong intellectual argument can be made for two or more conflicting positions, and the issue in dispute involves two or more parties with equal and competing interests" (p. 106). The criterion of reasonable positions on either side are commonly cited in relation to controversial issues.

Dearden (1981) also reinforces this: "a matter is controversial if contrary views can be held on it without those views being contrary to reason" (p. 38). For instance, abortion is a controversial issue because persuasive arguments can be made on either side of the issue: On one side, beliefs dictate that it is inappropriate to end a pregnancy because it is ending life; on the other side, the rights of women to have a choice of what happens in their bodies and futures is also persuasive. As news reporter Andy Rooney once said, controversial issues can often make someone "firmly of two minds" (cited in Malikow, 2006, p. 106). It is because different positions are justifiable and defensible based on different values, beliefs, and worldviews that controversial issues are enduring.

The goal of addressing controversial issues, then, is not to search for a universal truth or achieve consensus, but to understand different perspectives and the reasons behind these positions, to learn to respect differences, and to live together peacefully in spite of these contrary worldviews. None of these definitions, however, confronts what we view as an important aspect of which issues are deemed controversial—the fact that these topics are controversial because they are often related to equity and the uncomfortable issues of power, privilege, and oppression that underpin them. Controversial issues might be framed in terms of which group benefits to the detriment of others. However, this is not always the case. While particular issues are expected to elicit controversy (such as racism, sexism, and so on), all topics and disciplines (math, science) are potentially controversial because of the multiple identities and perspectives within classrooms (religious, political, philosophical, social).

1. Discussing Controversial Issues Is an Educational Imperative Because CIs Are Inevitable and Mirror Important Societal Issues

Discussing issues of diversity with students and teachers (especially in the pluralistic Canadian context) leads to conversations about conflict, controversial issues, and the recognition of difference. Discussing controversial issues is an educational imperative because CIs are inevitable and mirror important societal issues; in many cases these issues relate to equity. Controversy is embedded in human interaction and the social nature of our society; so too are diversity and conflict. It is our contention that controversial issues and conflict are an inevitable part of the human predicament more so in a country with many different groups who, by definition, hold many different values, beliefs, and perceptions about the world and the nature of education. In fact, addressing CIs is also necessary even where populations *seem* homogenous, as diversity of views and beliefs occurs both *within* and *between* different societal groups (Adams et al., 2007). Consequently, schools should appropriately deal with them. As one student aptly notes:

> We have to address conflict, because we can't just run around pretending things that aren't. There are issues in the school. When you get people from different countries coming together with different views, with different perspectives with different upbringings there will be conflicts, and if these are not addressed then they're just going to escalate and get worse so yeah, I think that's a must. (student, white male)

Emerging from the data were three perspectives on whether or not controversial issues should be discussed in schools: (1) avoidance of controversial issues, (2) denial of the existence of controversial issues, and (3) head-on confrontation with controversial issues.

Avoiding and Denying the Existence Controversial Issues

The first, and least pervasive, was the view that CIs should be avoided in schools: "Religion shouldn't even be discussed in schools" (white, female student). Participants who thought CIs should be avoided gave different reasons for their positions, including to minimize conflict and also because it was not fair to make students or teachers "uncomfortable." The assumption here is that conflict and "uncomfortableness" are necessarily not worthwhile. A common, but dangerous corollary to this perspective is the view that an expression of conflict or disagreements is disrespectful. The underlying fallacy is that disagreement and respect are in opposition to each other.

There are many reasons cited in the literature for avoiding CIs. Hess (2004), in her unequivocal argument for addressing CIs as part of a democratic education, outlines some of the reasons CIs are avoided in schools:

> Many adults either want schools to mirror their ideas, or fear that adding controversy to the curriculum *creates* controversy, as opposed to simply teaching young people how to deal more effectively with the kinds of political controversies that exist outside of school. . . . There are other barriers as well, including: (1) differing views about the purposes of democracy in education; (2) fears that teachers, other students, or instruments of the "official curriculum" (such as textbooks and films) will indoctrinate students into particular positions on issues; (3) and sharp conflicts about what should rightly be considered an issue in the first place. (p. 258)

Some of these concerns are legitimate, especially for professionals. Hess provides a number of examples in which teachers were reprimanded for addressing controversial issues in their classrooms: "In the most dramatic instances, teachers were disciplined and even fired for teaching about controversial political issues that involved September 11" (p. 258). So we want to respect the worries of some teachers about addressing these issues, especially when doing so often runs counter to the school culture. However, we do maintain that despite these concerns, teaching CIs is necessary in order to authentically prepare students for participation in our society, as well as to pursue equity and other democratic values.

The second view arising from the data, and perhaps more troubling, was that CIs did not exist in particular schools or settings. When we asked one student about her experiences with controversial issues in her school citing many examples, she quickly responded: "We've never really had, in all my years in school, problems with anything like that" (student, white female). There was also the feeling that particular controversial issues did not exist in certain homogenous settings:

> I really don't feel like racism is an issue at all in my school. Not that we have an overly large diversity in my school, but from what there is, I don't think there's a problem with that at all, whereas, I guess heterosexual/homosexuality, I think that's more of an issue if anything. (student, white female)

Just because the student population seems homogenous (for example, being predominantly white) does not mean that racism does not exist or that it should not be addressed with students. Simply ignoring or denying that controversial issues exist in schools will not make them disappear.

Addressing Controversial Issues

The third view, and the most pervasive among both teachers and students, was that controversial issues should be confronted head on in schools. One student highlighted that students needed to be equipped by education to make their own choices:

> I know for sure, in public schools anyways, you're educating for so many different kinds of people coming from all different kinds of backgrounds, cultures and everything, so I think that they should educate on all these controversial issues and allow these kids to make their own choices if anything. (student, white female)

Equipping students with information about CIs, as well as discussing the reasons behind different views on a particular issue, prepares students to deal with issues that will arise within their life. It also respects their right (and capacity) to make their own choices. Another student also thought that addressing CIs was important in order to recognize the way schools actually are:

> Well, I think the fact is you can't sort of dance around the issue. You've got to get right in and just say what the problem is and why it's there. Then, you need to look back and see how it started because, with most controversial issues, they have historical problems or historically inciting incidents that cause some sort of controversial issue. Until you look back at the history of the issue, you can't really solve it. (student, white male)

The historical underpinnings of controversial issues are important to understand issues of power and oppression and also how these factors influence the current societal context.

An aboriginal teacher also maintained that teaching about CIs in schools is necessary in order to adequately prepare students for the challenges they will inevitably face:

> We're the perfect institution for [controversial issues] to be brought up in, because we're educators. I was telling the kids today no subject is taboo if you use the correct terminology, if you're willing to do some research on it and you're willing to listen to others and to form an educated opinion. I said don't be spouting off on something if you don't know anything about it, and you've gone to redneck.com to get your information. And that's the thing, so I totally

believe in discussing "taboo subjects" . . . because I think the kids need to talk about these things. (teacher, aboriginal female)

Overwhelmingly, participants (both teachers and students alike) asserted that issues of controversy are to be expected within the school system; consequently, they need to be fully addressed. Most participants indicated that knowledge about a topic is integral to understanding the issue. Numerous participants also mentioned the importance of learning the historical context of controversial issues—many regarded learning the history of a problem as the first step in the process of tackling it. A majority of the participants emphasized that not only should these issues be explicitly dealt with, but schools have a responsibility to inform students on matters that will affect their lives. The arguments for the inclusion of controversial issues in the curriculum are compelling: "Education should not attempt to shelter our nation's children from even the harsher controversies of adult life, but should prepare them to deal with such controversies knowledgeably, sensibly, tolerantly and morally" (Qualification and Curriculum Authority, 1998, p. 56).

Issues associated with diversity, controversial issues, and conflict are inevitable and, as a result, need to be addressed: "The question is not one of teaching students to avoid conflict, for conflict and controversy are simply a part of human relationship. We all live in a world where beliefs, ideas, needs and wants differ among people and societies" (Soley, 1996, p. 12). So the question, rather than being whether or not CIs should be addressed, should be: How should controversial issues be addressed?

Most participants acknowledged that CIs, when dealt with, need to be dealt with in a particular way. Participants qualified their stance with various conditions, including the readiness of the students (age, maturity), the expertise of the teachers (knowledge, training), research of the issue's history, and the presentation of multiple perspectives; ultimately, participants listed many skills and dispositions necessary to engage in a critical dialogue on a particular issue (including respect, tolerance, open-mindedness, listening, compassion, empathy, and so on).

2. Discussing Controversial Issues Is an Educational Imperative for Democracy, Which, in Turn, Should be Founded on a Relentless Pursuit of Equity

Education and democracy are inextricably connected; so too are democracy and the relentless pursuit of equity rather than simply equality of opportunity. As Dewey (1958) states, "[i]t is obvious that the relation between democracy and education is a reciprocal one, a mutual one, and vitally so. Democracy is itself an educational principle, an educational measure and policy" (p. 294). Consequently, we argue that a crucial purpose of education is to bring about democratic transformation, "preparing students not to fit into a given world so much as to understand and transform the world as given" (Portelli & Solomon, 2001, p. 21). The goal of democratic transformation is equity. In order to prepare students to be actively engaged in democratic transformation, we need to encourage and foster skills and dispositions necessary to challenge inequitable societal institutions and structures (to be discussed more fully in the section of the chapter that argues for a curriculum of life). The process of engaging with CIs and the power and privilege associated with it unearths and brings to the forefront inequitable societal structures. Since we believe in education for democratic transformation, addressing these issues is paramount to equity.

Our conception of democracy is aligned with critical and interruptive models. Critical democracy is closely aligned to our view of the purpose of education:

> Critical democracy implies a significant expansion of democratic participation in the multiple realms of social life in which one takes part.... [It] also implies a moral commitment to promote "public good" over any individual's right to accumulate privilege and power. In this sense it suggests strong values for equality and social justice. As a result, critical democracy presupposes that social arrangements will be developed within a socio-historical context. (Goodman, 1992, pp. 7–8)

This conception of democracy does not attempt to conceal or bury difference; rather, the inevitable differences and conflict arising within communities are embraced as a central mechanism for constructive change. Difference is seen as an asset, rather than a deficit or something to be tolerated. Ongoing discussion through questioning, reflecting on, and analyzing the world is valued, and this democratic process is continuously unfolding and revisited, thereby negotiating and addressing shifting power differentials and societal problems. Similarly, interruptive democracy is "based on the disposition to challenge. It is founded on the principle of positive conflict" (Davies, 2007, p. 78). Conflict and disagreement are not "dirty words," nor are they synonymous with negativity. This conception of democracy is characterized as "the process whereby people are enabled to intervene in practices which continue injustice. Democracy by definition contains the seeds of conflict, as it is not an end-state but a process whereby people hold leaders accountable and argue for rights for themselves and others" (Davies, 2007, p. 72). Our understanding of democracy includes a process component, but it also includes substantive values such as equity that attempt to fulfill the different needs that arise not by applying a "one-size-fits-all" mentality. In short, democracy requires defiance and subversion, especially against inequitable societal structures. Schools are currently inequitable societal structures; hence, confronting controversial issues in schools is one way to contest the naturalization of inequitable outcomes and intervene (and teach students how to intervene, advocate, and mobilize around these critical and controversial equity issues).

Schools are entrusted with the task of preparing students for citizenship beyond the classroom and, in Canada, this citizenship occurs in an increasingly diverse society:

> As the cornerstone of our civil and democratic society, our public education systems are charged with the responsibility of educating our young people to take their place in society as productive citizens within the context of Canada's rich diversity.... It is therefore crucial at this time for extraordinary efforts to be made to ensure that all of our young people, including those who are most vulnerable, have the opportunity to succeed in school. To do this, however, we need an informed, open and broad-based discussion on the nature of these changes and how the needs of all students can be addressed. (Harvey & Houle, 2006, p. ii)

Addressing inequitable outcomes in education, which is a democratic imperative, requires delving into many issues that might be deemed "controversial" by some, because issues of equity are intimately related to who succeeds (and who does not) in our schools.

> The educational system of a given society reflects that society, and, at the same time, it is the main force perpetuating it. It may be perceived as the most powerful means of social control to which individuals must submit, and as one of the most universal models of social relationships to which they will refer later. (quoted by Michael Crozier in Smith, 1992, p. 11)

It is imperative for Canada to confront issues arising from diversity in order to find strategies and interventions that will ensure the equity required for democracy.

The justification to prioritize the correction of these inequities is one founded on human rights. The Canadian Charter of Rights and Freedoms guarantees equity for its citizens. Section 15 (Equality Rights), clearly outlines that:

> 15. (1) Every individual is equal before and under the law and has the right to the equal protection and equal benefit of the law without discrimination and, in particular, without discrimination based on race, national or ethnic origin, colour, religion, sex, age or mental or physical disability. (2) Subsection (1) does not preclude any law, program or activity that has as its object the amelioration of conditions of disadvantaged individuals or groups including those that are disadvantaged because of race, national or ethnic origin, colour, religion, sex, age or mental or physical disability. (Canada, 1982)

Our education system must reflect these inalienable rights by ensuring that all students have an equitable education. And as Ontario's (Ontario Ministry of Education, 2009) Equity Strategy clearly states, equity is "[a] condition or state of fair, inclusive, and respectful treatment of all people. Equity does not mean treating people the same without regard for individual differences" (p. 6).

Equity also entails that students are not constructed from a deficit mentality. Flutter and Rudduck (2004) maintain that many educators (including administrators) feel threatened by a process that may challenge their sense of expertise and may require them to relinquish (or share) power, control, and authority. The UN Convention of the Rights of the Child outlines that children have the rights to freedom of expression and to form associations, and hence, a right to participate in their education (Deuchar, 2008). A few teachers outlined that some students are simply not prepared to engage with controversial issues, highlighting that "it depends on where your students are at that particular time. If your group is mature enough to handle those types of things by all means" (administrator, white male). This is a common assumption that students are too young or ill-equipped to be able to discuss controversial issues, co-construct classroom instruction, and, of course, to take part in decision-making processes of schooling; however, this view is based on a deficit construction of students and underestimates their capacities. As Deuchar highlights, based on the work of Claire and Holden (2007), Clough and Holden (2002), and Hicks and Holden (1995, 2007), "evidence suggests that children as young as seven have concerns about the environment, poverty and injustice, that they are aware of global issues and have already developed a strong set of social and ethical values" (Deuchar, 2008, p. 21). We argue that respecting students means believing in their capability to handle important issues.

Acknowledging "the Controversial" Underlying Educational Inequities

Not all students enjoy or complete their secondary school education. Currently, school outcomes, educational attainment, and labor market success are largely correlated to ethnicity, race, socioeconomic status, and gender (Harvey & Houle, 2006). The majority of disengaged students have low socioeconomic status and "minority" group status (Ferguson, Tilleczek, Boydell, & Rummens, 2005, p. 14). It is no coincidence that the GM students are often at the bottom of the achievement gap and suspended more in comparison to white students; rather, these outcomes are a result of exclusionary and discriminatory practices based on race, gender, (dis)ability, sexuality and socioeconomic status (Dei, 1997). School factors related to disengagement include an "ineffective discipline system; lack of adequate counselling /referral; negative school climate; lack of relevant curriculum; passive instructional strategies; disregard of student learning styles; retentions or suspensions; streaming; and lack of assessment and support for students with disabilities" (Ferguson et al., 2005, p. 14). In a democratic country, freedom and equity among differently situated social groups must be a central pursuit; we argue that this pursuit requires transforming education so that we openly acknowledge the "controversial" underpinning educational inequities (racism, discrimination, Eurocentric curriculum and assessment, and so on) so that we can begin to change schools and curriculum to address these issues with a sense of urgency.

The Current Educational Climate: Sidelining Issues that Matter

Even though there was virtually unanimous agreement that CIs should be addressed in schools, the participants' common perception was that schools often curtail, sideline, and silence conversations about controversial issues and inequities. Some student leaders recognized, and disagreed with, the fact that aspects of their school cultures actually curtailed discussion of these issues: "Religion is a really big not-talk about it in our school, like in the public school, and I don't think that's right. I think every person should be able to say what they think about their religion and then if there's a problem you deal with it" (student, white female). In another example, an aboriginal teacher similarly notes that her school does not endorse the discussion of controversial issues:

> [Students have] been trying to do a sociology project, and it was about gay and lesbian issues. Our principal squashed that so friggen fast that your head would spin. We're not allowed to talk about gay/lesbian issues. I still do because we have some students that are in crisis, and if they're seeing their administrator say that it's a taboo subject how are they going to feel about themselves? I'm a taboo subject is how. They're going leave school thinking this school doesn't represent me, and this school doesn't welcome me. (teacher, aboriginal female)

The hidden lesson in schools not addressing certain issues (for instance, sexual orientation) alienates certain groups of students. The aboriginal teacher highlights the reluctance of her colleagues to confront controversial issues:

> Some of the teachers aren't prepared [to talk about controversial issues]. You have some teachers that won't put themselves out there to take a risk either and how sad, because teaching is taking a risk every day when you get up in front of the class, because you have no control over what you've got in front of you. You don't know what [students] just came from or how last night went or anything. (teacher, aboriginal female)

Teachers' ability to navigate these important issues influences the way in which students understand and approach diversity and difference. This aboriginal teacher also underscores the dire consequences of not dealing with topics of controversy by illustrating the ramifications of misinformation:

> If not in a school with education resources and people willing to talk about it, where are [students] going to learn about these subjects? Some girls think they can't get pregnant if they're on their period, because they're learning about sex in the bathroom. If teachers aren't willing to do it, get out of the way and let somebody that is. I'm sorry, but these kids they can't go to their parents. (teacher, aboriginal female)

Amy Gutmann (1999) also reinforces that schools are particularly well suited to addressing these issues as well as testing grounds for democratic practices: "Schools have a much greater capacity than most parents and voluntary associations for teaching children to reason out loud about disagreements that arise in democratic politics" (p. 58). The aboriginal teacher held school administrations responsible for sideling controversial issues:

> I think far too often, the people that have the power (the administrators) bring their own personal views in, and their view is the only view (which makes them a very poor administrator when they have the only view). So, if they don't agree with homosexuality, then it's wrong, it's evil, and we're not going to discuss it. That's certainly what's going on with our school is that [the administrators'] own personal views are clouding the judgment of everything, and I think their own fear, or their own associations with it, may cloud it as well. If they're not comfortable, personally I think that they feel intimidated by someone that can discuss it. I think that is their own failing. If you can't discuss it, that's fine, but don't squash other people that are talking about it and educating about it. We're not making it salacious and dirty, we're talking about it in an intellectual form. And why would you fear knowledge as an educator? (teacher, aboriginal female)

Positions of power can easily be abused in a hierarchal system. That is why it is important to have different groups represented in leadership roles. Key questions arising from the current educational climate, described in terms of sidelining issues that matter include the following: What do school systems gain by trivializing, silencing and preventing controversial issues from being discussed? What are the ramifications of this position for schools, educators, students, different social groups, and society at large?

The participants' common perception that schools often curtail, sideline, and silence conversations about controversial issues and inequities (including dialogues about race, ethnicity, gender, and sexual orientation, among others) is troubling at the turn of the 21st century in a country that claims to be free and democratic. Silence around these issues is prevalent in our current educational system. Shields (2004) aptly recognizes that:

Educational practices that ignore such inequities, either by essentializing difference or attempting to ignore it, are manifestations of firmly rooted and pervasive attitudes that may best be described as pathologizing the lived experiences
of students. I use the term pathologizing to denote a process of treating differences as deficits, a process that locates the responsibility for school success in
the lived experiences of children (home life, home culture, SES) rather than
situating responsibility in the education system itself. In large part because educators implicitly assign blame for school failure to children and to their families,
many students come to believe they are incapable of high-level academic performance. Pathologizing may be overt when, for example, policies, statements,
or practices use discriminatory language. However, it is equally common for
pathologizing to be covert and silent, engendering in students and their families feelings that, somehow, they and their lived experiences are abnormal and
unacceptable within the boundaries of the school community and their abilities
subnormal within the tightly prescribed bounds of core curriculum or transmis-
sive pedagogy still too common in many schools and classrooms. (p. 112)

It is precisely this silence that perpetuates inequities in our society. Participants from our study highlighted that discussion of certain issues was not
encouraged by their schools; in fact, in many cases, it was actively discour-
aged. The perplexing corollary of this position is that it in no way attempts
to solve the problem. Simply ignoring the situation often exacerbates it. As
an aboriginal teacher notes, her school's administration enacts the "See no
evil, speak no evil, hear no evil" philosophy. The strategy here is to "just
separate the groups, kick them out of school for a while, and [the admin-
istrator] thinks that's going to solve the problems. It doesn't, the conflict
just builds more" (teacher, aboriginal female). Not only does this type of
thinking (to close one's eyes, ears, and mouth to controversial issues and
conflict) not help the situation, it actually worsens it considerably.

We need to teach controversial issues in our schools in order to openly
acknowledge that these obstructions to equity (e.g., racism and heterosex-
ism) are, in fact, prevalent in our schools and society. It is only through
breaking these silences and generating open awareness that we can move
forward to correct injustices. Moreover, several studies have shown that one
of the major reasons for students' disengagement is the lack of discussion
on controversial issues (Portelli, Vibert, & Shields, 2007; Smith et al., 1998).

3. Addressing Controversial Issues Is an Educational Imperative for Student Engagement and Has Many Benefits for Students

The body of empirical research that exists on this topic consistently outlines that teaching CIs has many benefits for students; consequently, this is

another reason that teaching controversial issues is an educational imperative. Some of the benefits outlined in the literature include increased political participation; increased engagement with school; more exposure to CIs
in school results in students being more trusting of others and more socially
integrated; as well as higher levels of belief that people can actually affect
the surrounding system and society (Hess, 2004, 2005; Hicks & Holden,
2007; Soley, 1996).

Addressing controversial issues, since they often address the lived reality
of students, also increases student engagement in a curriculum of life—that
is, a curriculum that seriously deals with life including the substantive issues
that students encounter in their own lived experiences (Portelli & Vibert,
2001, 2002). Goodson (2008) argues that the current curricular content is
inadequate because it fails to deal with relevant issues to students:

> When we see learning as a response to actual events then the issue of engage-
> ment can be taken for granted. So much of the literature on learning fails to
> address this crucial question of *engagement,* and as a result learning is seen as
> some formal task that is unrelated to the needs and interests of the learner,
> hence so much of curriculum planning is based on prescriptive definitions
> of what is to be learnt without any understanding of the situation within the
> learners' lives. As a result a vast amount of curriculum planning is abortive
> because the learner simply does not engage; hence to see learning as located
> within a life history is to understand that learning is contextually situated
> and that it also has a history, both in terms of the individual's life story and
> the history and trajectories of the institutions that offer formal learning op-
> portunities, as well as the histories of the communities and locations in which
> informal learning takes place. (p. 133)

One student utilizes a real issue that has affected interactions in his school,
talking about the way that conflicts in schools mirror international conflicts:

> There will always be opposing views, and as long as these views are kept going,
> like I mean if you just even look once again going back to the Middle East, be-
> tween Israel and pretty much all the Arab nations, they hate each other, and
> as long as that keeps happening it's going to be a real tough cycle to break. So,
> what has to happen is it needs to start slow and it's a really tough thing to deal
> with because there are going to be people that just don't like each other. And
> to deal with that, you need to find something that is profound for both sides,
> and what that is I don't know but until that something is found, something
> profound that can be agreed upon and that can help unite people. (student,
> white male)

Because conflict was seen as unavoidable, many participants discussed the
benefits of addressing CIs and conflict:

> I think some of it can also be good to have some conflict because if you have someone who doesn't agree with your opinion, they might have an excellent idea of what to do then you could have two things on the go and it could be doubly as effective. (student, white female)

> Conflict is good in some ways because people are different and people have different opinions. (student, white male)

Another major benefit of discussing controversial issues with students is to develop critical thinking skills and dispositions. Critical thinking requires challenging issues: "There is no question that substantive knowledge is an essential ingredient of the learning process, for it is useless, and even impossible, to learn how to think unless there is something important to think about" (Soley, 1996, p. 10). It is not simply teaching about the context of CIs—although that is important as well—it is also about the process of engaging in critical thinking (Pinto & Portelli, 2009).

Addressing controversial issues in schools and classrooms is a way to transform the curriculum and teaching to reflect the understanding of the learning process as situated and contextualized within students' lived identities and experiences. Portelli and Vibert's (2002) "curriculum of life" encapsulates a similar understanding of teaching and learning in real-life contexts. They maintain that the curriculum of life "is unusual in that it is a view of curriculum as a dynamic relationship among teachers, students, knowledge, and contexts" (p. 36). This concept values and addresses issues of equity, difference, and social justice:

> A curriculum of life centres on the possibilities for the co-construction and co-production of knowledge, rather than on knowledge as simply teacher transmitted or simply student created.... [T]he curriculum of life makes explicit the kinds of issues usually associated with the "hidden curriculum." Hence, it takes substantive and possibly controversial issues in the students' personal, social and political lives very seriously. (Portelli & Vibert, 2002, p. 39)

This type of engagement with the curriculum of life is central to education in a genuine democracy. In order to illustrate this point, we utilize a real example of a controversial issue that emerged from the study.

RECOGNIZING DIFFERENCE: VARYING PERSPECTIVES AND NAVIGATING A CONTROVERSIAL ISSUE

In order to solidify what we mean by addressing controversial issues in schools and also to demonstrate the learning that can emerge from engaging with this curriculum of life, we are including the different perspectives of two teachers surrounding racism, equity and whether or not to recognizing difference. Racism was consistently cited as controversial by all participants in the study; however, there was a tension surrounding different viewpoints on whether to acknowledge race. Two participants' contrasting views illustrate the range of opinions that existed among those interviewed. While a white teacher saw not recognizing colour as equitable, another black teacher saw recognizing race as central to equity. The white male teacher took a stance of colour-blindness concerning race, a stance that is prevalent in school practices:

> A student leader at my school was Muslim and black, and I mean, I don't think the kids saw her as black or as Muslim in the school. I know when I see her, I don't see color, race, or religion. You know, because she's just such an outgoing person. She was an outstanding student president; kids loved her. You know? And one of the very few times that they had somebody of a different color, you know, running the school council, but I mean the kids loved her. When we talked about discrimination and things like that, she said "Well, I see it every day, and I feel it every day." Because, there were certain elements [and people] in the school that would make disparaging comments, but—for the most part—I'd say ninety eight, ninety nine percent of the students were totally, perfectly, one hundred percent accepting. She said [about how racist comments made her feel] "I put a lot of it to the fact that they just don't know me, and their lack of education, their ignorance in a sense." [As a teacher], if you see it, you try and say that's bad. (teacher, white male)

An analysis of the statement reveals many contradictions. If the teacher did not see color, race, or religion, why is this the way in which the student was first described? If other students did not "see her as black or Muslim," there would not have been disparaging comments made based on these categories of belonging. Likewise, the student's disclosure that she sees and feels discrimination every day stands in opposition to the teacher's assumption that 99% of students are accepting. And what would it mean to be "totally, perfectly, one hundred percent accepting"? In some ways, the assumption that students are accepting of difference is naïve, a product of these issues being continually sidelined, denied, and minimized in schools. Another interesting nuance of this interview excerpt, one evidenced by the lack of GM representation at the CSLC, was the fact that GM student leaders are rare. The same is true for representation of GM groups in educational administration leadership roles (Dei, 1997; Portelli & Campbell-Stevens, 2009). This is no coincidence. The reality is that social division happens early, even before high school, and these divisions are intensified as the dominant group is given opportunities that allow for the development of skills that ensure even more chances to assume leadership positions in adult life; meanwhile, GM groups are marginalized and do not have the same opportunities to cultivate these skills for future leadership roles even at the secondary school level.

A Black educator stood in direct opposition to the White educator on the issue of whether or not to acknowledge difference. He problematized the position of color-blindness, and its implications for his social group:

> Number one: understand that people are physically different. There's no such thing as being color blind. [Society needs] to recognize somebody in their difference. When you [consider] a person, no matter what race they are, the color comes with them, just like if you ask for water—you can't ask for water and say please hold the wet, because the wet is a characteristic of the water. What we try to do, is we try to let people know that it's not bad to acknowledge the fact that people are different as a starting point. You can't just say that everybody basically is the same.... Some of the challenges that people face are [that] communities can be marginalized and their voices are not necessarily heard. So providing them with an opportunity to speak...not just with their friends, but also with people that are in leadership and decision making capabilities, is critical. (teacher, black male)

To this educator, not recognizing race means disavowing the identity of an entire social group, and consequently marginalizing their experiences in the process. Creating opportunities for marginalized groups to influence people in positions of power becomes integral to disrupting oppression and building agency to become self-determining.

These excerpts illustrate the tension surrounding different controversial issues. In this case, one educator champions the focus on commonalities between groups, while the other insists that a recognition of differences is necessary in order to tackle racism. These viewpoints are influenced by the position each educator holds in different social groups—a values based difference that is not easy to overcome. This results in different groups experiencing controversial issues in very different ways based on their position within (or outside) the dominant group. Similarly, there are underlying assumptions about diversity and difference that go with each perspective that need to be discussed in schools. This example clearly demonstrates the need to deal with such issues, especially when teachers take such contrasting views. However, it is not sufficient to simply deal with these issues. We need to highlight that the way in which these issues are dealt with becomes crucial. The first teacher seems to be assuming that the educational process is a neutral one; the second teacher clearly conceptualizes education within the inevitable power dynamics context. In our view, a robust democracy cannot consider contexts to be neutral. Neutrality is self-contradictory and the presumption of neutrality mitigates against the success of democracy.

CONCLUSION

Education, above all else, is for equity and social justice. In order to address equity, controversial issues must be addressed in schools. Schools remain a potentially viable site to confront and dismantle hegemonic ideologies that reproduce societal inequities and confronting diversity and controversial issues are learning opportunities to address equity. Education for democratic transformation goes beyond conventional notions of teaching and learning. As Parker Palmer argued, "Education at its best—this profound human transaction called teaching and learning—is not just about getting information or getting a job. Education is about healing and wholeness. It is about empowerment, liberation, transcendence, about renewing the vitality of life. It is about finding and claiming ourselves and our place in the world" (as cited in hooks, 2003, p. 43). Equity has been sidelined for long enough in schools due to teachers and students feeling uncomfortable about the topics it raises. There are processes for preparing teachers to facilitate these important conversations. We cannot continue to be apathetic about controversial issues or equity. The time for change is now. It is crucial for policy makers to understand the necessity of dealing with controversial issues in a democracy that honors genuine student engagement rather than blind "on task work."

NOTE

1. We use the term "black and global majority" (GM) instead of "minority" because the latter term is contentious, and its meaning is often associated with being "subordinate" to the majority (Portelli & Campbell-Stevens, 2009). As Rosemary Campbell-Stevens highlights, "the [minority] term has outlived its usefulness because Black and GM groups are neither minorities numerically nor are they subordinate on the global stage or, increasingly, within the urban context of western countries. Three quarters of the world's population are of Asian and African extraction and our footprint is a large one" (Portelli & Campbell-Stevens, 2009, p. 1).

REFERENCES

Adams, M., Bell, L., & Griffin, P. (Eds.). (2007). *Teaching for diversity and social justice* (2nd ed.). New York, NY: Routledge.

Canada, Government of. (1982). The Canadian charter of rights and freedoms. Retrieved from http://laws.justice.gc.ca/en/charter

Claire, H., & Holden, C. (2007). The challenge of teaching controversial issues: Principles and practice. In H. Claire & C. Holden (Eds.), *The challenge of teaching controversial issues* (pp. 1–14). Stoke on Trent, UK: Trentham Books.

Clough, N., & Holden, C. (2002). *Education for citizenship: Ideas into action.* London: RoutlegeFalmer.

Cooper, A. (2008). *Student leadership for social justice in secondary schools: A Canadian perspective.* Unpublished master's thesis, University of Toronto, ON, Canada. Retrieved from https://tspace.library.utoronto.ca/bitstream/1807/17158/1/Cooper_Amanda-Mae_200811_MEd_Thesis.pdf

Crick, B. (1998). *Education for citizenship and the teaching of democracy in schools.* London, UK: Qualifications and Curriculum Authority.

Davies, L. (2007). Conflict resolution. In D. Hicks & C. Holden (Eds.), *Teaching the global dimension: Key principles and effective practices* (pp. 71–81). New York, NY: Routlege.

Dearden, R. F. (1981). Controversial issues in the curriculum. *Journal of Curriculum Studies, 13,* 37–44.

Dei, G. (1997). Understanding student disengagement. In G. Dei, J. Mazzuca, E. McIssac & J. Zine (Eds.), *Reconstructing "drop-out": A critical ethnography of the dynamics of Black students' disengagement from school* (pp. 64–84). Toronto, ON: University of Toronto Press.

Deuchar, R. (2008). 'All you need is an idea!': The impact of values-based participation on pupils' attitudes towards social activism enterprise. *Improving schools, 11*(1), 19–32.

Dewey, J. (1922). *Human nature and conduct: An introduction to social psychology.* New York, NY: Modern Library.

Dewey, J. (1958). *Experience and nature.* New York, NY: Dover Publications.

Ferguson, B., Tilleczek, K., Boydell, K., & Rummens, J. A. (2005). *Early school leavers: Understanding the lived reality of student disengagement from secondary school.* Toronto, ON: Ontario Ministry of Education. Retrieved from http://www.edu.gov.on.ca/eng/parents/schoolleavers.pdf

Flutter, J., & Rudduck, J. (2004). *Consulting pupils: What's in it for schools?* New York, NY: Routledge Falmer.

Goodman, J. (1992). *Elementary schooling for critical democracy.* Albany, NY: State University of New York Press.

Goodson, I. (2008). Schooling, curriculum, narrative and the social future. In C. Sugrue (Ed.), *The future of educational change: International perspectives* (pp.123–135). New York, NY: Routledge.

Gutmann, A. (1999). *Democratic education.* Princeton, NJ: Princeton University Press. (Original work published in 1987)

Harvey, E., & Houle R. (2006). *Demographic changes in Canada and their impact on public education: The learning partnership.* Retrieved from http://thelearning-partnership.ca/policy_research/RESEARCH_PAPER_06.pdf

Hess, D. (2004). Controversies about controversial issues in democratic education. *PS Online,* 257–261. Retrieved from http://www.apsanet.org

Hess, D. (2005). How do teachers' political views influence teaching about controversial issues? *Social Education, 69*(1), 47–48.

Hicks, D., & Holden, C. (1995) *Visions of the future: Why we need to teach for tomorrow.* Stoke-on-Trent: Trentham.

Hicks, D., & Holden, C. (Eds.). (2007). *Teaching the global dimension: Key principles and effective practices.* New York, NY: Routlege.

Holden, C. (2007). Teaching controversial issues. In D. Hicks & C. Holden (Eds.), *Teaching the global dimension: Key principles and effective practices* (pp. 55-67). London and New York: Routlege.

hooks, bell. (2003). *Teaching community: A pedagogy of hope.* New York, NY: Routledge.

Malikow, M. (2006). Engaging students in controversial issues. *Kappa Delta Pi Record, 42*(3), 106–108.

McLauglin, T. (2003). Teaching controversial issues in citizenship education. In A. Lockyer, B. Crick, & J. Annette (Eds.), *Education for democratic citizenship* (pp.149–160). Surrey, UK: Ashgate Publishing Limited.

McLauglin, T. H. (2005). What is education? In W. Hare & J. P. Portelli (Eds.), *Key questions for educators* (pp. 61–64). Halifax, NS: Edphil Books.

Noll, W. (1989). *Taking sides: Clashing views on controversial issues* (5th ed.). Guilford, CT: Dushkin Publishing Group.

Ontario Ministry of Education. (2009). *Realizing the promise of diversity: Ontario's equity and inclusive education strategy.* Toronto, ON: Author.

Oulton, C., Day, V., Dillon, J., & Grace, M. (2004). Controversial issues—Teachers' attitudes and practices in the context of citizenship education. *Oxford Review of Education, 30*(4), 489–507.

Oulton, C., Dillon, J., & Grace, M. (2004). Reconceptualizing the teaching of controversial issues. *International Journal of Science Education, 26*(4), 411–423.

Pinto, L., & Portelli, J.P. (2009). The role and impact of critical thinking in democratic education: Challenges and possibilities. In J. Sobocan & L. Groake (Eds.), *Critical thinking in an era of accountability: Can higher order thinking be tested?* (pp. 299–318). London, UK: Althouse Press.

Portelli, J. P., & Campbell-Stephens, R. (2009). *Leading for equity: The investing in equity approach.* Toronto, ON: Edphil Books.

Portelli, J. P., & Solomon, P. (Eds.). (2001). *The erosion of democracy in education: From critique to possibilities.* Calgary, AB: Detselig.

Portelli, J.P & Vibert A. (2001). Standards, equity, and the curriculum of life. *Analytic Teaching, 22*(1), 5–15.

Portelli, J. P., & Vibert, A. (2002). A curriculum of life. *Education Canada, 42*(2), 36–39.

Portelli, J. P., Vibert, A. B., & Shields, C. M (2007). *Toward an equitable education: Poverty, diversity, and students at risk.* Toronto, ON: BTT Communications.

Qualification and Curriculum Authority. (1998). *Education for citizenship and the teaching of democracy in schools.* London, UK: Author.

Ryan, J. (2006). *Inclusive leadership.* San Francisco, CA: Jossey-Bass.

Sechrest, L., & Sidani, S. (1995). Quantitative and qualitative methods: Is there an alternative? *Evaluation and Program Planning, 18*(1), 77–87.

Shields, C. M. (2004). Dialogic leadership for social justice: Overcoming pathologies of silence. *Educational Administration Quarterly, 40,* 109–134.

Smith, F. (1992, September). *Women in Educational Administration: Moving from a paradigm of power and control to empowerment and equality.* Paper presented at the Annual Meeting of Women in Educational Administration, Lincoln, NE. (ERIC Document Reproduction Service No. ED353675)

Smith, W., Butler-Kisber, L., LaRocque, L., Portelli, J., Shields, C., Sparkes, C., & Vibert, A. (1998). *Student engagement in learning and life: National Project Report.* Montreal, QB: Office of Research on Educational Policy, McGill University.

Soley, M. (1996). If it's controversial, why teach it? *Social Education, 60*(1), 9–14.

Stradling, B. (1985). Controversial issues in the curriculum. *Bulletin of Environmental Education, 170,* 9–13.

Stradling, R., Noctor, M., & Baines, B. (1984). *Teaching controversial issues.* London, UK: Arnold.

ABOUT THE CONTRIBUTORS

Amanda Cooper, Ontario Institute for Studies in Education (OISE) was a secondary school teacher (English, Science) in Trillium Lakelands District School Board, before enrolling in graduate studies, where she enjoyed coaching and was passionate about student engagement and equity issues. Her passion for teaching and learning led her to pursue a Master's degree, where she first became immersed in the world of educational research. Her qualitative Master's thesis, entitled *Student leadership for social justice in secondary schools: A Canadian perspective*, explores opportunities for schools to address equity issues through reconceptualising student leadership and its goals. Amanda's doctoral research maps the knowledge mobilization efforts of 44 intermediary organizations across Canada. Much of her work is available through the Research Supporting Practice in Education website at OISE: www.oise.utoronto.ca/rspe

Michael Fielding taught for 19 years in some of the UK's pioneer radical comprehensive schools and for a similar period and identical commitments at the universities of Cambridge, Sussex and London where he is currently Emeritus Professor of Education at the Institute of Education. Widely published in the fields of student voice, educational leadership and radical education, his latest book *Radical Education and the Common School—A Democratic Alternative* (Routledge 2011) co-authored with Peter Moss seeks to reclaim education as a democratic project and a community responsibility and the school as a public space of encounter for all citizens.

Student Engagement in Urban Schools, pages 197–201
Copyright © 2012 by Information Age Publishing

Trevor Gale holds a personal Chair in Education Policy and Social Justice at Deakin University, Australia. From 2008 to 2011, he was the founding director of Australia's National Centre for Student Equity in Higher Education. He is also the founding editor of *Critical Studies in Education* and a past President (2005) of the Australian Association for Research in Education (AARE). Trevor is a critical sociologist of education with research interests in social justice in education policy, particular in relation to schooling and higher education. His latest books are *Schooling in Disadvantaged Communities* (Springer 2010) with Carmen Mills and *Educational Research by Association* (Sense 2010) with Bob Lingard. He is the lead author of the national report on university outreach programs, *Interventions Early in School,* commissioned by the Australian Government. With Stephen Parker, he has recently completed a meta-analysis of research on students' transition into higher education, for the Australian Learning and Teaching Council.

Ben Kirshner is an Assistant Professor in Educational Psychology and Adolescent Development at CU-Boulder's School of Education. His research examines learning environments that enable youth to exercise social and political agency, including youth organizing, student voice, and participatory action research. Supported by the Spencer Foundation, he is currently collaborating with high school teachers to study processes of civic development by engaging students in critical inquiry and action research in alignment with curricular standards. In another study, Dr. Kirshner developed a participatory action research study in partnership with students to understand the impact of a school closure on students. Dr. Kirshner's publications have discussed youth civic engagement and activism, youth-adult research partnerships, and issues in urban education. From 1993 to 1997 he was education program manager in a youth organization in San Francisco's Mission District.

Brenda J. McMahon is an Associate Professor of Educational Leadership at the University of North Carolina at Charlotte. Her research focuses on educational leadership, student engagement, resilience, and the roles that race assumes within high schools. She is co-editor of the *Inclusion in urban educational environments: Addressing issues of diversity, equity, and social justice* series for Information Age Publishers. Dr. McMahon's single and co-authored publications include: White educational administrators: Working towards antiracism and social justice in the *Journal of Educational Administration;* Engagement for what? Beyond popular discourses on student engagement in *Leadership and Policy in Schools*; Putting the elephant in the refrigerator: Student engagement, critical pedagogy and antiracist education in the *McGill Journal of Educational Research*; and Engaged pedagogy: Valuing the strengths of students on the margins in the *Journal of Thought.*

Dana L. Mitra is Associate Professor in the Department of Education Policy Studies at the Pennsylvania State University. She holds a Ph.D. from Stanford University in Educational Administration and Policy Analysis. Her prior work experience includes teaching elementary school in the Washington, DC area and serving as the coordinator for two White House Conferences on Character Education. Dana's research interests include high school reform, student voice, and civic engagement. Among her publications, she has published articles in *Teachers College Record* entitled "The significance of students: Can increasing "student voice" in schools lead to gains in youth development?" and in *Applied Developmental Science* entitled "Providing spark and stability: The role of intermediary organizations in establishing school-based youth-adult partnerships." She also has published a book with SUNY Press entitled *Student voice in school reform: Building youth-adult partnerships that strengthen schools and empower youth.*

Geoff Munns is an Associate Professor, in the School of Education at the University of West Sydney, Australia. His research focuses on ways to improve social and academic outcomes for educationally disadvantaged students, including those from Indigenous backgrounds. He has a strong research record in ARC funded projects, and is currently Chief Investigator for 2 projects under the Discovery Indigenous Researcher Development Scheme, as well as Chief Investigator for 2 ARC Linkages Project. As leader of the Fair Go Project, Geoff Munns has developed the most significant and productive research activity around engagement for students in poverty in Australia. It is the major research project for the NSW DET's Priority Schools Programs, has had active research and professional development involvement in 10 educationally disadvantaged schools over an 8 year period and has a national and international publication reputation.

John P. Portelli is Professor and Co-Director of the Centre for Leadership and Diversity, Department of Theory and Policy Studies at OISE, University of Toronto. His research and teaching focus on: democratic values and educational policy, leadership and pedagogy; student engagement and the curriculum of life; standardization, equity and "students at risk". He has published eight books (including two collections of poetry). He has been involved in three major national Canadian projects. His latest book, co-authored with Rosemary Campbell Stephens, is entitled Leading for Equity (2009).

Sam Sellar is a Postdoctoral Research Fellow in the School of Education at The University of Queensland, Australia, and previously a Postdoctoral Research Fellow in the National Centre for Student Equity in Higher Education hosted at the University of South Australia. Sam's research spans the fields of cultural studies of education, sociology of education and education policy. He has recent publications in the *Cambridge Journal of Education* (with Trevor Gale and Stephen Parker), *Critical Studies in Education* (with Trevor Gale) and forthcoming articles in *Discourse: Studies in the Cultural Politics of Education* (sole author; and with Lew Zipin and Robert Hattam). He is also co-author of the recent report on university outreach programs commissioned by the Australian Government: *Interventions early in school as a means to improve higher education outcomes for disadvantaged (particularly low SES) students.*

Deborah Seltzer-Kelly is an Assistant Professor and member of the faculty of curriculum studies in the Department of Curriculum and Instruction at Southern Illinois University, Carbondale. Her earlier work in democratic and multicultural curricula and practices includes "Adventures in critical pedagogy: A lesson in U.S. history," which appeared in *Teacher Education Quarterly*, "and "Deweyan multicultural democracy, Rortian Solidarity, and the popular arts: Krumping into presence," in *Studies in Philosophy and Education*. Her research into scientific method as it is conceived in the sciences and its mistranslation to the field of education has focused upon the nature of method for teaching and research. Publications exploring these issues include: "Deweyan Darwinism for the 21st century: Toward an educational method for critical democratic engagement in the era of the Institute of Education Sciences," which appeared in *Educational Theory*; and "(Re) Imagining teacher preparation for conjoint democratic inquiry in complex classroom ecologies," a co-authored piece in *Complicity*.

John Smyth is Emeritus Professor, Flinders University of South Australian and Research Professor of Education, School of Education, University of Ballarat, Victoria, Australia where he is Director of the *Centre for Addressing Disadvantage and Inequality in Education and Health*. In 2011 he was elected as a Fellow of the Academy of Social Sciences of Australia. His research interests are in policy sociology, policy ethnography, social justice, and school and community capacity building. He is the author of 25 books the most recent of which is *Hanging in with Kids in Tough Times* (New York: Peter Lang Publishing, 2010).

David Zyngier is professor in the Faculty of Education at Monash University and a former school principal and state school teacher. His research focuses on Culturally, Linguistically and Economically Diverse (CLED) Learning Communities; Social Justice; Democratic Education; Teacher Knowledge and Beliefs. He has published widely on teacher pedagogies that improve outcomes for students from communities of promise. In 2010, the RUMAD program that he wrote received the prestigious Garth Boomer Award for its contribution to education in Australia. He developed the Enhanced Learning Improvement in Networked Communities program which gained a Schools First Award of $25,000 in 2010 for its contribution to students experiencing learning difficulties and school engagement problems. He is also a member of the Editorial Board of Teaching and Teacher Education (Elsevier). He is also Co-director (with Paul Carr) of the *Global Doing Democracy Research Project.*

CPSIA information can be obtained at www.ICGtesting.com
Printed in the USA
LVOW12s2348250714

396005LV00008B/116/P